Giants of America

★   ★   ★   ★

The Founding Fathers

Gouv Morris

★　★　★　★　★　★

GOUVERNEUR
MORRIS

The Home of Gouverneur Morris

THEODORE ROOSEVELT

ARLINGTON HOUSE　*New Rochelle, N.Y.*

Library of Congress Catalog Card Number: 79–111226

SBN 87000–090–x

MANUFACTURED IN THE UNITED STATES OF AMERICA

PREFACE

GOUVERNEUR MORRIS, like his far greater friend and political associate, Alexander Hamilton, had about him that " touch of the purple " which is always so strongly attractive. He was too unstable and erratic to leave a profound mark upon our political developments, but he performed two or three conspicuous feats, he rendered several marked services to the country, and he embodied to a peculiar degree both the qualities which made the Federalist party so brilliant and so useful, and those other qualities which finally brought about its downfall. Hamilton and even Jay represented better what was highest in the Federalist party. Gouverneur Morris stood for its weakness as well as for its strength. Able, fearless, and cultivated, deeply devoted to his people, and of much too tough fibre ever to be misled, into losing his affection for things American because of American faults and shortcomings, as was and is the case with weaker natures, he was able to render distinguished service to his country. Other American ministers have been greater and more successful

diplomats than Morris was ; but no one has better
represented those qualities of generous daring and
lofty disinterestedness which we like to associate
with the name American, than did the minister
who, alone among the foreign ministers, kept his
residence in Paris through the " Terror." He
stood for order. He stood for the honest payment of debts. Unlike many of his colleagues, he
was a polished man of the world, whose comments
on men and things showed that curious insight
and power of observation which come only when
to natural ability there is added special training.
But he distrusted the mass of the people, and especially the mass of the people in other sections of
the country than his own, who had not the habits
of refinement and the ways of looking at life
which he and his associates possessed ; and thus
it happened that, when the Federalists sank into
a secessionist faction, the name of Gouverneur
Morris was associated with the names of the others
who at that time lacked the power, but not the
will, to split a great nation into a chaos of feeble
and quarrelsome little states.

THEODORE ROOSEVELT.

WASHINGTON, April, 1898.

CONTENTS

ILLUSTRATIONS

GOUVERNEUR MORRIS

CHAPTER I

HIS YOUTH: COLONIAL NEW YORK

WHEN on January 31, 1752, Gouverneur Morris was born in the family manor-house at Morrisania, on the lands where his forefathers had dwelt for three generations, New York colony contained only some eighty thousand inhabitants, of whom twelve thousand were blacks. New York city was a thriving little trading town, whose people in summer suffered much from the mosquitoes that came back with the cows when they were driven home at nightfall for milking; while from among the locusts and water-beeches that lined the pleasant, quiet streets, the tree frogs sang so shrilly through the long, hot evenings that a man in speaking could hardly make himself heard.

Gouverneur Morris belonged by birth to that powerful landed aristocracy whose rule was known by New York alone among all the northern colonies. His great-grandfather, who had served in the Cromwellian armies, came to the seaport at the

mouth of the Hudson, while it was still beneath
the sway of Holland, and settled outside of Haer-
lem, the estate being invested with manorial privileges by the original grant of the governor. In the
next two generations the Morrises had played a
prominent part in colonial affairs, both the father
and grandfather of Gouverneur having been on the
bench, and having also been members of the provincial legislature, where they took the popular
side, and stood up stoutly for the rights of the
Assembly in the wearisome and interminable con-
flicts waged by the latter against the prerogatives
of the crown and the powers of the royal governors.
The Morrises were restless, adventurous men, of
erratic temper and strong intellect ; and, with far
more than his share of the family talent and brilliancy, young Gouverneur also inherited a certain
whimsical streak that ran through his character.
His mother was one of the Huguenot Gouverneurs,
who had been settled in New York since the revo-
cation of the Edict of Nantes ; and it was perhaps
the French blood in his veins that gave him the
alert vivacity and keen sense of humor that distinguished him from most of the great Revolutionary
statesmen who were his contemporaries.

He was a bright, active boy, fond of shooting
and out-door sports, and was early put to school at
the old Huguenot settlement of New Rochelle,
where the church service was still sometimes held
in French ; and he there learned to speak and
write this language almost as well as he could

English. Thence, after the usual preparatory instruction, he went to King's College — now, with
altered name and spirit, Columbia — in New York.
The years of his childhood were stirring ones for
the colonies; for England was then waging the
greatest and most successful of her colonial contests with France and Spain for the possession of
eastern North America. Such contests, with their
usual savage accompaniments in the way of Indian
warfare, always fell with especial weight on New
York, whose border lands were not only claimed,
but even held by the French, and within whose
boundaries lay the great confederacy of the Six
Nations, the most crafty, warlike, and formidable
of all the native races, infinitely more to be dreaded
than the Algonquin tribes with whom the other
colonies had to deal. Nor was this war any exception to the rule; for battle after battle was fought
on our soil, from the day when, unassisted, the
purely colonial troops of New York and New England at Lake George destroyed Baron Dieskau's
mixed host of French regulars, Canadian militia,
and Indian allies, to that still more bloody day
when, on the shores of Lake Champlain, Abercrombie's great army of British and Americans
recoiled before the fiery genius of Montcalm.

When once the war was ended by the complete
and final overthrow of the French power, and the
definite establishment of English supremacy along
the whole Atlantic seaboard, the bickering which
was always going on between Great Britain and

her American subjects, and which was but partially suppressed even when they were forced to join in common efforts to destroy a common foe, broke out far more fiercely than ever. While the colonists were still reaping the aftermath of the contest in the shape of desolating border warfare against those Indian tribes who had joined in the famous conspiracy of Pontiac, the Royal Parliament passed the Stamp Act, and thereby began the struggle thàt ended in the Revolution.

England's treatment of her American subjects was thoroughly selfish ; but that her conduct towards them was a wonder of tyranny will not now be seriously asserted ; on the contrary, she stood decidedly above the general European standard in such matters, and certainly treated her colonies far better than France and Spain did theirs ; and she herself had undoubted grounds for complaint in, for example, the readiness of the Americans to claim military help in time of danger, together with their frank reluctance to pay for it. It was impossible that she should be so far in advance of the age as to treat her colonists as equals ; they themselves were sometimes quite as intolerant in their behavior towards men of a different race, creed, or color. The New England Puritans lacked only the power, but not the will, to behave almost as badly towards the Pennsylvania Quakers as did the Episcopalian English towards themselves. Yet granting all this, the fact remains, that in the Revolutionary war the Americans stood towards

the British as the Protestant peoples stood towards
the Catholic powers in the sixteenth century, as the
Parliamentarians stood towards the Stuarts in the
seventeenth, or as the upholders of the American
Union stood towards the Confederate slaveholders
in the nineteenth; that is, they warred victoriously
for the right in a struggle whose outcome vitally
affected the welfare of the whole human race.
They settled, once for all, that thereafter the people of English stock should spread at will over the
world's waste spaces, keeping all their old liberties
and winning new ones; and they took the first and
longest step in establishing the great principle that
thenceforth those Europeans, who by their strength
and daring founded new states abroad, should be
deemed to have done so for their own profit as
freemen, and not for the benefit of their more
timid, lazy, or contented brethren who stayed
behind.

The rulers of Great Britain, and to a large extent
its people, looked upon the American colonies as
existing primarily for the good of the mother country: they put the harshest restrictions on American
trade in the interests of British merchants; they
discouraged the spread of the Americans westward;
and they claimed the right to decide for both parties
the proportions in which they should pay their
shares of the common burdens. The English and
Americans were not the subjects of a common sovereign; for the English were themselves the sovereigns, the Americans were the subjects. Whether

their yoke bore heavily or bore lightly, whether it galled or not, mattered little; it was enough that it was a yoke to warrant a proud, free people in throwing it off. We could not thankfully take as a boon part only of what we felt to be our lawful due. " We do not claim liberty as a privilege, but challenge it as a right," said the men of New York, through their legislature, in 1764; and all Americans felt with them.

Yet, for all this, the feeling of loyalty was strong and hard to overcome throughout the provinces, and especially in New York. The Assembly wrangled with the royal governor; the merchants and shipmasters combined to evade the intolerable harshness of the laws of trade that tried to make them customers of England only; the householders bitterly resented the attempts to quarter troops upon them; while the soldiers of the garrison were from time to time involved in brawls with the lower ranks of the people, especially the sailors, as the seafaring population was large, and much given to forcibly releasing men taken by the press-gang for the British warships; but in spite of everything there was a genuine sentiment of affection and respect for the British crown and kingdom. It is perfectly possible that if British statesmen had shown less crass and brutal stupidity, if they had shown even the wise negligence of Walpole, this feeling of loyalty would have been strong enough to keep England and America united until they had learned how to accommodate themselves to the rapidly changing conditions; but the chance was lost when once a prince like George the Third came to the throne. It has been the fashion to represent this king as a well meaning, though dull person, whose good morals and excellent intentions partially atoned for his mistakes of judgment; but such a view is curiously false. His private life, it is true, showed the very admirable but commonplace virtues, as well as the appalling intellectual littleness, barrenness, and stagnation, of the average British green-grocer; but in his public career, instead of rising to the level of harmless and unimportant mediocrity usually reached by the sovereigns of the House of Hanover, he fairly rivaled the Stuarts in his perfidy, wrongheadedness, political debauchery, and attempts to destroy free government, and to replace it by a system of personal despotism. It needed all the successive blunders both of himself and of his Tory ministers to reduce the loyal party in New York to a minority, by driving the moderate men into the patriotic or American camp; and even then the loyalist minority remained large enough to be a formidable power, and to plunge the embryonic state into a ferocious civil war, carried on, as in the Carolinas and Georgia, with even more bitterness than the contest against the British.

The nature of this loyalist party and the strength of the conflicting elements can only be understood after a glance at the many nationalities that in New York were being blended into one. The descendants of the old Dutch inhabitants were still more

numerous than those of any other one race, while the
French Huguenots, who, being of the same Calvinistic faith, were closely mixed with them, and had
been in the land nearly as long, were also plentiful;
the Scotch and Scotch- or Anglo-Irish, mostly Presbyterians, came next in point of numbers; the
English, both of Old and New England, next; there
were large bodies of Germans; and there were also
settlements of Gaelic Highlanders, and some Welsh,
Scandinavians, etc. Just prior to the Revolution
there were in New York city two Episcopalian
churches, three Dutch Reformed, three Presbyterian (Scotch and Irish), one French, two German
(one Lutheran and one Calvinistic, allied to the
Dutch Reformed); as well as places of worship for
the then insignificant religious bodies of the Meth-
odists, Baptists (largely Welsh), Moravians (German), Quakers, and Jews. There was no Roman
Catholic church until after the Revolution; in fact
before that date there were hardly any Roman
Catholics in the colonies, except in Maryland and
Pennsylvania, and in New York they did not acquire any strength until after the war of 1812.

This mixture of races is very clearly shown by
the ancestry of the half-dozen great men brought
forth by New York during the Revolution. Of
these, one, Alexander Hamilton, stands in the very
first class of American statesmen; two more, John
Jay and Gouverneur Morris, come close behind
him; the others, Philip Schuyler, Robert Livingston, and George Clinton, were of lesser, but still

of more than merely local, note. They were all born and bred on this side of the Atlantic. Hamilton's father was of Scotch, and his mother of French Huguenot, descent; Morris came on one side of English, and on the other of French Huguenot, stock; Jay, of French Huguenot blood, had a mother who was Dutch; Schuyler was purely Dutch; Livingston was Scotch on his father's, and Dutch on his mother's, side; the Clintons were of Anglo-Irish origin, but married into the old Dutch families. In the same way, it was Herkomer, of German parentage, who led the New York levies, and fell at their head in the bloody fight against the Tories and Indians at Oriskany; it was the Irishman Montgomery who died leading the New York troops against Quebec; while yet another of the few generals allotted to New York by the Continental Congress was MacDougall, of Gaelic Scotch descent. The colony was already developing an ethnic type of its own, quite distinct from that of England. No American State of the present day, not even Wisconsin or Minnesota, shows so many and important " foreign " or non-English elements as New York, and for that matter Pennsylvania and Delaware, did a century or so ago. In fact, in New York the English element in the blood has grown greatly during the past century, owing to the enormous New England immigration that took place during its first half; and the only important addition to the race conglomerate has been made by the Celtic Irish. The New Eng-

land element in New York in 1775 was small
and unimportant; on Long Island, where it was
largest, it was mainly Tory or neutral; in the city
itself, however, it was aggressively patriotic.

Recent English writers, and some of our own as
well, have foretold woe to our nation, because the
blood of the Cavalier and the Roundhead is being
diluted with that of " German boors and Irish cotters." The alarm is needless. As a matter of fact
the majority of the people of the middle colonies
at the time of the Revolution *were* the descendants of Dutch and German boors and Scotch and
Irish cotters; and in a less degree the same was
true of Georgia and the Carolinas. Even in New
England, where the English stock was purest, there
was plenty of other admixture, and two of her
most distinguished Revolutionary families bore,
one the Huguenot name of Bowdoin, and the other
the Irish name of Sullivan. Indeed, from the very
outset, from the days of Cromwell, there has been
a large Irish admixture in New England. When
our people began their existence as a nation, they
already differed in blood from their ancestral relatives across the Atlantic much as the latter did
from their forebears beyond the German Ocean;
and on the whole, the immigration since has not
materially changed the race strains in our nationality; a century back we were even less homoge-
neous than we are now. It is no doubt true that
we are in the main an offshoot of the English
stem; and cousins to our kinsfolk of Britain we

perhaps may be; but brothers we certainly are not.

But the process of assimilating, or as we should now say, of Americanizing, all foreign and non-English elements was going on almost as rapidly a hundred years ago as it is at present. A young Dutchman or Huguenot felt it necessary, then, to learn English, precisely as a young Scandinavian or German does now; and the churches of the former at the end of the last century were obliged to adopt English as the language for their ritual exactly as the churches of the latter do at the end of this. The most stirring, energetic, and progressive life of the colony was English; and all the young fellows of push and ambition gradually adopted this as their native language, and then refused to belong to congregations where the service was carried on in a less familiar speech. Accordingly the Dutch Reformed churches dwindled steadily, while the Episcopalian and Presbyterian swelled in the same ratio, until in 1764 the former gained a new and lasting lease of life by reluctantly adopting the prevailing tongue; though Dutch was also occasionally used until forty years later.

In fact, during the century that elapsed between the final British conquest of the colony and the Revolution, the New Yorkers — Dutch, French, German, Irish, and English — had become in the main welded into one people; they felt alike towards outsiders, having chronic quarrels with the

New England States as well as with Great Britain,
and showing, indeed, but little more jealous hostility
towards the latter than they did towards Connecticut and New Hampshire.

The religious differences no longer corresponded
to the differences of language. Half of the adherents of the Episcopalian Church were of Dutch or
Huguenot blood; the leading ministers of the Dutch
Church were of Scotch parentage; and the Presbyterians included some of every race. The colonists
were all growing to call themselves Englishmen;
when Mayor Cruger, and a board of aldermen with
names equally Dutch, signed the non-importation
agreement, they prefaced it by stating that they
claimed " their rights as Englishmen." But though
there were no rivalries of race, there were many
and bitter of class and religion, the different Protestant sects hating one another with a virulence
much surpassing that with which they now regard
even Catholics.

The colony was in government an aristocratic republic, its constitution modeled on that of England
and similar to it; the power lay in the hands of
certain old and wealthy families, Dutch and English, and there was a limited freehold suffrage.
The great landed families, the Livingstons, Van
Rensselaers, Schuylers, Van Cortlandts, Phillipses,
Morrises, with their huge manorial estates, their
riches, their absolute social preëminence and their
unquestioned political headship, formed a proud,
polished, and powerful aristocracy, deep rooted in

the soil; for over a century their sway was unbroken, save by contests between themselves or
with the royal governor, and they furnished the
colony with military, political, and social leaders for
generation after generation. They owned numerous black slaves, and lived in state and comfort on
their broad acres, tenant-farmed, in the great, roomy
manor-houses, with wainscoted walls and huge fire-
places, and round about the quaint old gardens,
prim and formal with their box hedges and precise
flower beds. They answered closely to the Whig
lords of England, and indeed were often connected
with the ruling orders abroad by blood or marriage;
as an example, Staats Long Morris, Gouverneur's
elder brother, who remained a royalist, and rose to
be a major-general in the British army, married
the Duchess of Gordon. Some of the manors were
so large that they sent representatives to the Albany legislature, to sit alongside of those from the
towns and counties.

Next in importance to the great manorial lords
came the rich merchants of New York; many
families, like the Livingstons, the most prominent
of all, had representatives in both classes. The
merchants were somewhat of the type of Frobisher,
Hawkins, Klaesoon, and other old English and
Dutch sea-worthies, who were equally keen as
fighters and traders. They were shrewd, daring,
and prosperous; they were often their own shipmasters, and during the incessant wars against the
French and Spaniards went into privateering ven-

tures with even more zest and spirit than into peaceful trading. Next came the smaller landed proprietors, who also possessed considerable local influence; such was the family of the Clintons. The law, too, was beginning to take high rank as an honorable and influential profession.

Most of the gentry were Episcopalians, theirs being practically the state church, and very influential and wealthy; some belonged to the Calvinistic bodies, — notably the Livingstons, who were in large part Presbyterians, while certain of their number were prominent members of the Dutch congregations. It was from among the gentry that the little group of New York revolutionary leaders came; men of singular purity, courage, and ability, who, if they could not quite rank with the brilliant Virginians of that date, nevertheless stood close behind, alongside of the Massachusetts men and ahead of those from any other colony; that, too, it must be kept in mind, at a time when New York was inferior in wealth and population to Massachusetts, Pennsylvania, or Virginia, and little, if at all, in advance of Maryland or Connecticut. The great families also furnished the leaders of the loyalists during the war; such were the De Lanceys, whose influence around the mouth of the Hudson was second to that of none others; and the Johnsons, who, in mansions that were also castles, held half-feudal, half-barbaric sway over the valley of the upper Mohawk, where they were absolute rulers, ready and willing to wage war on their own account, relying on their numerous kinsmen, their armed negro slaves, their trained bands of Gaelic retainers, and their hosts of savage allies, drawn from among the dreaded Iroquois.

The bulk of the people were small farmers in the country, tradesmen and mechanics in the towns. They were for the most part members of some of the Calvinistic churches, the great majority of the whole population belonging to the Presbyterian and Dutch Reformed congregations. The farmers were thrifty, set in their ways, and obstinate; the townsmen thrifty also, but restless and turbulent. Both farmers and townsmen were thoroughly independent and self-respecting, and were gradually getting more and more political power. They had always stood tenaciously by their rights, from the days of the early Stuart governors, who had complained loudly of the " Dutch Republicans." But they were narrow, jealous of each other, as well as of outsiders, and slow to act together.

The political struggles were very bitter. The great families, under whose banners they were carried on, though all intermarried, were divided by keen rivalries into opposing camps. Yet they joined in dreading too great an extension of democracy; and in return were suspected by the masses, who grumblingly followed their lead, of hostility to the popular cause. The Episcopalians, though greatly in the minority, possessed most power, and harassed in every way they dared the dissenting sects, especially the Presbyterians — for the

Dutch Reformed and Huguenot churches had certain rights guaranteed them by treaty. The Episcopalian clergy were royalists to a man, and it was in their congregations that the main strength of the Tories lay, although these also contained many who became the stanchest of patriots. King's College was controlled by trustees of this faith. They were busy trying to turn it into a diminutive imitation of Oxford, and did their best to make it, in its own small way, almost as much a perverse miracle of backward and invariable wrong-headedness as was its great model. Its president, when the Revolution broke out, was a real old wine-bibbing Tory parson, devoted to every worn-out theory that inculcated humble obedience to church and crown; and he was most summarily expelled by the mob.

Some important political consequences arose from the fact that the mass of the people belonged to some one or other of the branches of the Calvinistic faith — of all faiths the most republican in its tendencies. They were strongly inclined to put their republican principles into practice as well in state as in church; they tended towards hostility to the crown, and were strenuous in their opposition to the extension of the Episcopal power, always threatened by some English statesmen; their cry was against "the King and the Bishops." It is worth noting that the Episcopalian churches were shut up when the Revolution broke out, and were reopened when the British troops occupied

the city. The Calvinistic churches, on the contrary, which sided with the revolutionists, were
shut when the British came into New York, were
plundered by the troops, and were not reopened
until after the evacuation.

Thus three parties developed, although the third,
destined to overwhelm the others, had not yet come
to the front. The first consisted of the royalists,
or monarchists, the men who believed that power
came from above, from the king and the bishops,
and who were aristocratic in their sympathies ; who
were Americans only secondarily, and who stood
by their order against their country. This party
contained many of the great manorial families and
also of the merchants ; and in certain places, as in
Staten Island, the east end of Long Island, the
upper valley of the Mohawk, and part of Westchester County, the influence of the upper classes
combined with the jealousy and ignorance of large
sections of the lower to give it a clear majority
of the whole population. The second party was
headed by the great families of Whig or liberal
sympathies, who, when the split came, stood by
their country, although only very moderate republicans ; and it held also in its ranks the mass of
moderate men, who wished freedom, were resolute
in defense of their rights, and had republican leanings, but who also appreciated the good in the
system under which they were living. Finally
came the extremists, the men of strong republican
tendencies, whose delight it was to toast Pym,

Hampden, and the regicides. These were led by the agitators in the towns, and were energetic and active, but were unable to effect anything until the blunders of the British ministers threw the moderate men over to their side. They furnished none of the greater revolutionary leaders in New York, though the Clintons came near the line that divided them from the second party.

The last political contest carried on under the crown occurred in 1768, the year in which Morris graduated from college, when the last colonial legislature was elected. It reminds us of our own days when we read of the fears entertained of the solid German vote, and of the hostility to the Irish, who were hated and sneered at as " beggars " by the English party and the rich Episcopalians. The Irish of those days, however, were Presbyterians, and in blood more English than Gaelic. St. Patrick's Day was celebrated then as now, by public processions, as well as otherwise; but when, for instance, on March 17, 1766, the Irish residents of New York celebrated the day by a dinner, they gave certain toasts that would sound strangely in the ears of Milesian patriots of the present time, for they included " The Protestant Interest," and " King William, of glorious, pious, and immortal memory."

The royalist or conservative side in this contest in 1768 was led by the De Lanceys, their main support being drawn from among the Episcopalians, and most of the larger merchants helping them.

The Whigs, including those with republican leanings, followed the Livingstons, and were drawn
mainly from the Presbyterian and other Calvinistic
congregations. The moderate men on this occasion
went with the De Lanceys, and gave them the victory. In consequence the colonial legislature was
conservative and loyal in tone, and anti-republican,
although not ultra-Tory, as a whole ; and thus when
the Revolutionary outbreak began it went much
slower than was satisfactory to the patriot party,
and its actions were finally set aside by the people.

When Morris graduated from college, as mentioned above, he was not yet seventeen years old.
His college career was like that of any other bright,
quick boy, without over much industry or a passion
for learning. For mathematics he possessed a genuine taste; he was particularly fond of Shake-
speare ; and even thus early he showed great skill
in discussion and much power of argument. He
made the oration, or graduating address, of his class,
choosing for the subject " Wit and Beauty; " it was
by no means a noteworthy effort, and was couched
in the dreadful Johnsonian English of the period.
A little later, when he took his master's degree, he
again delivered an oration, — this time on " Love."
In point of style this second speech was as bad as
the first, disfigured by cumbrous Latinisms and a
hopeless use of the superlative ; but there were one
or two good ideas in it.

As soon as he graduated, he set to work to study
law, deciding on this profession at once as being

best suited for an active, hopeful, ambitious young
man of his social standing and small fortune, who
was perfectly self-confident and conscious of his
own powers. He soon became interested in his
studies, and followed them with great patience,
working hard and mastering both principles and
details with ease. He was licensed to practice as
an attorney in 1771, just three years after another
young man, destined to stand as his equal in the
list of New York's four or five noted statesmen,
John Jay, had likewise been admitted to the bar;
and among the very few cases in which Morris was
engaged of which the record has been kept is one
concerning a contested election, in which he was
pitted against Jay, and bore himself well.

Before this, and while not yet of age, he had
already begun to play a part in public affairs. The
colony had been run in debt during the French and
Indian wars, and a bill was brought forward in the
New York Assembly to provide for this by raising
money through the issue of interest-bearing bills of
credit. The people, individually, were largely in
debt, and hailed the proposal with much satisfaction,
on the theory that it would "make money more
plenty;" our Revolutionary forefathers being unfortunately not much wiser or more honest in their
ways of looking at the public finances than we ourselves, in spite of our state repudiators, national
greenbackers, and dishonest silver men.

Morris attacked the bill very forcibly, and with
good effect, opposing any issue of paper money,

which could bring no absolute relief, but merely a
worse catastrophe of bankruptcy in the end; he
pointed out that it was nothing but a mischievous
pretense for putting off the date of a payment that
would have to be met anyhow, and that ought rather
to be met at once with honest money gathered from
the resources of the province. He showed the bad
effects such a system of artificial credit would have
on private individuals, the farmers and tradesmen,
by encouraging them to speculate and go deeper
into debt; and he criticised unsparingly the attitude of the majority of his fellow citizens in wishing
such a measure of relief, not only for their short-
sighted folly, but also for their criminal and selfish
dishonesty in trying to procure a temporary benefit
for themselves at the lasting expense of the community; finally he strongly advised them to bear
with patience small evils in the present rather than
to remedy them by inflicting infinitely greater ones
on themselves and their descendants in the future.

At the law he did very well, having the advantages of his family name, and of his own fine
personal appearance. He was utterly devoid of
embarrassment, and his perfect self-assurance and
freedom from any timidity or sense of inferiority
left his manner without the least tinge of awkwardness, and gave clear ground for his talents and
ambition to make their mark.

However, hardworking and devoted to his profession though he was, he had the true family rest-
lessness and craving for excitement, and soon after

he was admitted to the bar he began to long for
foreign travel, as was natural enough in a young
provincial gentleman of his breeding and education.
In a letter to an old friend (William Smith, a
man of learning, the historian of the colony, and
afterwards its chief justice), in whose office he had
studied law, he asks advice in the matter, and
gives as his reasons for wishing to make the trip
the desire " to form my manners and address by
the example of the truly polite, to rub off in the
gay circle a few of the many barbarisms which
characterize a provincial education, and to curb
the vain self-sufficiency which arises from comparing ourselves with companions who are inferior to
us." He then anticipates the objections that may
be made on the score of the temptations to which
he will be exposed by saying: " If it be allowed
that I have a *taste* for pleasure, it may naturally
follow that I shall avoid those low pleasures which
abound on this as well as on the other side of the
Atlantic. As for these poignant joys which are
the lot of the affluent, like Tantalus I may grasp at
them, but they will certainly be out of my reach."
In this last sentence he touches on his narrow
means; and it was on this point that his old pre-
ceptor harped in making his reply, cunningly in-
stilling into his mind the danger of neglecting his
business, and bringing up the appalling example of
an " Uncle Robin," who, having made three pleasure trips to England, " began to figure with thirty
thousand pounds, and did not leave five thousand;"

going on: "What! '*Virtus post nummos?* Curse
on inglorious wealth?' Spare your indignation.
I, too, detest the ignorant miser; but both virtue
and ambition abhor poverty, or they are mad.
Rather imitate your grandfather [who had stayed
in America and prospered] than your uncle."

The advice may have had its effect; at any rate
 Morris stayed at home, and, with an occasional trip
to Philadelphia, got all he could out of the society
of New York, which, little provincial seaport though
it was, was yet a gay place, gayer than any other
American city save Charleston, the society consisting of the higher crown officials, the rich merchants, and the great landed proprietors. Into
this society Morris, a handsome, high-bred young
fellow, of easy manners and far from puritanical
morals, plunged with a will, his caustic wit and
rather brusque self-assertion making him both admired and feared. He enjoyed it all to the full,
and in his bright, chatty letters to his friends pic-
tures himself as working hard, but gay enough
also: "up all night — balls, concerts, assemblies —
all of us. mad in the pursuit of pleasure."

But the Revolution was at hand; and both pleasure and office-work had to give way to something
more important.

CHAPTER II

THE OUTBREAK OF THE REVOLUTION: MORRIS IN THE PROVINCIAL CONGRESS

DURING the years immediately preceding the outbreak of the Revolution, almost all people were utterly in the dark as to what their future conduct should be. No responsible leader thought seriously of separation from the mother country, and the bulk of the population were still farther from supposing such an event to be possible. Indeed it must be remembered that all through the Revolutionary war not only was there a minority actively favorable to the royal cause, but there was also a minority — so large that, added to the preceding, it has been doubted whether it was not a majority — that was but lukewarm in its devotion to the American side, and was kept even moderately patriotic almost as much by the excesses of the British troops and blunders of the British generals and ministers as by the valor of our own soldiers, or the skill of our own statesmen. We can now see clearly that the right of the matter was with the patriotic party; and it was a great thing for the whole English-speaking race that that section of it which was destined to be the most numerous and

powerful should not be cramped and fettered by
the peculiarly galling shackles of provincial de-
pendency; but all this was not by any means so
clear then as now, and some of our best citizens
thought themselves in honor bound to take the
opposite side, — though of necessity those among
our most high-minded men, who were also far-
sighted enough to see the true nature of the struggle, went with the patriots.

That the loyalists of 1776 were wrong is beyond
question; but it is equally beyond question that
they had greater grounds for believing themselves
right than had the men who tried to break up the
Union three quarters of a century later.   That
these latter had the most hearty faith in the justice
of their cause need not be doubted; and he is but
a poor American whose veins do not thrill with
pride as he reads of the deeds of desperate prowess
done by the Confederate armies; but it is most
unfair to brand the " Tory" of 1776 with a shame
no longer felt to pertain to the " rebel" of 1860.
Still, there is no doubt, not only that the patriots
were right, but also that they were as a whole
superior to the Tories; they were the men with a
high ideal of freedom, too fond of liberty, and
too self-respecting, to submit to foreign rule; they
included the mass of hard-working, orderly, and yet
high-spirited yeomen and freeholders.   The Tories
included those of the gentry who were devoted to
aristocratic principles; the large class of timid and
prosperous people (like the Pennsylvania Qua-

kers) ; the many who feared above all things disorder ; also the very lowest sections of the community, the lazy, thriftless, and vicious, who hated
their progressive neighbors, as in the Carolinas ;
and finally the men who were really principled in
favor of a kingly government.

Morris was at first no more sure of his soundings
than were the rest of his companions.   He was
a gentleman of old family, and belonged to the
ruling Episcopalian Church.   He was no friend
to tyranny, and he was a thorough American, but
he had little faith in extreme democracy.   The
Revolution had two sides ; in the northern Atlantic
States at least it was almost as much an uprising
of democracy against aristocracy as it was a contest
between America and England ; and the patriotic
Americans, who nevertheless distrusted ultra-democratic ideas, suffered many misgivings when they
let their love for their country overcome their pride
of caste.   The "Sons of Liberty," a semi-secret
society originating among the merchants, and very
powerful in bringing discontent to a head, now
showed signs of degenerating into a mob ; and for
mobs Morris, like other clear-headed men, felt the
most profound dislike and contempt.

Throughout 1774 he took little part in the various commotions, which kept getting more and more
violent.   He was angered by the English encroachments, and yet was by no means pleased with the
measures taken to repel them.   The gentry, and
the moderate men generally, were at their wits'

ends in trying to lead the rest of the people, and
were being pushed on farther and farther all the
time; the leadership, even of the Revolutionary
party, still rested in their hands; but it grew continually less absolute. Said Morris: "The spirit
of the English Constitution has yet a little influence left, and but a little. The remains of it, however, will give the wealthy people a superiority this
time; but, would they secure it, they must banish
all schoolmasters and confine all knowledge to
themselves. . . . The gentry begin to fear this.
Their committee will be appointed; they will
deceive the people, and again forfeit a share of
their confidence. And if these instances of what
with one side is policy, with the other perfidy, shall
continue to increase and become more frequent,
farewell, aristocracy. I see, and see it with fear
and trembling, that if the dispute with Britain continues, we shall be under the worst of all possible
dominions; we shall be under the dominion of a
riotous mob. It is the interest of all men, therefore, to seek for reunion with the parent state."
He then goes on to discuss the terms which will
make this reunion possible, and evidently draws
ideas from sources as diverse as Rousseau and
Pitt, stating, as preliminaries, that when men come
together in society, there must be an implied contract that "a part of their freedom shall be given
up for the security of the remainder. But what
part? The answer is plain. The least possible,
considering the circumstances of the society, which

constitute what may be called its political necessity; " and again : " In every society the members
have a right to the utmost liberty that can be
enjoyed consistent with the general safety; " while
he proposes the rather wild remedy of divorcing
the taxing and the governing powers, giving America the right to lay her own imposts, and regulate
her internal police, and reserving to Great Britain
that to regulate the trade for the entire empire.

Naturally there was no hope of any compromise of this sort. The British ministry grew more
imperious, and the colonies more defiant. At last
the clash came, and then Morris's thorough Amer-
icanism and inborn love of freedom and impatience of tyranny overcame any lingering class
jealousy, and he cast in his lot with his countrymen. Once in, he was not of the stuff to waver or
look back ; but like most other Americans, and
like almost all New Yorkers, he could not for some
little time realize how hopeless it was to try to
close the breach with Great Britain. Hostilities
had gone on for quite a while before even Washington could bring himself to believe that a lasting separation was inevitable.

The Assembly, elected, as shown in the previous
chapter, at a moment of reaction, was royalist in
tone. It contained several stanch patriots, but the
majority, although unwilling to back up the British
ministers in all their doings, were still more hostile
to the growing body of republican revolutionists.
They gradually grew wholly out of sympathy with

the people; until the latter at last gave up all attempts to act through their ordinary representatives, and set about electing delegates who should prove more faithful. Thereupon, in April, 1775, the last colonial legislature adjourned for all time, and was replaced by successive bodies more in touch with the general sentiment of New York; that is, by various committees, by a convention to elect delegates to the Continental Congress, and then by the Provincial Congress. The lists of names in these bodies show not only how many leading men certain families contributed, but also how mixed the lineage of such families was; for among the numerous Jays, Livingstons, Ludlows, Van Cortlandts, Roosevelts, Beekmans, and others of Dutch, English, and Huguenot ancestry, appear names as distinctly German, Gaelic-Scotch, and Irish, like Hoffman, Mulligan, MacDougall, Connor.[1]

---

[1] The habit of constantly importing indentured Irish servants, as well as German laborers, under contract, prevailed throughout the colonies; and the number of men thus imported was quite sufficient to form a considerable element in the population, and to add a new, although perhaps not very valuable, strain to our already mixed blood. In taking up at random the file of the *New York Gazette* for 1766, we find among the advertisements many offering rewards for runaway servants; such as " three pounds for the runaway servant Conner O'Rourke," " ten pounds for the runaway Irish servant, Philip Maginnis," " five pounds apiece for certain runaway German miners — Bruderlein, Baum, Ostmann, etc. — imported under contract; " all this mixed in with advertisements of rewards of about the same money value for " the mulatto man named Tom," or the " negroes Nero and Pompey." Still, in speaking of the Revolutionary armies, the word "Irish" must almost always be understood as meaning Presbyterian Irish; the

To the Provincial Congress, from thenceforth on the regular governmental body of the colony, eighty-one delegates were elected, including Gouverneur Morris from the county of Westchester, and seventy were present at the first meeting, which took place on May 22 at New York. The voting in the Congress was done by counties, each being allotted a certain number of votes roughly approximating to its population.

Lexington had been fought, and the war had already begun in Massachusetts; but in New York, though it was ablaze with sympathy for the insurgent New Englanders, the royal authority was still nominally unquestioned, and there had been no collision with the British troops. Few, if any, of the people of the colony as yet aimed at more than a redress of their grievances and the restoration of their rights and liberties; they had still no idea of cutting loose from Great Britain. Even such an avowedly popular and revolutionary body as the Provincial Congress contained some few out and out Tories and very many representatives of that timid, wavering class which always halts midway

Catholic Irish had but little hand in the war, and that little was limited to furnishing soldiers to some of the British regiments. The Presbyterian Irish, however, in the Revolutionary armies, played a part as manful and valiant as, and even more important than, that taken by the Catholic Irish soldiers who served so bravely during the great contest between the North and South. The few free Catholic Irish already in America in 1776 were for the most part heartily loyal; but they were not numerous enough to be of the least consequence.

in any course of action, and is ever prone to adopt
half measures, — a class which in any crisis works
quite as much harm as the actively vicious, and is
almost as much hated and even more despised by
the energetic men of strong convictions. The timid
good are never an element of strength in a community; but they have always been well represented in New York. During the Revolutionary
war, it is not probable that much more than half of
her people were ever in really hearty and active
sympathy with the patriots.

Morris at once took a prominent place in the
Congress, and he showed the national bent of his
mind when he seconded a resolution to the effect
that implicit obedience ought to be rendered to the
Continental Congress in all matters pertaining to
the general regulation of the associated colonies.
The Assembly, however, was by no means certain
how far it would be well to go; and the majority
declined either to approve or disapprove of the proceedings of the late Continental Congress. They
agreed to subscribe to the association, and recommended the same course to their constituents, but
added that they did not believe the latter should
be forced to do so.

Still, with all their doubting and faint-hearted-
ness, they did set about preparing for resistance,
and for at least the possibility of concerted action
with the other colonies. The first step, of course,
was to provide for raising funds; this was considered by a committee of which Morris was a mem-

ber, and he prepared and drew up their report. In the state of public feeling, which was nearly a unit against " taxation without representation " abroad, but was the reverse of unanimous as to submitting even to taxation with representation at home, it was impossible to raise money by the ordinary method ; indeed, though the mass of active patriots were willing to sacrifice much, perhaps all, for the cause, yet there were quite as many citizens whose patriotism was lukewarm enough already, and could not stand any additional chilling. Such people are always willing to face what may be called a staved-off sacrifice, however ; and promises to pay in the future what they can, but will not pay in the present, come under this head. Besides, there would have been other difficulties in the way, and in fact it was impossible to raise the amount needed by direct taxation. Accordingly Morris, in his report on behalf of the committee, recommended an issue of paper money, and advised that this should not be done by the colony itself, but that the Continental Congress should strike the whole sum needed, and apportion the several shares to the different colonies, each of them being bound to discharge its own particular part, and all together to be liable for whatever any particular colony was unable to pay. This plan secured a wide credit and circulation to the currency, and, what was equally desirable, created throughout the colonies a common interest and common responsibility on a most important point, and greatly strengthened the bonds of their union. Morris even thus early showed the breadth of his far-seeing patriotism; he was emphatically an American first, a New Yorker next; the whole tone of his mind was thoroughly national. He took the chief part in urging the adoption of the report, and made a most telling speech in its favor before the Assembly, a mixed audience of the prominent men of the colony being also present. The report was adopted and forwarded to the Continental Congress; Morris was felt on all sides to have already taken his place among the leaders, and from thenceforth he was placed on almost every important committee of the Provincial Congress.

This body kept on its course, corresponding with the other colonies, exchanging thinly veiled threats with the Johnsons, the powerful Tory overlords of the upper Mohawk, and preparing rather feebly for defense, being hampered by a total lack of funds or credit until the Continental currency was coined. But they especially busied themselves with a plan of reconciliation with England; and in fact were so very cautious and moderate as to be reproached by their chosen agent in England, Edmund Burke, for their " scrupulous timidity." The Congress, by the way, showed some symptoms of an advance in toleration, at least so far as the Protestant sects went; for it was opened and closed by ministers of the Episcopalian, Dutch Reformed, Presbyterian, Baptist, and other sects, each in turn; but, as will shortly be seen, the feeling against Catholics was quite as narrow-minded and intense as ever. This was natural enough in colonial days, when Protestantism and national patriotism were almost interchangeable terms; for the hereditary and embittered foes of the Americans, the French and Spaniards, were all Catholics, and even many of the Indians were of the same faith; and undoubtedly the wonderful increase in the spirit of tolerance shown after the Revolution was due in part to the change of the Catholic French into our allies, and of the Protestant English into our most active foes. It must be remembered, however, that the Catholic gentry of Maryland played the same part in the Revolution that their Protestant neighbors did. One of the famous Carroll family was among the signers of the Declaration of Independence; and, on the other hand, one of the Cliftons was a noted loyalist leader.

Morris took a prominent part, both in and out of committee, in trying to shape the plan of reconciliation, although utterly disapproving of many of the ways in which the subject was handled; for he had all the contempt natural to most young men of brains, decision, and fiery temper for his timid, short-sighted, and prolix colleagues. The report was not all to his taste in the final shape in which it was adopted. It consisted of a series of articles recommending the repeal of the obnoxious statutes of the Imperial Parliament, the regulation of trade for the benefit of the whole empire, the establishment of triennial colonial legislatures, and also asserting the right of the colonies to manage their internal polity to suit themselves, and their willingness to do their part, according to their capacities, for the general defense of the empire. The eighth article contained a denial of the right of " Great Britain, or any other earthly legislature or tribunal, to interfere in the ecclesiastical or religious concerns of the colonies," together with a " protest against the indulgence and establishment of popery all along their interior confines ; " this being called forth by what was known as the " Quebec Bill," whereby the British Parliament had recently granted extraordinary powers and privileges to the Canadian clergy, with the obvious purpose of conciliating that powerful priesthood, and thereby converting — as was actually done — the recently conquered French of the St. Lawrence valley into efficient allies of the British government against the old Protestant colonies.

This eighth article was ridiculous, and was especially objected to by Morris. In one of his vigorous, deliciously fresh, and humorous letters, dated June 30, 1775, and addressed to John Jay, then in the Continental Congress, he writes : —

" The foolish religious business I opposed until I was weary ; it was carried by a very small majority, and my dissent entered. . . . The article about religion is most arrant nonsense, and would do as well in a high Dutch Bible as the place it now stands in.

" I drew a long report for our committee, to which they could make no objections excepting that none of them could understand it. . . . I was pleased at the rejection, because, as I observed to you before, I think the question ought to be simplified.

"I address this letter to you, but I shall be glad [if] you will read it to Livingston, for I intend it for both of you; make my compliments to him, and tell him that I shall write to him when I have time to write a good letter — this is a damned bad one, and would not exist, if I did not think it a duty to myself to show my friends that I had no hand in that foolish religious business. I am, as you well know, your friend, etc."

Morris did not believe in a colonial assembly making overtures for a reconciliation, as he thought this was the province of the Continental Congress. The majority was against him, but he was a clever politician and parliamentary tactician, as well as a great statesman, and he fairly outwitted and hood-winked his opponents, persuading them finally to adopt the report in the form of a mere expression of opinions to be sent to their congressional delegates, with a prayer that the latter would "use every effort for the compromising of this unnatural quarrel between the parent and child." In this shape it was forwarded to the delegates, who answered that they would do all in their power to compromise the quarrel, and added a postscript, written by Jay himself, to the effect that they deemed it better not to make any mention of the religious article before the Congress, as they thought it wise to bury "all disputes on ecclesiastical points, which have for ages had no other tendency than

that of banishing peace and charity from the
world."

While all this was pending, and though Bunker
Hill had been fought, and the war was in full progress round Boston, New York yet maintained
what might almost be described as an attitude of
armed neutrality.   The city was so exposed to the
British warships in the bay, and the surrounding
population was so doubtful, that the patriot party
dared not take the deciding steps, especially as so
many of its members still clung to the hope of a
peaceful settlement.   Morris announced frankly
that he did not believe in breaking the peace until
they were prepared to take the consequences.   Indeed, when the few British troops left the city to
join the garrison in Boston, he strongly opposed
the action of the Sons of Liberty, who gathered
hastily together, and took away the cartloads of
arms and ammunition that the soldiers were taking
with them.   The Congress, to their honor, discouraged, to the best of their power, the rioting and
mobbing of Tories in the city.

In fact, New York's position was somewhat like
that of Kentucky at the outbreak of the civil war.
Her backwardness in definitely throwing in her lot
with the revolutionists was clearly brought out by
a rather ludicrous incident.   General Washington,
on his way to take command of the Continental
army round Boston, passed through New York the
same day the royal governor, Tryon, arrived by
sea, and the authorities were cast into a great

quandary as to how they should treat two such kings of Brentford when the one rose was so small. Finally they compromised by sending a guard of honor to attend each; Montgomery and Morris, as delegates from the Assembly, received Washington and brought him before that body, which addressed him in terms of cordial congratulation, but ended with a noteworthy phrase, — that "when the contest should be decided by an accommodation with the mother country, he should deliver up the important deposit that had been confided to his hands."

These words give us the key to the situation. Even the patriots of the colony could not realize that there was no hope of an "accommodation;" and they were hampered at every step by the fear of the British frigates, and of the numerous Tories. The latter were very bold and defiant; when Congress tried to disarm them, they banded themselves together, bade the authorities defiance, and plainly held the upper hand on Staten Island and in Queens County. New York furnished many excellent soldiers to the royal armies during the war, and from among her gentry came the most famous of the Tory leaders, — such as Johnson and De Lancey, whose prowess was felt by the hapless people of their own native province; De Peyster, who was Ferguson's second in command at King's Mountain; and Cruger, who, in the Carolinas, inflicted a check upon Greene himself. The Tories were helped also by the jealousy felt towards some of the other colonies, especially Connecticut, whose people took the worst possible course for the patriot side by threatening to "crush down" New York, and by finally furnishing an armed and mounted mob which rode suddenly into the city, and wrecked the office of an obnoxious loyalist printer named Rivington. This last proceeding caused great indignation, and nearly made a split in the Revolutionary camp.

New York had thus some cause for her inaction; nevertheless, her lack of boldness and decision were not creditable to her, and she laid herself open to just reproaches. Nor can Morris himself be altogether freed from the charge of having clung too long to the hope of a reconciliation and to a policy of half measures. He was at that time chairman of a legislative committee which denounced any projected invasion of Canada (therein, however, only following the example of the Continental Congress), and refused to allow Ethan Allen to undertake one, as that adventurous partisan chieftain requested. But Morris was too clear-sighted to occupy a doubtful position long; and he now began to see things clearly as they were, and to push his slower or more timid associates forward along the path which they had set out to tread. He was instrumental in getting the militia into somewhat better shape; and, as it was found impossible to get enough Continental money, a colonial paper currency was issued. In spite of the quarrel with Connecticut, a force from that province moved in to take part in the defense of New York.

Yet, in the main, the policy of the New York
Congress still continued both weak and changeable,
and no improvement was effected when it was dissolved and a second elected. To this body the
loyalist counties of Richmond and Queens refused
to return delegates, and throughout the colony affairs grew more disorderly, and the administration
of justice came nearly to a standstill. Finding
that the local congress seemed likely to remain
unable to make up its mind how to act, the Continental leaders at last took matters into their own
hands, and marched a force into New York city
early in February, 1776. This had a most bracing
effect upon the provincial authorities; yet they still
continued to allow the British warships in the bay
to be supplied with provisions, nor was this attitude altered until in April Washington arrived
with the main Continental army. He at once
insisted that a final break should be made; and
about the same time the third Provincial Congress
was elected. Morris, again returned for Westchester, headed the bolder spirits, who had now
decided that the time had come to force their associates out of their wavering course, and to make
them definitely cast in their lot with their fellow
Americans. Things had come to a point which
made a decision necessary; the gathering of the
Continental forces on Manhattan Island and the
threatening attitude of the British fleet and army
made it impossible for even the most timid to keep
on lingering in a state of uncertainty. So the

Declaration of Independence was ratified, and a state constitution organized; then the die was cast, and thereafter New York manfully stood by the result of the throw.

The two Provincial Congresses that decided on this course held their sessions in a time of the greatest tumult, when New York was threatened hourly by the British; and long before their work was ended they had hastily to leave the city. Before describing what they did, a glance should .be taken at the circumstances under which it was done.

The peaceable citizens, especially those with any property, gradually left New York; and it remained in possession of the raw levies of the Continentals, while Staten Island received Howe with open arms, and he was enabled without difficulty to disembark his great force of British and German mercenaries on Long Island. The much smaller, motley force opposed to him, unorganized, ill-armed, and led by utterly inexperienced men, was beaten, with hardly an effort, in the battle that followed, and only escaped annihilation through the skill of Washington and the supine blundering of Howe. Then it was whipped up the Hudson and beyond the borders of the State, the broken remnant fleeing across New Jersey; and though the brilliant feats of arms at Trenton and Princeton enabled the Americans to reconquer the latter province, southern New York lay under the heel of the British till the close of the war.

Thus Morris, Jay, and the other New York leaders were obliged for six years to hold up their cause in a half-conquered State, a very large proportion of whose population was lukewarm or hostile. The odds were heavy against the patriots, because their worst foes were those of their own household. English writers are fond of insisting upon the alleged fact that America only won her freedom by the help of foreign nations. Such help was certainly most important, but, on the other hand, it must be remembered that during the first and vital years of the contest the Revolutionary colonists had to struggle unaided against the British, their mercenary German and Indian allies, Tories, and even French Canadians. When the French court declared in our favor the worst was already over; Trenton had been won, Burgoyne had been captured, and Valley Forge was a memory of the past.

We did not owe our main disasters to the might of our foes, nor our final triumph to the help of our friends. It was on our own strength that we had to rely, and it was with our own folly and weakness that we had to contend. The Revolutionary leaders can never be too highly praised; but taken in bulk the Americans of the last quarter of the eighteenth century do not compare to advantage with the Americans of the third quarter of the nineteenth. In our civil war it was the people who pressed on the leaders, and won almost as much in spite of as because of them; but the leaders of the Revolution had to goad the rank and file into line. They were forced to contend not only with the active hostility of the Tories, but with the passive neutrality of the indifferent, and the selfishness, jealousy, and short-sightedness of the patriotic. Had the Americans of 1776 been united, and had they possessed the stubborn, unyielding tenacity and high devotion to an ideal shown by the North, or the heroic constancy and matchless valor shown by the South, in the civil war, the British would have been driven off the continent before three years were over.

It is probable that nearly as great a proportion of our own people were actively or passively opposed to the formation of our Union originally as were in favor of its dissolution in 1860. This was one of the main reasons why the war dragged on so long. It may be seen by the fact, among others, that when in the Carolinas and Georgia a system of relentless and undying partisan warfare not only crushed the Tories, but literally destroyed them from off the face of the earth, then the British, though still victorious in almost every pitched battle, were at once forced to abandon the field.

Another reason was the inferior military capacity of the Revolutionary armies. The Continental troops, when trained, were excellent; but in almost every battle they were mixed with more or less worthless militia; and of the soldiers thus obtained all that can be said is that their officers could never be sure that they would fight, nor their ene-

mies that they would run away. The Revolutionary
troops certainly fell short of the standard reached
by the volunteers who fought Shiloh and Gettys-
burg.   The British rarely found them to be such
foes as they afterwards met at New Orleans and
Lundy's Lane. Throughout the Revolution the
militia were invariably leaving their posts at critical times; they would grow either homesick or
dejected, and would then go home at the very
crisis of the campaign; they did not begin to show
the stubbornness and resolution to " see the war
through " so common among their descendants in
the contending Federal and Confederate armies.

The truth is that in 1776 our main task was to
shape new political conditions, and then to reconcile our people to them; whereas in 1860 we had
merely to fight fiercely for the preservation of
what was already ours.   In the first emergency we
needed statesmen, and in the second warriors; and
the statesmen and warriors were forthcoming.   A
comparison of the men who came to the front
during these, the two heroic periods of the republic, brings out this point clearly.

Washington, alike statesman, soldier, and patriot, stands alone. He was not only the greatest
American; he was also one of the greatest men
the world has ever known. Few centuries and
few countries have ever seen his like. Among the
people of English stock there is none to compare
with him, unless perhaps Cromwell, utterly different though the latter was. Of Americans, Lincoln
alone is worthy to stand even second.

As for our other statesmen: Franklin, Hamilton, Jefferson, Adams, and their fellows most surely stand far above Seward, Sumner Chase, Stanton, and Stevens, great as were the services which these, and those like them, rendered.

But when we come to the fighting men, all this is reversed. As a mere military man, Washington himself cannot rank with the wonderful war-chief who for four years led the Army of Northern Virginia; and the names of Washington and Greene fill up the short list of really good Revolutionary generals. Against these the civil war shows a roll that contains not only Lee, but also Grant and Sherman, Jackson and Johnson, Thomas, Sheridan, and Farragut, — leaders whose volunteer soldiers and sailors, at the end of their four years' service, were ready and more than able to match themselves against the best regular forces of Europe.

CHAPTER III

INDEPENDENCE: FORMING THE STATE CONSTITUTION

THE third Provincial Congress, which came together in May, and before the close of its sessions was obliged to adjourn to White Plains, had to act on the Declaration of Independence, and provide for the foundation of a new state government.

Morris now put himself at the head of the patriotic party, and opened the proceedings by a long and very able speech in favor of adopting the recommendation of the Continental Congress that the colonies should form new governments. In his argument he went at length into the history and growth of the dispute with Great Britain; spoke of the efforts made in the past for reconciliation, and then showed clearly how such efforts were now not only hopeless, but also no longer compatible with the dignity and manhood of Americans. He sneered at those who argued that we ought to submit to Great Britain for the sake of the protection we got from her. "Great Britain will not fail to bring us into a war with some of her neighbors, and then protect us as a lawyer defends a suit, — the client paying for it. This is quite in form, but a wise man would, I think, get rid of the suit and the lawyer together. Again, how are we to be protected? If a descent is made upon our coasts and the British navy and army are three thousand miles off, we cannot receive very great benefit from them on that occasion. If, to obviate this inconvenience, we have an army and navy constantly among us, who can say that we shall not need a little protection against *them?*" He went on to point out the hopelessness of expecting Great Britain to keep to any terms which would deprive Parliament of its supremacy over America; for no succeeding Parliament could be held bound by the legislation of its predecessor, and the very acknowledgment of British supremacy on the part of the Americans would bind them as subjects, and make the supremacy of Parliament legitimate. He bade his hearers remember the maxim " that no faith is to be kept with rebels," and said: " In this case, or in any other case, if we fancy ourselves hardly dealt with, I maintain there is no redress but by arms. For it never yet was known that, when men assume power, they will part with it again, unless by compulsion."

He then took up the subject of independence; showed, for the benefit of the good but timid men who were frightened at the mere title, that, in all but name, it already existed in New York, and proved that its maintenance was essential to our well-being. " My argument, therefore, stands thus: As a connection with Great Britain cannot again exist without enslaving America, an independence is absolutely necessary. I cannot balance between the two. We run a hazard in one path, I confess; but then we are infallibly ruined if we pursue the other. . . . We find the characteristic marks and insignia of independence in this society, considered in itself and compared with other societies. The enumeration is conviction. Coining moneys, raising armies, regulating commerce, peace, war, — all these things you are not only adepts in, but masters of. Treaties alone remain, and even those you have dabbled at. Georgia you put under the ban of empire, and received her upon repentance as a member of the flock. Canada you are now treating with. France and Spain you ought to treat with, and the rest is but a name. I believe, sir, the Romans were as much governed, or rather oppressed, by their emperors, as ever any people were by their king. But emperor was more agreeable to their ears than king. [So] some, nay, many, persons in America dislike the word independence."

He then went on to show how independence would work well alike for our peace, liberty, and security. Considering the first, he laughed at the apprehensions expressed by some that the moment America was independent all the powers of Europe would pounce down on her, to parcel out the country among themselves; and showed clearly that to a European power any war of conquest in America would be " tedious, expensive, uncertain, and ruinous," and that none of the country could be kept

even if it should come to pass that some little portion of it were conquered. " But I cannot think it
will ever come to this. For when I turn my eyes to
the means of defense, I find them amply sufficient.
We have all heard that in the last war America
was conquered in Germany. I hold the converse of
this to be true, namely, that in and by America his
majesty's German dominions were secured. . . . I
expect a full and lasting defense against any and
every part of the earth." After thus treating of the
advantages to be hoped for on the score of peace, he
turns attention "to a question of infinitely greater
importance, namely, the liberty of this country;"
and afterwards passes to the matter of security,
which, " so long as the system of laws by which we
are now governed shall prevail, is amply provided
for in every separate colony. There may indeed
arise an objection because some gentlemen suppose
that the different colonies will carry on a sort of
land piracy against one another. But how this can
possibly happen when the idea of separate colonies
no longer exists I cannot for my soul comprehend.
That something very like this has already been
done I shall not deny, but the reason is as evident
as the fact. We never yet had a government in
this country of sufficient energy to restrain the law-
less and indigent. Whenever a form of government is established which deserves the name, these
insurrections must cease. But who is the man so
hardy as to affirm that they will not grow with our
growth, while on every occasion we must resort to

an English judicature to terminate differences which
the maxims of policy will teach them to leave undetermined? By degrees we are getting beyond the
utmost pale of English government. Settlements
are forming to the westward of us, whose inhabitants acknowledge no authority but their own." In
one sentence he showed rather a change of heart,
as regarded his former aristocratic leanings; for
he reproached those who were "apprehensive of
losing a little consequence and importance by living
in a country where all are on an equal footing,"
and predicted that we should " cause all nations to
resort hither as an asylum from oppression."

The speech was remarkable for its incisive directness and boldness, for the exact clearness with
which it portrayed things as they were, for the
broad sense of American nationality that it displayed, and for the accurate forecasts that it contained as to our future course in certain particulars,
— such as freedom from European wars and en-
tanglements, a strong but purely defensive foreign
policy, the encouragement of the growth of the
West, while keeping it united to us, and the throwing open our doors to the oppressed from abroad.

Soon after the delivery of this speech news came
that the Declaration of Independence had been
adopted by the Continental Congress; and Jay,
one of the New York delegates to this body, and
also a member of the Provincial Congress, drew
up for the latter a resolution emphatically indorsing
the declaration, which was at once adopted without

a dissenting voice. At the same time the Provincial Congress changed its name to that of "The Convention of the Representatives of the State of New York."

These last acts were done by a body that had been elected, with increased power, to succeed the third Provincial Congress and provide for a new constitution. Just before this, Morris had been sent to the Continental Congress in Philadelphia to complain that the troops from New England were paid more largely than those from the other colonies; a wrong which was at once redressed, the wages of the latter being raised, and Morris returned to New York in triumph after only a week's absence.

The Constitutional Convention of New York led a most checkered life; for the victorious British chevied it up and down the State, hunting it in turn from every small town in which it thought to have found a peaceful haven of refuge. At last it rested in Fishkill, such an out-of-the-way place as to be free from danger. The members were obliged to go armed, so as to protect themselves from stray marauding parties; and the number of delegates in attendance alternately dwindled and swelled in a wonderful manner, now resolving themselves into a committee of safety, and again resuming their functions as members of the convention.

The most important duties of the convention were intrusted to two committees. Of the first, which was to draft a plan for the Constitution,

Morris, Jay, and Livingston were the three leading members, upon whom all the work fell; of the second, which was to devise means for the establishment of a state fund, Morris was the chairman and moving spirit.

He was also chairman of a committee which was appointed to look after the Tories, and prevent them from joining together and rising; and so numerous were they that the jails were soon choked with those of their number who, on account of their prominence or bitterness, were most obnoxious to the patriots. Also a partial system of confiscation of Tory estates was begun. So greatly were the Tories feared and hated, and so determined were the attempts to deprive them of even the shadow of a chance to do harm, by so much as a word, that the convention sent a memorial, drafted by Morris, to the Continental Congress, in which they made the very futile suggestion that it should take " some measures for expunging from the Book of Common Prayer such parts, and discontinuing in the congregations of all other denominations all such prayers, as interfere with the interests of the American cause." The resolution was not acted on; but another part of the memorial shows how the Church of England men were standing by the mother country, for it goes on to recite that " the enemies of America have taken great pains to insinuate into the minds of the Episcopalians that the church is in danger. We could wish the Congress would pass some resolve to quiet their fears,

and we are confident that it would do essential
service to the cause of America, at least in this
State."

Morris's position in regard to the Tories was a
peculiarly hard one, because among their number
were many of his own relatives, including his elder
brother. The family house, where his mother
resided, was within the British lines; and not only
did he feel the disapproval of such of his people as
were loyalists, on the one side, but, on the other,
his letters to his family caused him to be regarded
with suspicion by the baser spirits in the American
party. About this time one of his sisters died;
the letter he then wrote to his mother is in the
usual formal style of the time, yet it shows marks
of deep feeling, and he takes occasion, while ad-
mitting that the result of the war was uncertain,
to avow, with a sternness unusual to him, his intention to face all things rather than abandon the
patriot cause. "The worst that can happen is to
fall on the last bleak mountain of America; and
he who dies there in defense of the injured rights
of mankind is happier than his conqueror, more
beloved by mankind, more applauded by his own
heart." The letter closes by a characteristic touch,
when he sends his love to "such as deserve it.
The number is not great."

The committee on the Constitution was not ready
to report until March, 1777. Then the convention devoted itself solely to the consideration of
the report, which, after several weeks' discussion,

was adopted with very little change. Jay and
Morris led the debate before the convention, as
they had done previously in committee. There
was perfect agreement upon the general principles.
Freehold suffrage was adopted, and a majority of
the freeholders of the State were thus the ultimate governing power. The executive, judicial,
and legislative powers were separated sharply, as
was done in the other States, and later on in the
federal Constitution as well. The legislative body
was divided into two chambers.

It was over the executive branch that the main
contest arose. It was conceded that this should be
nominally single-headed; that is, that there should
be a governor. But the members generally could
not realize how different was a governor elected
by the people, and responsible to them, from one
appointed by an alien and higher power to rule
over them, as in the colonial days. The remembrance of the contests with the royal governors
was still fresh; and the mere name of governor
frightened them. They had the same illogical fear
of the executive that the demagogues of to-day
(and some honest but stupid people, as well) pro-
fess to feel for a standing army. Men often let
the dread of the shadow of a dead wrong frighten
them into courting a living evil.

Morris himself was wonderfully clear - sighted
and cool-headed. He did not let the memory of
the wrong-doing of the royal governors blind him;
he saw that the trouble with them lay, not in the

power that they held, but in the source from which
that power came. Once the source was changed,
the power was an advantage, not a harm, to the
State. Yet few or none of his companions could
see this; and they nervously strove to save their
new State from the danger of executive usurpation
by trying to make the executive practically a board
of men instead of one man, and by crippling it
so as to make it ineffective for good, while at the
same time dividing the responsibility, so that no
one need be afraid to do evil. Above all, they
were anxious to take away from the governor the
appointment of the military and civil servants of
the State.

Morris had persuaded the committee to leave
the appointment of these officials to the governor,
the legislature retaining the power of confirmation
or rejection; but the convention, under the lead of
Jay, rejected this proposition, and after some discussion adopted in its place the cumbrous and foolish plan of a " council of appointment," to consist
of the governor and several senators. As might
have been expected, this artificial body worked
nothing but harm, and became simply a peculiarly
odious political machine.

Again, Morris advocated giving the governor a
qualified veto over the acts passed by the legislature; but instead of such a simple and straightforward method of legislative revision, the convention
saw fit to adopt a companion piece of foolishness
to the council of appointment, in the shape of the

equally complicated and anomalous council of revision, consisting of the governor, chancellor, and
judges of the Supreme Court, by whom all the acts
of the legislature had to be revised before they
could become laws. It is marvelous that these
two bodies should have lived on so long as they
did, — over forty years.

The convention did one most praiseworthy thing
in deciding in favor of complete religious toleration. This seems natural enough now; but at
that time there was hardly a European state that
practiced it. Great Britain harassed her Catholic
subjects in a hundred different ways; while in
France Protestants were treated far worse, and, in
fact, could scarcely be regarded as having any
legal standing whatever. On no other one point
do the statesmen of the Revolution show to more
marked advantage when compared with their European compeers than in this of complete religious
toleration. Their position was taken, too, simply
because they deemed it to be the right and proper
one; they had nothing to fear or hope from Catholics, and their own interests were in no wise advanced by what they did in the matter.

But in the New York convention toleration was
not obtained without a fight. There always ran-
kled in Jay's mind the memory of the terrible
cruelty wrought by Catholics on his Huguenot
forefathers; and he introduced into the article on
toleration an appendix, which discriminated against
the adherents of the Church of Rome, denying

them the rights of citizenship until they should solemnly swear before the Supreme Court, first, " that they verily believe in their conscience that no pope, priest, or foreign authority on earth has power to absolve the subjects of this State from their allegiance to the same ; " and, second, " that they renounce . . . the dangerous and damnable doctrine that the Pope or any other earthly authority has power to absolve men from sins described in and prohibited by the Holy Gospel." This second point, however important, was of purely theological interest, and had absolutely nothing to do with the state Constitution ; as to the first proposition, it might have been proper enough had there been the least chance of a conflict between the Pope, either in his temporal or his ecclesiastical capacity, and the United States ; but as there was no possibility of such a conflict arising, and as, if it did arise, there would not be the slightest danger of the United States receiving any damage, to put the sentence in would have been not only useless, but exceedingly foolish and harmful, on account of the intense irritation it would have excited.

The whole clause was rejected by a two to one vote, and then all the good that it aimed at was accomplished by the adoption, on the motion of Morris, of a proviso that the toleration granted should not be held to " justify practices inconsistent with the peace and safety of this State." This proviso of Morris remains in the Constitution to this day ; and thus, while absolute religious liberty is guaranteed, the State reserves to itself full right of protection, if necessary, against the adherents of any religious body, foreign or domestic, if they menace the public safety.

On a question even more important than religious toleration, namely, the abolition of domestic slavery, Jay and Morris fought side by side; but though the more enlightened of their fellow members went with them, they were a little too much in advance of the age, and failed. They made every effort to have a clause introduced into the Constitution recommending to the future legislature of New York to abolish slavery as soon as it could be done consistently with the public safety and the rights of property; "so that in future ages every human being who breathes the air of this State shall enjoy the privileges of a free man." Although they failed in their immediate purpose, yet they had much hearty support, and by the bold stand they took and the high ground they occupied they undoubtedly brought nearer the period when the abolition of slavery in New York became practicable.

The Constitution was finally adopted by the convention almost unanimously, and went into effect forthwith, as there was no ratification by the people at large.

As soon as it was adopted a committee, which included Morris, Jay, and Livingston, was appointed to start and organize the new government. The courts of justice were speedily put in running order, and thus one of the most crying evils that affected the State was remedied. A council of safety of fifteen members — again including Morris — was established to act as the provincial government, until the regular legislature should convene. An election for governor was also held almost immediately, and Clinton was chosen. He was then serving in the field, where he had done good work, and, together with his brother James, had fought with the stubborn valor that seems to go with Anglo-Irish blood. He did not give up his command until several months after he was elected, although meanwhile keeping up constant communication with the Council of Safety, through whom he acted in matters of state.

Meanwhile Burgoyne, with his eight or nine thousand troops, excellently drilled British and Hessians, assisted by Tories, Canadians, and Indians, had crossed the northern frontier, and was moving down towards the heart of the already disorganized State, exciting the wildest panic and confusion. The Council of Safety hardly knew how to act, and finally sent a committee of two, Morris being one, to the headquarters of General Schuyler, who had the supreme command over all the troops in the northern part of New York.

On Morris's arrival he found affairs at a very low ebb, and at once wrote to describe this condition to the president of the Council of Safety. Burgoyne's army had come steadily on. He first destroyed Arnold's flotilla on Lake Champlain.

Then he captured the forts along the Lakes, and
utterly wrecked the division of the American army
that had been told off to defend them, under the
very unfortunate General St. Clair. He was now
advancing through the great reaches of wooded
wilderness towards the head of the Hudson. Schuyler, a general of fair capacity, was doing what he
could to hold the enemy back; but his one efficient
supporter was the wilderness itself, through which
the British army stumbled painfully along. Schuyler had in all less than five thousand men, half of
them short service Continental troops, the other
half militia. The farmers would not turn out until
after harvest home; all the bodies of militia, especially those from New England, were very insubor-
dinate and of most fickle temper, and could not be
depended on for any sustained contest; as an example, Stark, under whose nominal command the
northern New Englanders won the battle of Bennington, actually marched off his whole force the
day before the battle of Stillwater, alleging the
expiration of the term of service of his soldiers as
an excuse for what looked like gross treachery or
cowardice, but was probably merely sheer selfish
wrong-headedness and mean jealousy. Along the
Mohawk valley the dismay was extreme, and the
militia could not be got out at all. Jay was so
angered by the abject terror in this quarter that
he advised leaving the inhabitants to shift for
themselves; sound advice, too, for when the pinch
came and they were absolutely forced to take arms,

they did very fairly at Oriskany. It was even feared that the settlers of the region which afterwards became Vermont would go over to the enemy; still, time and space were in our favor, and Morris was quite right when he said in his first letter (dated July 16, 1777): "Upon the whole I think we shall do very well, but this opinion is founded merely upon the barriers which nature has raised against all access from the northward." As he said of himself, he was "a good guesser."

He outlined the plan which he thought the Americans should follow. This was to harass the British in every way, without risking a stand-up fight, while laying waste the country through which they were to pass so as to render it impossible for an army to subsist on it. For the militia he had the most hearty contempt, writing: "Three hundred of the militia of Massachusetts Bay went off this morning, in spite of the opposition — we should have said, entreaties — of their officers. All the militia on the ground are so heartily tired, and so extremely desirous of getting home, that it is more than probable that none of them will remain here ten days longer. One half was discharged two days ago, to silence, if possible, their clamor; and the remainder, officers excepted, will soon discharge themselves."

The Council of Safety grew so nervous over the outlook that their letters became fairly querulous; and they not unnaturally asked Morris to include in his letters some paragraphs that could be given to the public. To this that rather quick-tempered gentleman took exceptions, and replied caustically in his next letter, the opening paragraph being: "We have received yours of the 19th, which has afforded us great pleasure, since we are enabled in some measure to collect from it our errand to the northward, one of the most important objects of our journey being, in the opinion of your honorable body, to write the news," and he closes by stating that he shall come back to wait upon them, and learn their pleasure, at once.

Meanwhile the repeated disasters in the north had occasioned much clamor against Schuyler, who, if not a brilliant general, had still done what he could in very trying circumstances, and was in no wise responsible for the various mishaps that had occurred. The New England members of Congress, always jealous of New York, took advantage of this to begin intriguing against him, under the lead of Roger Sherman and others, and finally brought about his replacement by Gates, a much inferior man, with no capacity whatever for command. Morris and Jay both took up Schuyler's cause very warmly, seeing clearly, in the first place, that the disasters were far from ruinous, and that a favorable outcome was probable; and, in the second place, that it was the people themselves who were to blame and not Schuyler. They went on to Philadelphia to speak for him, but they arrived just a day too late, Gates having been appointed twenty-four hours previous to their coming.

When Gates reached his army the luck had already begun to turn. Burgoyne's outlying parties had been destroyed, his Indians and Canadians had left him, he had been disappointed in his hopes of a Tory uprising in his favor, and, hampered by his baggage-train, he had been brought almost to a standstill in the tangled wilds through which he had slowly ploughed his way. Schuyler had done what he could to hinder the foe's progress, and had kept his own army together as a rallying point for the militia, who, having gathered in their harvests, and being inspirited by the outcome of the fights at Oriskany and Bennington, flocked in by hundreds to the American standard. Gates himself did literally nothing; he rather hindered his men than otherwise; and the latter were turbulent and prone to disobey orders. But they were now in fine feather for fighting, and there were plenty of them. So Gates merely sat still, and the levy of backwoods farmers, all good individual fighters, and with some excellent brigade and regimental commanders, such as Arnold and Morgan, fairly mobbed to death the smaller number of dispirited and poorly led regulars against whom they were pitted. When the latter were at last fought out and forced to give in, Gates allowed them much better terms than he should have done; and the Continental Congress, to its shame, snatched at a technicality, under cover of which to break the faith plighted through its general, and to avoid fulfilling the conditions to which he had so foolishly agreed.

Morris and Jay, though unable to secure the retention of Schuyler, had, nevertheless, by their representations while at Philadelphia, prevailed on the authorities largely to reinforce the army which was about to be put under Gates. Morris was very angry at the intrigue by which the latter had been given the command; but what he was especially aiming at was the success of the cause, not the advancement of his friends. Once Gates was appointed he did all in his power to strengthen him, and, with his usual clear-sightedness, he predicted his ultimate success.

Schuyler was a man of high character and public spirit, and he behaved really nobly in the midst of his disappointment; his conduct throughout affording a very striking contrast to that of McClellan, under somewhat similar circumstances in the civil war. Morris wrote him, sympathizing with him, and asking him to sink all personal feeling and devote his energies to the common weal of the country while out of power just as strenuously as he had done when in command. Schuyler responded that he should continue to serve his country as zealously as before, and he made his words good; but Gates was jealous of the better man whose downfall he had been the instrument of accomplishing, and declined to profit by his help.

In a later letter to Schuyler, written September 18, 1777, Morris praised the latter very warmly for the way he had behaved, and commented roughly on Gates's littleness of spirit. He considered that with such a commander there was nothing to be hoped for from skillful management, and that Burgoyne would have to be simply tired out. Alluding to a rumor that the Indians were about to take up the hatchet for us, he wrote, in the humorous vein he adopted so often in dealing even with the most pressing matters: "If this be true, it would be infinitely better to wear away the enemy's army by a scrupulous and polite attention, than to violate the rules of decorum and the laws of hospitality by making an attack upon strangers in our own country!" He gave Schuyler the news of Washington's defeat at the battle of Brandywine, and foretold the probable loss of Philadelphia and a consequent winter campaign.

In ending he gave a thoroughly characteristic sketch of the occupations of himself and his colleagues. "The chief justice (Jay) is gone to fetch his wife. The chancellor (Livingston) is solacing himself with his wife, his farm, and his imagination. Our Senate is doing, I know not what. In Assembly we wrangle long to little purpose. . . . We have some principles of fermentation which must, if it be possible, evaporate before business is entered upon."

CHAPTER IV

IN THE CONTINENTAL CONGRESS

AT the end of 1777, while still but twenty-five years old, Morris was elected to the Continental Congress, and took his seat in that body at York-town in the following January.

He was immediately appointed as one of a committee of five members to go to Washington's headquarters at Valley Forge and examine into the condition of the Continental troops.

The dreadful suffering of the American army in this winter camp was such that its memory has literally eaten its way into the hearts of our people, and it comes before our minds with a vividness that dims the remembrance of any other disaster. Washington's gaunt, half-starved Continentals, shoeless and ragged, shivered in their crazy huts, worn out by want and illness, and by the bitter cold ; while the members of the Continental Congress not only failed to support them in the present, but even grudged them the poor gift of a promise of half-pay in the future. Some of the delegates, headed by Samuel Adams, were actually caballing against the great chief himself, the one hope of America. Meanwhile the States looked askance at each other, and each sunk into supine indifference when its own borders were for the moment left unthreatened by the foe. Throughout the Revolutionary war our people hardly once pulled with a will together; although almost every locality in turn, on some one occasion, varied its lethargy by a spasm of terrible energy. Yet, again, it must be remembered that we were never more to be dreaded than when our last hope seemed gone; and if the people were unwilling to show the wisdom and self-sacrifice that would have insured success, they were equally determined under no circumstances whatever to acknowledge final defeat.

To Jay, with whom he was always intimate, Morris wrote in strong terms from Valley Forge, painting things as they were, but without a shadow of doubt or distrust; for he by this time saw clearly enough that in American warfare the darkest hour was often followed close indeed by dawn. "The skeleton of an army presents itself to our eyes in a naked, starving condition, out of health, out of spirits. But I have seen Fort George in 1777." The last sentence refers to what he saw of Schuyler's forces, when affairs in New York State were at the blackest, just before the tide began to turn against Burgoyne. He then went on to beseech Jay to exert himself to the utmost on the great question of taxation, the most vital of all. Morris himself was so good a financier that Revolutionary financial economics drove him almost

wild. The Continental Congress, of which he had
just become a member, he did not esteem very
highly, and dismissed it, as well as the currency,
as having "both depreciated." The State of Pennsylvania, he remarked, was "sick unto death;"
and added that "Sir William [the British general]
would prove a most damnable physician."

Most wisely, in examining and reporting, he
paid heed almost exclusively to Washington's re-
commendations, and the plan he and his colleagues
produced was little more than an enlargement of
the general's suggestions as to filling out the regiments, regulating rank, modeling the various
departments, etc. In fact, Morris now devoted
himself to securing the approval of Congress for
Washington's various plans.

In urging one of the most important of these he
encountered very determined opposition. Washington was particularly desirous of securing a per-
manent provision for the officers by the establishment of a system of half-pay, stating that without
some such arrangement he saw no hope whatever
for the salvation of the cause; for as things then
were the officers were leaving day by day; and of
those who went home on furlough to the Eastern
and Southern States, many, instead of returning,
went into some lucrative employment. This fact,
by the way, while showing the difficulties with
which Washington had to deal, and therefore his
greatness, since he successfully dealt with them, at
the same time puts the officers of the Revolution

in no very favorable light as compared with their
descendants at the time of the great rebellion; and
the Continental Congress makes a still worse showing.

When Morris tried to push through a measure
providing for half-pay for life, he was fought, tooth
and nail, by many of his colleagues, including, to
their lasting discredit be it said, every delegate
from New England. The folly of these ultra-
democratic delegates almost passes belief. They
seemed incapable of learning how the fight for liberty should be made. Their leaders, like Samuel
Adams and John Hancock, did admirable service
in exciting the Americans to make the struggle;
but once it was begun, their function ended, and
from thence onward they hampered almost as much
as they helped the patriot cause. New England,
too, had passed through the period when its patriotic fervor was at white heat. It still remained as
resolute as ever; and if the danger had been once
more brought home to its very door-sill, then it
would have risen again as it had risen before; but
without the spur of an immediate necessity it
moved but sluggishly.

The New Englanders were joined by the South
Carolina delegates. Morris was backed by the
members from New York, Virginia, and the other
States, and he won the victory, but not without
being obliged to accept amendments that took
away some of the good of the measure. Half-pay
was granted, but it was only to last for seven years

after the close of the war; and the paltry bounty of eighty dollars was to be given to every soldier who served out his time to the end.

At the same period Morris was engaged on numerous other committees, dealing chiefly with the finances, or with the remedy of abuses that had crept into the administration of the army. In one of his reports he exposed thoroughly the frightful waste in the purchase and distribution of supplies, and, what was much worse, the accompanying frauds. These frauds had become a most serious evil; Jay, in one of his letters to Morris, had already urgently requested him to turn his attention especially to stopping the officers, in particular those of the staff, from themselves engaging in trade, on account of the jobbing and swindling that it produced. The shoddy contractors of the civil war had plenty of predecessors in the Revolution.

When these events occurred, in the spring of 1778, it was already three years after the fight at Lexington; certainly, the Continental armies of that time do not compare favorably, even taking all difficulties into account, with the Confederate forces which in 1864, three years after the fall of Sumter, fronted Grant and Sherman. The men of the Revolution failed to show the capacity to organize for fighting purposes, and the ability to bend all energies towards the attainment of a given end, which their great-grandsons of the civil war, both at the North and the South, possessed. Yet,

after all, their very follies sprang from their virtues, from their inborn love of freedom, and their
impatience of the control of outsiders. So fierce
had they been in their opposition to the rule of
foreigners that they were now hardly willing to
submit to being ruled by themselves; they had
seen power so abused that they feared its very use;
they were anxious to assert their independence of
all mankind, even of each other. Stubborn, honest,
and fearless, they were taught with difficulty, and
only by the grinding logic of an imperious necessity, that it was no surrender of their freedom to
submit to rulers chosen by themselves, through
whom alone that freedom could be won. They had
not yet learned that right could be enforced only
by might, that union was to the full as important as liberty, because it was the prerequisite condition for the establishment and preservation of
liberty.

But if the Americans of the Revolution were
not perfect, how their faults dwindle when we stand
them side by side with their European compeers!
What European nation then brought forth rulers
as wise and pure as our statesmen, or masses as
free and self-respecting as our people? There was
far more swindling, jobbing, cheating, and stealing
in the English army than in ours; the British king
and his ministers need no criticism; and the outcome of the war proves that their nation as a whole
was less resolute than our own. As for the other
European powers, the faults of our leaders sink

out of sight when matched against the ferocious
frivolity of the French noblesse, or the ignoble,
sordid, bloody baseness of those swinish German
kinglets who let out their subjects to do hired
murder, and battened on the blood and sweat of
the wretched beings under them, until the whirlwind of the French Revolution swept their car-
casses from off the world they cumbered.

We must needs give all honor to the men who
founded our Commonwealth ; only in so doing let
us remember that they brought into being a government under which their children were to grow
better and not worse.

Washington at once recognized in Morris a man
whom he could trust in every way, and on whose
help he could rely in other matters besides getting
his officers half-pay. The young New Yorker was
one of the great Virginian's warmest supporters
in Congress, and took the lead in championing his
cause at every turn. He was the leader in putting
down intrigues like that of the French-Irish adventurer Conway, his ready tongue and knowledge of
parliamentary tactics, no less than his ability, ren-
dering him the especial dread and dislike of the
anti-Washington faction.

Washington wrote to Morris very freely, and in
one of his letters complained of the conduct of
some of the officers who wished to resign when
affairs looked dark, and to be reinstated as soon as
they brightened a little. Morris replied with one

of his bright caustic letters, sparing his associates very little, their pompous tediousness and hesitation being peculiarly galling to a man so far-seeing and so prompt to make up his mind. He wrote: "We are going on with the regimental arrangements as fast as possible, and I think the day begins to appear with respect to that business. Had our Saviour addressed a chapter to the rulers of mankind, as he did many to the subjects, I am persuaded his good sense would have dictated this text: *Be not wise overmuch.* Had the several members who compose our multifarious body been only wise *enough,* our business would long since have been completed. But our superior abilities, or the desire of appearing to possess them, lead us to such exquisite tediousness of debate that the most precious moments pass unheeded away. . . . As to what you mention of the extraordinary demeanor of some gentlemen, I cannot but agree with you that such conduct is not the most *honorable.* But, on the other hand, you must allow that it is the most *safe,* and certainly you are not to learn that, however ignorant of that happy art in your own person, the bulk of us bipeds know well how to balance solid pudding against empty praise. There are other things, my dear sir, beside virtue, which are their own *reward.*"

Washington chose Morris as his confidential friend and agent to bring privately before Congress a matter in reference to which he did not consider it politic to write publicly. He was at

that time annoyed beyond measure by the shoals
of foreign officers who were seeking employment
in the army, and he wished Congress to stop giving them admission to the service. These foreign
officers were sometimes honorable men, but more
often adventurers ; with two or three striking exceptions, they failed to do as well as officers of
native birth ; and, as later in the civil war, so in
the Revolution, it appeared that Americans could
be best commanded by Americans. Washington
had the greatest dislike for these adventurers,
stigmatizing them as " men who in the first instance tell you that they wish for nothing more
than the honor of serving in so glorious a cause as
volunteers, the next day solicit rank without pay,
the day following want money advanced to them,
and in the course of a week want further promo-
tion, and are not satisfied with anything you can
do for them." He ended by writing: " I do most
devoutly wish that we had not a single foreigner
among us, except the Marquis de Lafayette, who
acts upon very different principles from those
which govern the rest." To Lafayette, indeed,
America owes as much as to any of her own children, for his devotion to us was as disinterested
and sincere as it was effective ; and it is a pleasant
thing to remember that we, in our turn, not only
repaid him materially, but, what he valued far
more, that our whole people yielded him all his
life long the most loving homage a man could
receive. No man ever kept pleasanter relations

with a people he had helped than Lafayette did
with us.

Morris replied to Washington that he would do
all in his power to aid him.   Meanwhile he had
also contracted a very warm friendship for Greene,
then newly appointed quartermaster-general of the
army, and proved a most useful ally, both in and
out of Congress, in helping the general to get his
department in good running order, and in extricat-
ing it from the frightful confusion in which it had
previously been plunged.

He also specially devoted himself at this time to
an investigation of the finances, which were in a
dreadful condition; and by the ability with which
he performed his very varied duties he acquired
such prominence that he was given the chairman-
ship of the most important of all the congressional
committees.   This was the committee to which was
confided the task of conferring with the British
commissioners, who had been sent over, in the
spring of 1778, to treat with the Americans, in
accordance with the terms of what were known as
Lord North's conciliatory bills.   These bills were
two in number, the first giving up the right of
taxation, about which the quarrel had originally
arisen, and the second authorizing the commissioners to treat with the revolted colonies on all
questions in dispute.   They were introduced in
Parliament on account of the little headway made
by the British in subduing their former subjects,
and were pressed hastily through because of the

fear of an American alliance with France, which was then, indeed, almost concluded.

Three years before, these bills would have achieved their end; but now they came by just that much time too late. The embittered warfare had lasted long enough entirely to destroy the old friendly feelings; and the Americans having once tasted the "perilous pleasure" of freedom, having once stretched out their arms and stood before the world's eyes as their own masters, it was certain that they would never forego their liberty, no matter with what danger it was fraught, no matter how light the yoke, or how kindly the bondage, by which it was to be replaced.

Two days after the bills were received, Morris drew up and presented his report, which was unanimously adopted by Congress. Its tenor can be gathered from its summing up, which declared that the indispensable preliminaries to any treaty would have to be the withdrawal of all the British fleets and armies, and the acknowledgment of the independence of the United States; and it closed by calling on the several States to furnish without delay their quotas of troops for the coming campaign.

This decisive stand was taken when America was still without allies in the contest; but ten days afterwards messengers came to Congress bearing copies of the treaty with France. It was ratified forthwith, and again Morris was appointed chairman of a committee, this time to issue an address on the subject to the American people at large. He penned this address himself, explaining fully the character of the crisis, and going briefly over the events that had led to it; and shortly afterwards he drew up, on behalf of Congress, a sketch of all the proceedings in reference to the British commissioners, under the title of " Observations on the American Revolution," giving therein a masterly outline not only of the doings of Congress in the particular matter under consideration, but also an account of the causes of the war, of the efforts of the Americans to maintain peace, and of the chief events that had taken place, as well as a comparison between the contrasting motives and aims of the contestants.

Morris was one of the committee appointed to receive the French minister, M. Gérard. Immediately afterwards he was also selected by Congress to draft the instructions which were to be sent to Franklin, the American minister at the court of Versailles. As a token of the closeness of our relations with France, he was requested to show these instructions to M. Gérard, which he accordingly did; and some interesting features of the conversation between the two men have been preserved for us in the dispatches of Gérard to the French court. The Americans were always anxious to undertake the conquest of Canada, although Washington did not believe the scheme feasible; and the French strongly, although secretly, opposed it, as it was their policy from the beginning that

Canada should remain English. Naturally the
French did not wish to see America transformed
into a conquering power, a menace to themselves
and to the Spaniards as well as to the English;
nor can they be criticised for feeling in this way,
or taunted with acting only from motives of self-
interest. It is doubtless true that their purposes
in going into the war were mixed; they unquestionably wished to benefit themselves, and to hurt
their old and successful rival; but it is equally
unquestionable that they were also moved by a
generous spirit of sympathy and admiration for
the struggling colonists. It would, however, have
been folly to let this sympathy blind them to the
consequences that might ensue to all Europeans
having possessions in America, if the Americans
should become not only independent, but also
aggressive; and it was too much to expect them
to be so far-sighted as to see that, once independent, it was against the very nature of things that
the Americans should *not* be aggressive, and impossible that they should be aught but powerful and
positive instruments, both in their own persons and
by their example, in freeing the whole western
continent from European control.

Accordingly M. Gérard endeavored, though
without success, to prevail on Morris not to mention the question of an invasion of Canada in the
instructions to Franklin. He also warned the
American of the danger of alarming Spain by
manifesting a wish to encroach on its territory in

the Mississippi valley, mentioning and condemn-
ing the attitude taken by several members of Congress to the effect that the navigation of the
Mississippi should belong equally to the English
and Americans.

Morris's reply showed how little even the most
intelligent American of that time — especially if he
came from the Northern or Eastern States — could
appreciate the destiny of his country. He stated
that his colleagues favored restricting the growth
of our country to the south and west, and believed
that the navigation of the Mississippi, from the
Ohio down, should belong exclusively to the Spaniards, as otherwise the western settlements springing up in the valley of the Ohio, and on the shores
of the Great Lakes, would not only domineer over
Spain, but also over the United States, and would
certainly render themselves independent in the end.
He further said that some at least of those who were
anxious to secure the navigation of the Mississippi
were so from interested motives, having money ventures in the establishments along the river.   However, if he at this time failed fully to grasp his
country's future, he was, later on, one of the first
in the Northern States to recognize it; and once
he did see it he promptly changed, and became the
strongest advocate of our territorial expansion.

Accompanying his instructions to Franklin,
Morris sent a pamphlet entitled " Observations on
the Finances of America," to be laid before the
French ministry. Practically, all that the pam-

phlet amounted to was a most urgent begging
letter, showing that our own people could not, or
would not, either pay taxes or take up a domestic
loan, so that we stood in dire need of a subsidy
from abroad.   The drawing up of such a document
could hardly have been satisfactory employment
for a high-spirited man who wished to be proud of
his country.

All through our negotiations with France and
England, Morris's views coincided with those of
Washington, Hamilton, Jay, and the others who
afterwards became leaders of the Federalist party.
Their opinions were well expressed by Jay in a letter to Morris written about this time, which ran:
" I view a return to the domination of Britain with
horror, and would risk all for independence ; but
that point ceded, . . . the destruction of Old England would hurt me; I wish it well ; it afforded
my ancestors an asylum from persecution." The
rabid American adherents of France could not
understand such sentiments, and the more mean-
spirited among them always tried to injure Morris
on account of his loyalist relatives, although so
many families were divided in this same way,
Franklin's only son being himself a prominent
Tory. So bitter was this feeling that when, later
on, Morris's mother, who was within the British
lines, became very ill, he actually had to give up
his intended visit to her, because of the furious
clamor that was raised against it. He refers bitterly, in one of his letters to Jay, to the "malevo-

lence of individuals," as something he had to
expect, but which he announced that he would conquer by so living as to command the respect of
those whose respect was worth having.

When, however, his foes were of sufficient importance to warrant his paying attention to them
individually, Morris proved abundantly able to
take care of himself, and to deal heavier blows than
he received. This was shown in the controversy
which convulsed Congress over the conduct of Silas
Deane, the original American envoy to France.
Deane did not behave very well, but at first he was
certainly much more sinned against than sinning,
and Morris took up his cause warmly. Thomas
Paine, the famous author of "Common Sense,"
who was secretary of the Committee of Foreign
Affairs, attacked Deane and his defenders, as well
as the court of France, with peculiar venom, using
as weapons the secrets he became acquainted with
through his official position, and which he was in
honor bound not to divulge. For this Morris had
him removed from his secretaryship, and in the
debate handled him extremely roughly, character-
izing him with contemptuous severity as "a mere
adventurer from England . . . ignorant even of
grammar," and ridiculing his pretensions to importance. Paine was an adept in the art of invective;
but he came out second best in this encounter, and
never forgot or forgave his antagonist.

As a rule, however, Morris was kept too busily
at work to spare time for altercations. He was

chairman of three important standing committees,
those on the commissary, quartermaster's, and medi-
cal departments, and did the whole business for
each. He also had more than his share of special
committee work, besides playing his full part in
the debates and consultations of the Congress itself. Moreover, his salary was so small that he
had to eke it out by the occasional practice of his
profession. He devoted himself especially to the
consideration of our finances and of our foreign
relations; and, as he grew constantly to possess
more and more weight and influence in Congress,
he was appointed, early in 1779, as chairman of a
very important committee, which was to receive
communications from our ministers abroad, as well
as from the French envoy. He drew out its report,
together with the draft of instructions to our foreign ministers, which it recommended. Congress
accepted the first, and adopted the last, without
change, whereby it became the basis of the treaty
by which we finally won peace. In his draft he
had been careful not to bind down our representatives on minor points, and to leave them as large
liberty of action as was possible; but the main
issues, such as the boundaries, the navigation of
the Mississippi, and the fisheries, were discussed at
length and in order.

At the time this draft of instructions for a treaty
was sent out, there was much demand among certain members in Congress that we should do all in
our power to make foreign alliances, and to pro-

cure recognitions of our independence in every
possible quarter.   To this Morris was heartily opposed, deeming that this " rage for treaties," as he
called it, was not very dignified on our part.   He
held rightly that our true course was to go our
own gait, without seeking outside favor, until we
had shown ourselves able to keep our own place
among nations, when the recognitions would come
without asking.   Whether European nations recognized us as a free people, or not, was of little
moment so long as we ourselves knew that we had
become one in law and in fact, through the right
of battle and the final arbitrament of the sword.

Besides these questions of national policy, Morris
also had to deal with an irritating matter affecting
mainly New York.   This was the dispute of that
State with the people of Vermont, who wished to
form a separate commonwealth of their own, while
New York claimed that their lands came within its
borders.   Even the fear of their common foe, the
British, against whom they needed to employ their
utmost strength, was barely sufficient to prevent
the two communities from indulging in a small
civil war of their own ; and they persisted in
pressing their rival claims upon the attention of
Congress, and clamoring for a decision from that
harassed and overburdened body.   Clinton, who
was much more of a politician than a statesman,
led the popular party in this foolish business, the
majority of the New Yorkers being apparently
nearly as enthusiastic in asserting their sovereignty

over Vermont as they were in declaring their independence of Britain.   Morris, however, was very
half-hearted in pushing the affair before Congress.
He doubted if Congress had the power, and he
knew it lacked the will, to move in the matter at
all; and besides he did not sympathize with the
position taken by his State.   He was wise enough
to see that the Vermonters had much of the right
on their side in addition to the great fact of possession; and that New York would be probably
unable to employ force enough to conquer them.
Clinton was a true type of the separatist or states'-
rights politician of that day: he cared little how
the national weal was affected by the quarrel; and
he was far more anxious to bluster than to fight
over the matter, to which end he kept besieging
the delegates in Congress with useless petitions.
In a letter to him, Morris put the case with his
usual plainness, telling him that it was perfectly
idle to keep worrying Congress to take action, for
it would certainly not do so, and, if it did render a
decision, the Vermonters would no more respect it
than they would the Pope's Bull.   He went on to
show his characteristic contempt for half measures,
and capacity for striking straight at the root of
things: " Either let these people alone, or conquer
them.   I prefer the latter; but I doubt the means.
If we have the means let them be used, and let
Congress deliberate and decide, or deliberate without deciding, — it is of no consequence.   Success
will sanctify every operation. . . . If we have not

Geor: Clinton.

the means of conquering these people we must let them alone. We must continue our impotent threats, or we must make a treaty. . . . If we continue our threats they will either hate or despise us, and perhaps both. . . . On the whole, then, my conclusion is here, as on most other human affairs, act decisively, fight or submit, — conquer or treat." Morris was right; the treaty was finally made, and Vermont became an independent State.

But the small politicians of New York would not forgive him for the wisdom and the broad feeling of nationality he showed on this and so many other questions; and they defeated him when he was a candidate for reëlection to Congress at the end of 1779. The charge they urged against him was that he devoted his time wholly to the service of the nation at large, and not to that of New York in particular; his very devotion to the public business, which had kept him from returning to the State, being brought forward to harm him. Arguments of this kind are common enough even at the present day, and effective too, among that numerous class of men with narrow minds and selfish hearts. Many an able and upright Congressman since Morris has been sacrificed because his constituents found he was fitted to do the exact work needed; because he showed himself capable of serving the whole nation, and did not devote his time to advancing the interests of only a portion thereof.

CHAPTER V

AT the end of 1779 Morris was thus retired to private life; and, having by this time made many friends in Philadelphia, he took up his abode in that city. His leaving Congress was small loss to himself, as that body was rapidly sinking into a condition of windy decrepitude.

He at once began working at his profession, and also threw himself with eager zest into every attainable form of gayety and amusement, for he was of a most pleasure-loving temperament, very fond of society, and a great favorite in the little American world of wit and fashion. But although in private life, he nevertheless kept his grip on public affairs, and devoted himself to the finances, which were in a most wretched state. He could not keep out of public life; he probably agreed with Jay, who, on hearing that he was again a private citizen, wrote him to "remember that Achilles made no figure at the spinning-wheel." At any rate, as early as February, 1780, he came to the front once more as the author of a series of essays on the finances. They were published in Philadelphia, and attracted the attention of all

thinking men by their soundness. In fact it was
in our monetary affairs that the key to the situation was to be found ; for, had we been willing to
pay honestly and promptly the necessary war ex-
penses, we should have ended the struggle in short
order. But the niggardliness as well as the real
poverty of the people, the jealousies of the States,
kept aflame by the states'-rights leaders for their
own selfish purposes, and the foolish ideas of most
of the congressional delegates on all money matters, combined to keep our treasury in a pitiable
condition.

Morris tried to show the people at large the
advantage of submitting to reasonable taxation,
while at the same time combating some of the
theories entertained as well by themselves as by
their congressional representatives. He began by
discussing with great clearness what money really
is, how far coin can be replaced by paper, the
interdependence of money and credit, and other ele-
mentary points in reference to which most of his
fellow citizens seemed to possess wonderfully mixed
ideas. He attacked the efforts of Congress to
make their currency legal tender, and then showed
the utter futility of one of the pet schemes of Revolutionary financial wisdom, the regulation of prices
by law. Hard times, then as now, always produced not only a large debtor class, but also a corresponding number of political demagogues who
truckled to it; and both demagogue and debtor,
when they clamored for laws which should " re-

lieve " the latter, meant thereby laws which would
enable him to swindle his creditor. The people,
moreover, liked to lay the blame for their misfortunes neither on fate nor on themselves, but on
some unfortunate outsider; and they were especially apt to attack as " monopolists " the men who
had purchased necessary supplies in large quanti-
ties to profit by their rise in price. Accordingly
they passed laws against them; and Morris showed
in his essays the unwisdom of such legislation,
while not defending for a moment the men who
looked on the misfortunes of their country solely
as offering a field for their own harvesting.

He ended by drawing out an excellent scheme
of taxation; but, unfortunately, the people were
too short-sighted to submit to any measure of the
sort, no matter how wise and necessary. One of
the pleas he made for his scheme was, that something of the sort would be absolutely necessary for
the preservation of the Federal Union, " which,"
he wrote, " in my poor opinion, will greatly depend upon the management of the revenue." He
showed with his usual clearness the need of obtain-
ing, for financial as well as for all other reasons,
a firmer union, as the existing confederation bade
fair to become, as its enemies had prophesied, a
rope of sand. He also foretold graphically the
misery that would ensue — and that actually did
ensue — when the pressure from a foreign foe
should cease, and the States should be resolved
into a disorderly league of petty, squabbling com-

munities. In ending he remarked bitterly : " The Articles of Confederation were formed when the attachment to Congress was warm and great. The framers of them, therefore, seem to have been only solicitous how to provide against the power of that body, which, by means of their foresight and care, now exists by mere courtesy and sufferance."

Although Morris was not able to convert Congress to the ways of sound thinking, his ability and clearness impressed themselves on all the best men, notably on Robert Morris, — who was no relation of his, by the way, — the first in the line of American statesmen who have been great in finance ; a man whose services to our treasury stand on a par, if not with those of Hamilton, at least with those of Gallatin and John Sherman. Congress had just established four departments, with secretaries at the head of each. The two most important were the Departments of Foreign Affairs and of Finance. Livingston was given the former, while Robert Morris received the latter ; and immediately afterwards appointed Gouverneur Morris as assistant financier, at a salary of eighteen hundred and fifty dollars a year.

Morris accepted this appointment, and remained in office for three years and a half, until the beginning of 1785. He threw himself heart and soul into the work, helping his chief in every way ; and in particular giving him invaluable assistance in the establishment of the " Bank of North America," which Congress was persuaded to incorporate, — an

institution which was the first of its kind in the
country. It was of wonderful effect in restoring
the public credit, and was absolutely invaluable
in the financial operations undertaken by the secretary.

When, early in 1782, the secretary was directed
by Congress to present to that body a report on
the foreign coins circulating in the country, it was
prepared and sent in by Gouverneur Morris, and
he accompanied it with a plan for an American
coinage. The postscript was the really important
part of the document, and the plan therein set forth
was made the basis of our present coinage system,
although not until several years later, and then
only with important modifications, suggested, for
the most part, by Jefferson.

Although his plan was modified, it still remains
true that Gouverneur Morris was the founder of
our national coinage. He introduced the system
of decimal notation, invented the word "cent" to
express one of the smaller coins, and nationalized
the already familiar word "dollar." His plan,
however, was a little too abstruse for the common
mind, the unit being made so small that a large
sum would have had to be expressed in a very great
number of figures, and there being five or six different kinds of new coins, some of them not simple
multiples of each other. Afterwards he proposed
as a modification a system of pounds, or dollars,
and doits, the doit answering to our present mill,
while providing also an ingenious arrangement by

which the money of account was to differ from the
money of coinage. Jefferson changed the system
by grafting on it the dollar as a unit, and simplify-
ing it; and Hamilton perfected it further.

To understand the advantage, as well as the boldness, of Morris's scheme, we must keep in mind the
horrible condition of our currency at that time.
We had no proper coins of our own; nothing but
hopelessly depreciated paper bills, a mass of copper,
and some clipped and counterfeited gold and silver
coin from the mints of England, France, Spain, and
even Germany. Dollars, pounds, shillings, doub-
loons, ducats, moidores, joes, crowns, pistareens,
coppers, and sous circulated indifferently, and with
various values in each colony. A dollar was worth
six shillings in Massachusetts, eight in New York,
seven and sixpence in Pennsylvania, six again in
Virginia, eight again in North Carolina, thirty-two
and a half in South Carolina, and five in Georgia.
The government itself had to resort to clipping in
one of its most desperate straits; and at last people would only take payment by weight of gold or
silver.

Morris, in his report, dwelt especially on three
points: first, that the new money should be easily
intelligible to the multitude, and should, therefore,
bear a close relation to the coins already existing,
as otherwise its sudden introduction would bring
business to a standstill, and would excite distrust
and suspicion everywhere, particularly among the
poorest and most ignorant, the day-laborers, the

farm servants, and the hired help; second, that its lowest divisible sum, or unit, should be very small, so that the price and the value of little things could be made proportionate; and third, that as far as possible the money should increase in decimal ratio. The Spanish dollar was the coin most widely circulated, while retaining everywhere about the same value. Accordingly he took this, and then sought for a unit that would go evenly into it, as well as into the various shillings, disregarding the hopelessly aberrant shilling of South Carolina. Such a unit was a quarter of a grain of pure silver, equal to the one fourteen hundred and fortieth part of a dollar; it was not, of course, necessary to have it exactly represented in coin. On the contrary, he proposed to strike two copper pieces, respectively of five and eight units, to be known as *fives* and *eights*. Two *eights* would then make a penny in Pennsylvania, and three *eights* one in Georgia, while three *fives* would make one in New York, and four would make one in Massachusetts. Morris's great aim was, while establishing uniform coins for the entire Union, to get rid of the fractional remainders in translating the old currencies into the new; and in addition his reckoning adapted itself to the different systems in the different States, as well as to the different coins in use. But he introduced an entirely new system of coinage, and moreover used therein the names of several old coins while giving them new values. His originally proposed table of currency was as follows: —

One crown = ten dollars, or . . . 10,000 units.
One dollar = ten bills, or . . . . 1,000 "
One bill = ten pence, or . . . . 100 "
One penny = ten quarters, or . . 10 "
One quarter = ... 1 "

But he proposed that for convenience other coins
should be struck, like the copper *five* and *eight*
above spoken of, and he afterwards altered his
names. He then called the bill of one hundred
units a *cent*, making it consist of twenty-five grains
of silver and two of copper, being thus the lowest
silver coin. Five *cents* were to make a *quint*, and
ten a *mark*.

Congress, according to its custom, received the
report, applauded it, and did nothing in the matter.
Shortly afterwards, however, Jefferson took it up,
when the whole subject was referred to a committee
of which he was a member. He highly approved
of Morris's plan, and took from it the idea of a
decimal system, and the use of the words "dollar"
and "cent." But he considered Morris's unit too
small, and preferred to take as his own the Spanish
dollar, which was already known to all the people,
its value being uniform and well understood. Then,
by keeping strictly to the decimal system, and dividing the dollar into one hundred parts, he got
cents for our fractional currency. He thus introduced a simpler system than that of Morris, with
an existing and well-understood unit, instead of an
imaginary one that would have to be, for the first
time, brought to the knowledge of the people, and

which might be adopted only with reluctance. On the other hand, Jefferson's system failed entirely to provide for the extension of the old currencies in the terms of the new without the use of fractions. On this account Morris vehemently opposed it, but it was nevertheless adopted. He foretold, what actually came to pass, that the people would be very reluctant to throw away their local moneys in order to take up a general money which bore no special relation to them. For half a century afterwards the people clung to their absurd shillings and sixpences, the government itself, in its post-office transactions, being obliged to recognize the obsolete terms in vogue in certain localities. Some curious pieces circulated freely up to the time of the civil war. Still, Jefferson's plan worked admirably in the end.

All the time he was working so hard at the finances, Morris nevertheless continued to enjoy himself to the full in the society of Philadelphia. Imperious, light-hearted, good-looking, well-dressed, he ranked as a wit among men, as a beau among women. He was equally sought for dances and dinners. He was a fine scholar and a polished gentleman; a capital story-teller; and had just a touch of erratic levity that served to render him still more charming. Occasionally he showed whimsical peculiarities, usually about very small things, that brought him into trouble; and one such freak cost him a serious injury. In his capacity of young man of fashion, he used to drive

about town in a phaeton with a pair of small, spirited horses; and because of some whim, he would
not allow the groom to stand at their heads. So
one day they took fright, ran, threw him out, and
broke his leg. The leg had to be amputated, and
he was ever afterwards forced to wear a wooden
one. However, he took his loss with most philosophic cheerfulness, and even bore with equanimity
the condolences of those exasperating individuals,
of a species by no means peculiar to Revolutionary
times, who endeavored to prove to him the mani-
fest falsehood that such an accident was " all for
the best." To one of these dreary gentlemen he
responded, with disconcerting vivacity, that his
visitor had so handsomely argued the advantage of
being entirely legless as to make him almost tempted
to part with his remaining limb; and to another he
announced that at least there was the compensation
that he would be a *steadier* man with one leg than
with two. Wild accounts of the accident got about,
which rather irritated him, and in answer to a letter from Jay he wrote: " I suppose it was Deane
who wrote to you from France about the loss of
my leg. His account is facetious. Let it pass.
The leg is gone, and there is an end of the matter."
His being crippled did not prevent him from going
about in society very nearly as much as ever; and
society in Philadelphia was at the moment gayer
than in any other American city. Indeed Jay, a
man of Puritanic morality, wrote to Morris somewhat gloomily to inquire about " the rapid progress

of luxury at Philadelphia;" to which his younger friend, who highly appreciated the good things of life, replied light-heartedly: "With respect to our taste for luxury, do not grieve about it. Luxury is not so bad a thing as it is often supposed to be; and if it were, still we must follow the course of things, and turn to advantage what exists, since we have not the power to annihilate or create. The very definition of 'luxury' is as difficult as the suppression of it." In another letter he remarked that he thought there were quite as many knaves among the men who went on foot as there were among those who drove in carriages.

Jay at this time, having been successively a member of the Continental Congress, the New York legislature, and the State Constitutional Convention, having also been the first chief justice of his native State, and then president of the Continental Congress, had been sent as our minister to Spain. Morris always kept up an intimate correspondence with him. It is noticeable that the three great Revolutionary statesmen from New York, Hamilton, Jay, and Morris, always kept on good terms, and always worked together; while the friendship between two, Jay and Morris, was very close.

The two men, in their correspondence, now and then touched on other than state matters. One of Jay's letters which deals with the education of his children would be most healthful reading for those Americans of the present day who send their chil-

dren to be brought up abroad in Swiss schools, or
English and German universities. He writes: " I
think the youth of every free, civilized country
should be educated in it, and not permitted to
travel out of it until age has made them so cool
and firm as to retain their national and moral
impressions. American youth may possibly form
proper and perhaps useful friendships in European
seminaries, but I think not so *probably* as among
their fellow citizens, with whom they are to grow
up, whom it will be useful for them to know and
be early known to, and with whom they are to be
engaged in the business of active life. . . . I do
not hesitate to prefer an American education."
The longer Jay stayed away, the more devoted he
became to America. He had a good, hearty, honest contempt for the miserable " cosmopolitanism "
so much affected by the feebler folk of fashion.
As he said, he " could never become so far a citizen of the world as to view every part of it with
equal regard," for " his affections were deep-rooted
in America," and he always asserted that he had
never seen anything in Europe to cause him to
abate his prejudices in favor of his own land.

Jay had a very hard time at the Spanish court,
which, he wrote Morris, had " little money, less
wisdom, and no credit." Spain, although fighting
England, was bitterly jealous of the United States,
fearing most justly our aggressive spirit, and desiring to keep the lower Mississippi valley entirely
under its own control. Jay, a statesman of in-

tensely national spirit, was determined to push our
boundaries as far westward as possible; he insisted on their reaching to the Mississippi, and on
our having the right to navigate that stream.
Morris did not agree with him, and on this subject, as has been already said, he for once showed
less than his usual power of insight into the future. He wrote Jay that it was absurd to quarrel
about a country inhabited only by red men, and to
claim "a territory we cannot occupy, a navigation
we cannot enjoy." He also ventured the curiously
false prediction that, if the territory beyond the
Alleghanies should ever be filled up, it would be
by a population drawn from the whole world, not
one hundredth part of it American, which would
immediately become an independent and rival nation. However, he could not make Jay swerve a
hand's breadth from his position about our western
boundaries, though on every other point the two
were in hearty accord.

In relating and forecasting the military situation, Morris was more happy. He was peculiarly
interested in Greene, and from the outset foretold
the final success of his southern campaign. In a
letter written March 31, 1781, after the receipt of
the news of the battle of Guilford Court House, he
describes to Jay Greene's forces and prospects.
His troops included, he writes, "from 1500 to
2000 Continentals, many of them raw, and somewhat more of militia than regular troops, — the
whole of these almost in a state of nature, and of

whom it ought to be said, as by Hamlet to Hora-
tio, ' Thou hast no other revenue but thy good
spirits to feed and clothe thee.' " The militia he
styled the "*fruges consumere nati* of an army."
He then showed the necessity of the battle being
fought, on account of the fluctuating state of the
militia, the incapacity of the state governments to
help themselves, the poverty of the country (" so
that the very teeth of the enemy defend them,
especially in retreat "), and, above all, because a
defeat was of little consequence to us, while it
would ruin the enemy. He wrote : " There is no
loss in fighting away two or three hundred men
who would go home if they were not put in the
way of being knocked on the head. . . . These
are unfeeling reflections. I would apologize for
them to any one who did not know that I have at
least enough of sensibility. The gush of sentiment
will not alter the nature of things, and the business of the statesman is more to reason than to
feel." Morris was always confident that we should
win in the end, and sometimes thought a little
punishment really did our people good. When
Cornwallis was in Virginia he wrote : " The enemy
are scourging the Virginians, at least those of
Lower Virginia. This is distressing, but will have
some good consequences. In the mean time the
delegates of Virginia make as many lamentations
as ever Jeremiah did, and to as good purpose perhaps."

The war was drawing to an end. Great Britain

had begun the struggle with everything — allies, numbers, wealth — in her favor; but now, towards the close, the odds were all the other way. The French were struggling with her on equal terms for the mastery of the seas; the Spaniards were helping the French, and were bending every energy to carry through successfully the great siege of Gibraltar; the Dutch had joined their ancient enemies, and their fleet fought a battle with the English, which, for bloody indecisiveness, rivaled the actions when Van Tromp and De Ruyter held the Channel against Blake and Monk. In India the name of Hyder Ali had become a very nightmare of horror to the British. In America, the centre of the war, the day had gone conclusively against the Island folk. Greene had doggedly fought and marched his way through the southern States with his ragged, under-fed, badly armed troops; he had been beaten in three obstinate battles, had each time inflicted a greater relative loss than he received, and, after retiring in good order a short distance, had always ended by pursuing his lately victorious foes; at the close of the campaign he had completely reconquered the southern States by sheer capacity for standing punishment, and had cooped up the remaining British force in Charleston. In the northern States the British held Newport and New York, but could not penetrate, elsewhere; while at Yorktown their ablest general was obliged to surrender his whole army to the overwhelming force brought against him by Washington's masterly strategy.

Yet England, hemmed in by the ring of her foes, fronted them all with a grand courage. In her veins the Berserker blood was up, and she hailed each new enemy with grim delight, exerting to the full her warlike strength. Single-handed she kept them all at bay, and repaid with crippling blows the injuries they had done her. In America alone the tide ran too strongly to be turned. But Holland was stripped of all her colonies; in the East, Sir Eyre Coote beat down Hyder Ali, and taught Moslem and Hindoo alike that they could not shake off the grasp of the iron hands that held India. Rodney won back for his country the supremacy of the ocean in that great sea-fight where he shattered the splendid French navy; and the long siege of Gibraltar closed with the crushing overthrow of the assailants. So, with bloody honor, England ended the most disastrous war she had ever waged.

The war had brought forth many hard fighters, but only one great commander, — Washington. For the rest, on land, Cornwallis, Greene, Rawdon, and possibly Lafayette and Rochambeau, might all rank as fairly good generals, probably in the order named, although many excellent critics place Greene first. At sea, Rodney and the Bailli de Suffren won the honors; the latter stands beside Duquesne and Tourville in the roll of French admirals; while Rodney was a true latter-day buccaneer, as fond of fighting as of plundering, and a first-rate hand at both. Neither ranks with such mighty sea-chiefs as Nelson, nor yet with Blake, Farragut, or Tegethof.

All parties were tired of the war; peace was essential to all. But of all, America was most resolute to win what she had fought for; and America had been the most successful so far. English historians — even so generally impartial a writer as Mr. Lecky — are apt greatly to exaggerate our relative exhaustion, and try to prove it by quoting from the American leaders every statement that shows despondency and suffering. If they applied the same rule to their own side, they would come to the conclusion that the British empire was at that time on the brink of dissolution. Of course we had suffered very heavily, and had blundered badly; but in both respects we were better off than our antagonists. Mr. Lecky is right in bestowing unstinted praise on our diplomatists for the hardihood and success with which they insisted on all our demands being granted; but he is wrong when he says or implies that the military situation did not warrant their attitude. Of all the contestants, America was the most willing to continue the fight rather than yield her rights. Morris expressed the general feeling when he wrote to Jay, on August 6, 1782: "Nobody will be thankful for any peace but a very good one. This *they* should have thought on who made war with the republic. I am among the number who would be extremely ungrateful for the grant of a bad peace. My public and private character

will both concert to render the sentiment coming
from me unsuspected. Judge, then, of others,
judge of the many-headed fool who can feel no
more than his own sorrowing. . . . I wish that
while the war lasts it may be real war, and that
when peace comes it may be real peace." As to
our military efficiency, we may take Washington's
word (in a letter to Jay of October 18, 1782) :
" I am certain it will afford you pleasure to know
that our army is better organized, disciplined, and
clothed than it has been at any period since the
commencement of the war. This you may be assured is the fact."

Another mistake of English historians — again
likewise committed by Mr. Lecky — comes in their
laying so much stress on the help rendered to the
Americans by their allies, while at the same time
speaking as if England had none. As a matter of
fact, England would have stood no chance at all
had the contest been strictly confined to British
troops on the one hand, and to the rebellious colonists on the other. There were more German
auxiliaries in the British ranks than there were
French allies in the American; the loyalists, including the regularly enlisted loyalists as well as
the militia who took part in the various Tory up-
risings, were probably more numerous still. The
withdrawal of all Hessians, Tories, and Indians
from the British army would have been cheaply
purchased by the loss of our own foreign allies.

The European powers were even a shade more

anxious for peace than we were ; and to conduct the negotiations for our side, we chose three of our greatest statesmen, — Franklin, Adams, and Jay.

Congress, in appointing our commissioners, had, with little regard for the national dignity, given them instructions which, if obeyed, would have rendered them completely subservient to France ; for they were directed to undertake nothing in the negotiations without the knowledge and concurrence of the French cabinet, and in all decisions to be ultimately governed by the advice of that body. Morris fiercely resented such servile subservience, and in a letter to Jay denounced Congress with well-justified warmth, writing : " That the proud should prostitute the very little dignity this poor country is possessed of would be indeed astounding, if we did not know the near alliance between pride and meanness. Men who have too little spirit to demand of their constituents that they do their duty, who have sufficient humility to beg a paltry pittance at the hands of any and every sovereign, — such men will always be ready to pay the price which vanity shall demand from the vain." Jay promptly persuaded his colleagues to unite with him in disregarding the instructions of Congress on this point; had he not done so, the dignity of our government would, as he wrote Morris, " have been in the dust." Franklin was at first desirous of yielding obedience to the command, but Adams immediately joined Jay in repudiating it.

We had waged war against Britain, with France

and Spain as allies; but in making peace we had
to strive for our rights against our friends almost
as much as against our enemies.   There was much
generous and disinterested enthusiasm for America
among Frenchmen individually ; but the French
government, with which alone we were to deal in
making peace, had acted throughout from purely
selfish motives, and in reality did not care an atom
for American rights.   We owed France no more
gratitude for taking our part than she owed us for
giving her an opportunity of advancing her own
interests, and striking a severe blow at an old-time
enemy and rival.   As for Spain, she disliked us
quite as much as she did England.

The peace negotiations brought all this out very
clearly.   The great French minister, Vergennes,
who dictated the policy of his court all through the
contest, cared nothing for the Revolutionary colonists themselves ; but he was bent upon securing
them their independence, so as to weaken England,
and he was also bent upon keeping them from
gaining too much strength, so that they might
always remain dependent allies of France.   He
wished to establish the " balance of power " system
in America.   The American commissioners he at
first despised for their blunt, truthful straightforwardness, which he, trained in the school of deceit,
and a thorough believer in every kind of finesse
and double-dealing, mistook for boorishness ; later
on, he learned to his chagrin that they were able
as well as honest, and that their resolution, skill,

and far-sightedness made them, where their own
deepest interests were concerned, over-matches for
the subtle diplomats of Europe.

America, then, was determined to secure not only
independence, but also a chance to grow into a
great continental nation; she wished her boundaries fixed at the Great Lakes and the Mississippi;
she also asked for the free navigation of the latter
to the Gulf, and for a share in the fisheries. Spain
did not even wish that we should be made independent; she hoped to be compensated at our expense
for her failure to take Gibraltar; and she desired
that we should be kept so weak as to hinder us
from being aggressive. Her fear of us, by the
way, was perfectly justifiable, for the greatest part
of our present territory lies within what were nominally Spanish limits a hundred years ago. France,
as the head of a great coalition, wanted to keep on
good terms with both her allies; but, as Gérard,
the French minister at Washington, said, if France
had to choose between the two, " the decision would
not be in favor of the United States." She wished
to secure for America independence, but she wished
also to keep the new nation so weak that it would
" feel the need of sureties, allies, and protectors."
France desired to exclude our people from the fisheries, to deprive us of half our territories by making the Alleghanies our western boundaries, and to
secure to Spain the undisputed control of the navigation of the Mississippi. It was not to the interest of France and Spain that we should be a great

and formidable people, and very naturally they would not help us to become one. There is no need of blaming them for their conduct, but it would have been rank folly to have been guided by their wishes. Our true policy was admirably summed up by Jay in his letters to Livingston, where he says: " Let us be honest and grateful to France, but let us think for ourselves. . . . Since we have assumed a place in the political firmament, let us move like a primary and not a secondary planet." Fortunately, England's own self-interest made her play into our hands; as Fox put it, it was necessary for her to " insist in the strongest manner that, if America is independent, she must be so of the whole world. No secret, tacit, or ostensible connection with France."

Our statesmen won; we got all we asked, as much to the astonishment of France as of England; we proved even more successful in diplomacy than in arms. As Fox had hoped, we became independent not only of England, but of all the world; we were not entangled as a dependent subordinate in the policy of France, nor did we sacrifice our western boundary to Spain. It was a great triumph, — greater than any that had been won by our soldiers. Franklin had a comparatively small share in gaining it; the glory of carrying through successfully the most important treaty we ever negotiated belongs to Jay and Adams, and especially to Jay.

CHAPTER VI

THE FORMATION OF THE NATIONAL CONSTITUTION

BEFORE peace was established, Morris had been appointed a commissioner to treat for the exchange of prisoners. Nothing came of his efforts, however, the British and Americans being utterly unable to come to any agreement. Both sides had been greatly exasperated, — the British by the Americans' breach of faith about Burgoyne's troops, and the Americans by the inhuman brutality with which their captive countrymen had been treated. An amusing feature of the affair was a conversation between Morris and the British general, Dalrymple, wherein the former assured the latter rather patronizingly that the British "still remained a great people, a very great people," and that "they would undoubtedly still hold their rank in Europe." He would have been surprised had he known not only that the stubborn Island folk were destined soon to hold a higher rank in Europe than ever before, but that from their loins other nations, broad as continents, were to spring, so that the South Seas should become an English ocean, and that over a fourth of the

world's surface there should be spoken the tongue
of Pitt and Washington.

No sooner was peace declared, and the immediate and pressing danger removed, than the confederation relapsed into a loose knot of communities,
as quarrelsome as they were contemptible. The
states'-rights men for the moment had things all
their own way, and speedily reduced us to the level
afterwards reached by the South American republics. Each commonwealth set up for itself, and
tried to oppress its neighbors; not one had a creditable history for the next four years; while the
career of Rhode Island in particular can only be
properly described as infamous. We refused to
pay our debts, we would not even pay our army;
and mob violence flourished rankly. As a natural
result, the European powers began to take advantage of our weakness and division.

All our great men saw the absolute need of
establishing a National Union — not a league or a
confederation — if the country was to be saved.
None felt this more strongly than Morris, and no
one was more hopeful of the final result. Jay had
written to him as to the need of " raising and maintaining a national spirit in America; " and he
wrote in reply, at different times: " Much of con-
vulsion will yet ensue, yet it must terminate in
giving to government that power without which
government is but a name. . . . This country has
never yet been known to Europe, and God knows
whether it ever will be. To England it is less

known than to any other part of Europe, because
they constantly view it through a medium of either
prejudice or faction. True it is that the general
government wants energy, and equally true it is
that the want will eventually be supplied. A national spirit is the natural result of national existence; *and although some of the present generation may feel the result of colonial oppositions of
opinion, that generation will die away and give
place to a race of Americans.*[1] On this occasion,
as on others, Great Britain is our best friend; and,
by seizing the critical moment when we were about
to divide, she has shown us the dreadful consequences of division. . . . Indeed, my friend, nothing can do us so much good as to convince the
eastern and southern States how necessary it is
to give proper force to the federal government,
and nothing will so soon operate that conviction
as foreign efforts to restrain the navigation of the
one and the commerce of the other." The last
sentence referred to the laws aimed at our trade
by Great Britain, and by other powers as well, —
symptoms of outside hostility which made us at
once begin to draw together again.

Money troubles grew apace, and produced the
usual crop of crude theories and of vicious and dishonest legislation in accordance therewith. Law-
less outbreaks became common, and in Massachusetts culminated in actual rebellion. The mass of
the people were rendered hostile to any closer

[1] The italics are mine.

union by their ignorance, their jealousy, and the general particularistic bent of their minds, — this last being merely a vicious graft on, or rather outgrowth of, the love of freedom inborn in the race. Their leaders were enthusiasts of pure purpose and unsteady mental vision; they were followed by the mass of designing politicians, who feared that their importance would be lost if their sphere of action should be enlarged. Among these leaders the three most important were, in New York, George Clinton, and, in Massachusetts and Virginia, two much greater men, — Samuel Adams and Patrick Henry. All three had done excellent service at the beginning of the Revolutionary troubles. Patrick Henry lived to redeem himself, almost in his last hour, by the noble stand he took in aid of Washington against the democratic nullification agitation of Jefferson and Madison; but the usefulness of each of the other two was limited to the early portion of his career.

Like every other true patriot and statesman, Morris did all in his power to bring into one combination the varied interests favorable to the formation of a government that should be strong and responsible as well as free. The public creditors and the soldiers of the army — whose favorite toasts were, " A hoop to the barrel," and " Cement to the union " — were the two classes most sensible of the advantages of such a government; and to each of these Morris addressed himself when he proposed to consolidate the public debt, both to private citizens and to the soldiers, and to make it a charge on the United States, and not on the several separate States.

In consequence of the activity and ability with which he advocated a firmer union, the extreme states'-rights men were especially hostile to him; and certain of their number assailed him with bitter malignity, both then and afterwards. One accusation was, that he had improper connections with the public creditors. This was a pure slander, absolutely without foundation, and not supported by even the pretense of proof. Another accusation was that he favored the establishment of a monarchy. This was likewise entirely untrue. Morris was not a sentimental political theorist; he was an eminently practical — that is, useful — statesman, who saw with unusual clearness that each people must have a government suited to its own individual character, and to the stage of political and social development it had reached. He realized that a nation must be governed according to the actual needs and capacities of its citizens, not according to any abstract theory or set of ideal principles. He would have dismissed with contemptuous laughter the ideas of those Americans who at the present day believe that Anglo-Saxon democracy can be applied successfully to a half-savage negroid people in Hayti, or of those Englishmen who consider seriously the proposition to renovate Turkey by giving her representative institutions and a parliamentary government. He understood and stated that a monarchy "did not consist with the taste and temper of the people" in America, and he believed in establishing a form of government that did. Like almost every other statesman of the day, the perverse obstinacy of the extreme particularist section at times made him downhearted, and caused him almost to despair of a good government being established ; and like every sensible man he would have preferred almost any strong, orderly government to the futile anarchy towards which the ultra states'-rights men or separatists tended. Had these last ever finally obtained the upper hand, either in Revolutionary or post-Revolutionary times, either in 1787 or 1861, the fact would have shown conclusively that Americans were unfitted for republicanism and self-government. An orderly monarchy would certainly be preferable to a republic of the epileptic Spanish-American type. The extreme doctrinaires, who are fiercest in declaiming in favor of freedom, are in reality its worst foes, far more dangerous than any absolute monarchy ever can be. When liberty becomes license, some form of one-man power is not far distant.

The one great reason for our having succeeded as no other people ever has, is to be found in that common sense which has enabled us to preserve the largest possible individual freedom on the one hand, while showing an equally remarkable capacity for combination on the other. We have committed plenty of faults, but we have seen and rem-

edied them. Our very doctrinaires have usually
acted much more practically than they have talked.
Jefferson, when in power, adopted most of the Federalist theories, and became markedly hostile to the
nullification movements at whose birth he had himself officiated. We have often blundered badly in
the beginning, but we have always come out well
in the end. The Dutch, when they warred for freedom from Spanish rule, showed as much short-
sighted selfishness and bickering jealousy as even
our own Revolutionary ancestors, and only a part
remained faithful to the end : as a result, but one
section won independence, while the Netherlands
were divided, and never grasped the power that
should have been theirs. As for the Spanish-
Americans, they split up hopelessly almost before
they were free, and, though they bettered their
condition a little, yet lost nine tenths of what they
had gained. Scotland and Ireland, when independent, were nests of savages. All the follies our
forefathers committed can be paralleled elsewhere,
but their successes are unique.

So it was in the few years immediately succeeding the peace by which we won our independence.
The mass of the people wished for no closer union
than was to be found in a lax confederation ; but
they had the good sense to learn the lesson taught
by the weakness and lawlessness they saw around
them ; they reluctantly made up their minds to the
need of a stronger government, and when they had
once come to their decision, neither demagogue nor
doctrinaire could swerve them from it.

The national convention to form a constitution met in May, 1787 ; and rarely in the world's history has there been a deliberative body which contained so many remarkable men, or produced results so lasting and far-reaching. The Congress whose members signed the Declaration of Independence had but cleared the ground on which the framers of the Constitution were to build. Among the delegates in attendance, easily first stood Washington and Franklin, — two of that great American trio in which Lincoln is the third. Next came Hamilton from New York, having as colleagues a couple of mere obstructionists sent by the Clintonians to handicap him.   From Pennsylvania came Robert Morris and Gouverneur Morris ; from Virginia, Madison ; from South Carolina, Rutledge and the Pinckneys ; and so on through the other States. Some of the most noted statesmen were absent, however. Adams and Jefferson were abroad. Jay was acting as secretary for foreign affairs, in which capacity, by the way, he had shown most unlooked-for weakness in yielding to Spanish demands about the Mississippi.

Two years after taking part in the proceedings of the American Constitutional Convention, Morris witnessed the opening of the States General of France. He thoroughly appreciated the absolute and curious contrast offered by these two bodies, each so big with fate for all mankind. The men who predominated in and shaped the actions of

the first belonged to a type not uncommonly
brought forth by a people already accustomed to
freedom at a crisis in the struggle to preserve or
extend its liberties. During the past few centuries
this type had appeared many times among the liberty-loving nations who dwelt on the shores of the
Baltic and the North Sea; and our forefathers represented it in its highest and most perfect shapes.
It is a type only to be found among men already
trained to govern themselves as well as others. The
American statesmen were the kinsfolk and fellows
of Hampden and Pym, of William the Silent and
John of Barneveldt. Save love of freedom, they
had little in common with the closet philosophers,
the enthusiastic visionaries, and the selfish demagogues who in France helped pull up the flood-
gates of an all-swallowing torrent. They were
great men; but it was less the greatness of mere
genius than that springing from the union of strong,
virile qualities with steadfast devotion to a high
ideal. In certain respects they were ahead of all
their European compeers; yet they preserved virtues forgotten or sneered at by the contempora-
neous generation of trans-Atlantic leaders. They
wrought for the future as surely as did the French
Jacobins; but their spirit was the spirit of the
Long Parliament. They were resolute to free
themselves from the tyranny of man; but they had
not unlearned the reverence felt by their fathers
for their fathers' God. They were sincerely religious. The advanced friends of freedom abroad

scoffed at religion, and would have laughed outright at a proposition to gain help for their cause
by prayer ; but to the founders of our Constitution,
when matters were at a deadlock, and the outcome
looked almost hopeless, it seemed a most fit and
proper thing that one of the chief of their number
should propose to invoke to aid them a wisdom
greater than the wisdom of human beings.   Even
those among their descendants who no longer share
their trusting faith may yet well do regretful homage to a religious spirit so deep-rooted and so
strongly tending to bring out a pure and high
morality.   The statesmen who met in 1787 were
earnestly patriotic.   They unselfishly desired the
welfare of their countrymen.   They were cool,
resolute men, of strong convictions, with clear insight into the future.   They were thoroughly acquainted with the needs of the community for
which they were to act.   Above all, they possessed
that inestimable quality, so characteristic of their
race, hard-headed common sense.   Their theory of
government was a very high one ; but they understood perfectly that it had to be accommodated to
the shortcomings of the average citizen.   Small
indeed was their resemblance to the fiery orators
and brilliant pamphleteers of the States General.
They were emphatically good men; they were no
less emphatically practical men.   They would have
scorned Mirabeau as a scoundrel; they would have
despised Sieyès as a vain and impractical theorist.
   The deliberations of the convention in their

result illustrated in a striking manner the truth
of the American principle, that — for deliberative,
not executive, purposes — the wisdom of many
men is worth more than the wisdom of any one
man. The Constitution that the members assem-
bled in convention finally produced was not only
the best possible one for America at that time, but
it was also, in spite of its shortcomings, and taking
into account its fitness for our own people and conditions, as well as its accordance with the principles of abstract right, probably the best that any
nation has ever had, while it was beyond question
a very much better one than any single member
could have prepared. The particularist statesmen
would have practically denied us any real union or
efficient executive power; while there was hardly
a Federalist member who would not, in his anxiety
to avoid the evils from which we were suffering,
have given us a government so centralized and
aristocratic that it would have been utterly un-
suited to a proud, liberty-loving, and essentially
democratic race, and would have infallibly pro-
voked a tremendous reactionary revolt.

It is impossible to read through the debates of
the convention without being struck by the innumerable shortcomings of each individual plan proposed by the several members, as divulged in their
speeches, when compared with the plan finally
adopted. Had the result been in accordance with
the views of the strong-government men like Hamilton on the one hand, or of the weak-government

men like Franklin on the other, it would have been equally disastrous for the country. The men who afterwards naturally became the chiefs of the Federalist party, and who included in their number the bulk of the great Revolutionary leaders, were the ones to whom we mainly owe our present form of government; certainly we owe them more, both on this and on other points, than we do their rivals, the after-time Democrats. Yet there were some articles of faith in the creed of the latter so essential to our national well-being, and yet so counter to the prejudices of the Federalists, that it was inevitable they should triumph in the end. Jefferson led the Democrats to victory only when he had learned to acquiesce thoroughly in some of the fundamental principles of Federalism, and the government of himself and his successors was good chiefly in so far as it followed out the theories of the Hamiltonians; while Hamilton and the Federalists fell from power because they could not learn the one great truth taught by Jefferson, — that in America a statesman should trust the people, and should endeavor to secure to each man all possible individual liberty, confident that he will use it aright. The old-school Jeffersonian theorists believed in "a strong people and a weak government." Lincoln was the first who showed how a strong people might have a strong government and yet remain the freest on the earth. He seized — half unwittingly — all that was best and wisest in the traditions of Federalism; he was the true successor of the Federalist leaders; but he grafted on their system a profound belief that the great heart of the nation beat for truth, honor, and liberty.

This fact, that in 1787 all the thinkers of the day drew out plans that in some respects went very wide of the mark, must be kept in mind, or else we shall judge each particular thinker with undue harshness when we examine his utterances without comparing them with those of his fellows. But one partial exception can be made. In the Constitutional Convention Madison, a moderate Federalist, was the man who, of all who were there, saw things most clearly as they were, and whose theories most closely corresponded with the principles finally adopted; and although even he was at first dissatisfied with the result, and both by word and by action interpreted the Constitution in widely different ways at different times, still this was Madison's time of glory: he was one of the statesmen who do extremely useful work, but only at some single given crisis. While the Constitution was being formed and adopted, he stood in the very front; but in his later career he sunk his own individuality, and became a mere pale shadow of Jefferson.

Morris played a very prominent part in the convention. He was a ready speaker, and among all the able men present there was probably no such really brilliant thinker. In the debates he spoke more often than any one else, although Madison was not far behind him; and his speeches

betrayed, but with marked and exaggerated emphasis, both the virtues and the shortcomings of the
Federalist school of thought.   They show us, too,
why he never rose to the first rank of statesmen.
His keen, masterful mind, his far-sightedness, and
the force and subtlety of his reasoning were all
marred by his incurable cynicism and deep-rooted
distrust of mankind.   He throughout appears as
advocatus diaboli ; he puts the lowest interpreta-
tion upon every act, and frankly avows his disbe-
lief in all generous and unselfish motives.   His
continual allusions to the overpowering influence
of the baser passions, and to their mastery of the
human race at all times, drew from Madison, although the two men generally acted together, a
protest against his " forever inculcating the utter
political depravity of men, and the necessity for
opposing one vice and interest as the only possible
check to another vice and interest."

Morris championed a strong national government, wherein he was right ; but he also championed a system of class representation, leaning
towards aristocracy, wherein he was wrong.   Not
Hamilton himself was a firmer believer in the
national idea.   His one great object was to secure
a powerful and lasting Union, instead of a loose
federal league.   It must be remembered that in
the convention the term " federal " was used in
exactly the opposite sense to the one in which it
was taken afterwards ; that is, it was used as the
antithesis of " national," not as its synonym.   The

states'-rights men used it to express a system of government such as that of the old federation of the thirteen colonies; while their opponents called themselves Nationalists, and only took the title of Federalists after the Constitution had been formed, and then simply because the name was popular with the masses. They thus appropriated their adversaries' party name, bestowing it on the organization most hostile to their adversaries' party theories. Similarly, the term " Republican Party," which was originally in our history merely another name for the Democracy, has in the end been adopted by the chief opponents of the latter.

The difficulties for the convention to surmount seemed insuperable; on almost every question that came up, there were clashing interests. Strong government and weak government, pure democracy or a modified aristocracy, small States and large States, North and South, slavery and freedom, agricultural sections as against commercial sections, — on each of twenty points the delegates split into hostile camps, that could only be reconciled by concessions from both sides. The Constitution was not one compromise; it was a bundle of compromises, all needful.

Morris, like every other member of the convention, sometimes took the right and sometimes the wrong side on the successive issues that arose. But on the most important one of all he made no error; and he commands our entire sympathy for his thorough-going nationalism. As was to be expected, he had no regard whatever for states' rights. He wished to deny to the small States the equal representation in the Senate finally allowed them; and he was undoubtedly right theoretically. No good argument can be adduced in support of the present system on that point. Still, it has thus far worked no harm; the reason being that our States have merely artificial boundaries, while those of small population have hitherto been distributed pretty evenly among the different sections, so that they have been split up like the others on every important issue, and thus have never been arrayed against the rest of the country.

Though Morris and his side were defeated in their efforts to have the States represented proportionally in the Senate, yet they carried their point as to representation in the House. Also, on the general question of making a national government, as distinguished from a league or federation, the really vital point, their triumph was complete. The Constitution they drew up and had adopted no more admitted of legal or peaceable rebellion — whether called secession or nullification — on the part of the State than on the part of a county or an individual.

Morris expressed his own views with his usual clear-cut, terse vigor when he asserted that " state attachments and state importance had been the bane of the country," and that he came, not as a mere delegate from one section, but " as a representative of America, — a representative in some

degree of the whole human race, for the whole
human race would be affected by the outcome of
the convention." And he poured out the flood
of his biting scorn on those gentlemen who came
there "to truck and bargain for their respective
States," asking what man there was who could tell
with certainty the State wherein he — and even
more wherein his children — would live in the
future; and reminding the small States, with cavalier indifference, that, "if they did not like the
Union, no matter, — they would have to come in,
and that was all there was about it; for if per-
suasion did not unite the country, then the sword
would." His correct language and distinct enun-
ciation — to which Madison has borne witness —
allowed his grim truths to carry their full weight;
and he brought them home to his hearers with a
rough, almost startling earnestness and directness.
Many of those present must have winced when he
told them that it would matter nothing to America
"if all the charters and constitutions of the States
were thrown into the fire, and all the demagogues
into the ocean," and asserted that "any particular
State *ought* to be injured, for the sake of a majority of the people, in case its conduct showed
that it deserved it." He held that we should create a national government, to be the one and only
supreme power in the land, — one which, unlike a
mere federal league, such as we then lived under,
should have complete and compulsive operation;
and he instanced the examples as well of Greece

as of Germany and the United Netherlands, to prove that local jurisdiction destroyed every tie of nationality.

It shows the boldness of the experiment in which we were engaged, that we were forced to take all other nations, whether dead or living, as warnings, not examples; whereas, since we succeeded, we have served as a pattern to be copied, either wholly or in part, by every other people that has followed in our steps. Before our own experience, each similar attempt, save perhaps on the smallest scale, had been a failure. Where so many other nations teach by their mistakes, we are among the few who teach by their successes.

Be it noted also that, the doctrinaires to the contrary notwithstanding, we proved that a strong central government was perfectly compatible with absolute democracy. Indeed, the separatist spirit does not lead to true democratic freedom. Anarchy is the handmaiden of tyranny. Of all the States, South Carolina has shown herself (at least throughout the greater part of the present century) to be the most aristocratic, and the most wedded to the separatist spirit. The German masses were never so ground down by oppression as when the little German principalities were most independent of each other and of any central authority.

Morris believed in letting the United States interfere to put down a rebellion in a State, even though the executive of the State himself should be at the head of it; and he was supported in his views by Pinckney, the ablest member of the brilliant and useful but unfortunately short-lived school of South Carolina Federalists. Pinckney was a thorough-going Nationalist; he wished to go a good deal farther than the convention actually went in giving the central government complete control. Thus he proposed that Congress should have power to negative by a two thirds vote all State laws inconsistent with the harmony of the Union. Madison also wished to give Congress a veto over state legislation. Morris believed that a national law should be allowed to repeal any state law, and that Congress should legislate in all cases where the laws of the States conflicted among themselves.

Yet Morris, on the very question of nationalism, himself showed the narrowest, blindest, and least excusable sectional jealousy on one point. He felt as an American for all the Union, as it then existed; but he feared and dreaded the growth of the Union in the West, the very place where it was inevitable, as well as in the highest degree desirable, that the greatest growth should take place. He actually desired the convention to commit the criminal folly of attempting to provide that the West should always be kept subordinate to the East. Fortunately he failed; but the mere attempt casts the gravest discredit alike on his far-sightedness and on his reputation as a statesman. It is impossible to understand how one who was usually so cool and clear-headed an observer could have blundered so flagrantly on a point hardly less vital than the establishment of the Union itself. Indeed, had his views been carried through, they would in the end have nullified all the good bestowed by the Union.   In speaking against state jealousy, he had shown its foolishness by observing that no man could tell in what State his children would dwell; and the folly of the speaker himself was made quite as clear by his not perceiving that their most likely dwelling-place was in the West. This jealousy of the West was even more discreditable to the Northeast than the jealousy of America had been to England; and it continued strong, especially in New England, for very many years. It was a mean and unworthy feeling; and it was greatly to the credit of the Southerners that they shared it only to a very small extent.   The South, in fact, originally was in heartiest sympathy with the West; it was not until the middle of the present century that the country beyond the Alleghanies became preponderatingly Northern in sentiment.   In the Constitutional Convention itself, Butler of South Carolina pointed out " that the people and strength of America were evidently tending westwardly and southwestwardly."

Morris wished to discriminate against the West by securing to the Atlantic States the perpetual control of the Union.   He brought this idea up again and again, insisting that we should reserve to ourselves the right to put conditions on the Western States when we should admit them.   He

dwelt at length on the danger of throwing the pre-
ponderance of influence into the Western scale;
stating his dread of the " back members," who were
always the most ignorant, and the opponents of all
good measures. He foretold with fear that some
day the people of the West would outnumber the
people of the East, and he wished to put it in
the power of the latter to keep a majority of the
votes in their own hands. Apparently he did not
see that, if the West once became as populous as
he predicted, its legislators would forthwith cease
to be " back members." The futility of his fears,
and still more of his remedies, was so evident that
the convention paid very little heed to either.

On one point, however, his anticipations of harm
were reasonable, and indeed afterwards came true
in part. He insisted that the West, or interior,
would join the South and force us into a war with
some European power, wherein the benefits would
accrue to them and the harm to the Northeast.
The attitude of the South and West already clearly
foreshadowed a struggle with Spain for the Mississippi valley; and such a struggle would surely
have come, either with the French or Spaniards,
had we failed to secure the territory in question by
peaceful purchase. As it was, the realization of
Morris's prophecy was only put off for a few years;
the South and West brought on the war of 1812,
wherein the East was the chief sufferer.

On the question as to whether the Constitution should be made absolutely democratic or not,

Morris took the conservative side.   On the suffrage
his views are perfectly defensible : he believed that
it should be limited to freeholders.   He rightly
considered the question as to how widely it should
be extended to be one of expediency merely.   It
is simply idle folly to talk of suffrage as being an
" inborn " or " natural " right.   There are enormous communities totally unfit for its exercise ;
while true universal suffrage never has been, and
never will be, seriously advocated by any one.
There must always be an age limit, and such a limit
must necessarily be purely arbitrary.   The wildest
democrat of Revolutionary times did not dream of
doing away with the restrictions of race and sex
which kept most American citizens from the ballot-
box ;   and there is certainly much less abstract
right in a system which limits the suffrage to people of a certain color than there is in one which
limits it to people who come up to a given standard
of thrift and intelligence.   On the other hand, our
experience has not proved that men of wealth make
any better use of their ballots than do, for instance,
mechanics and other handicraftsmen.   No plan
could be adopted so perfect as to be free from all
drawbacks.   On the whole, however, and taking
our country in its length and breadth, manhood
suffrage has worked well, better than would have
been the case with any other system ; but even here
there are certain localities where its results have
been evil, and must simply be accepted as the
blemishes inevitably attendant upon, and marring,

any effort to carry out a scheme that will be widely applicable.

Morris contended that his plan would work no novel or great hardship, as the people in several States were already accustomed to freehold suffrage. He considered the freeholders to be the best guardians of liberty, and maintained that the restriction of the right to them was only creating a necessary safeguard "against the dangerous influence of those people, without property or principle, with whom, in the end, our country, like all other countries, was sure to abound." He did not believe that the ignorant and dependent could be trusted to vote. Madison supported him heartily, likewise thinking the freeholders the safest guardians of our rights; he indulged in some gloomy (and fortunately hitherto unverified) forebodings as to our future, which sound strangely coming from one who was afterwards an especial pet of the Jeffersonian democracy. He said: "In future times a great majority of the people will be without landed or any other property. They will then either combine under the influence of their common situation, — in which case the rights of property and the public liberty will not be safe in their hands, — or, as is more probable, they will become the tools of opulence and ambition."

Morris also enlarged on this last idea. "Give the votes to people who have no property, and they will sell them to the rich," said he. When taunted with his aristocratic tendencies, he answered that he had long ceased to be the dupe of words, that the mere sound of the name "aristocracy" had no terrors for him, but that he did fear lest harm should result to the people from the unacknowledged existence of the very thing they feared to mention. As he put it, there never was or would be a civilized society without an aristocracy, and his endeavor was to keep it as much as possible from doing mischief. He thus professed to be opposed to the existence of an aristocracy, but convinced that it would exist anyhow, and that therefore the best thing to be done was to give it a recognized place, while clipping its wings so as to prevent its working harm. In pursuance of this theory, he elaborated a wild plan, the chief feature of which was the provision for an aristocratic senate, and a popular or democratic house, which were to hold each other in check, and thereby prevent either party from doing damage. He believed that the senators should be appointed by the national executive, who should fill up the vacancies that occurred. To make the upper house effective as a checking branch, it should be so constituted as to have a personal interest in checking the other branch; it should be a senate for life, it should be rich, it should be aristocratic. He continued: It would then do wrong? He believed so; he hoped so. The rich would strive to enslave the rest; they always did. The proper security against them was to form them into a separate interest. The two forces would then con-

trol each other. By thus combining and setting
apart the aristocratic interest, the popular interest
would also be combined against it. There would
be mutual check and mutual security. If, on the
contrary, the rich and poor were allowed to mingle,
then, if the country were commercial, an oligarchy
would be established; and if it were not, an unlimited democracy would ensue. It was best to
look truth in the face. The loaves and fishes
would be needed to bribe demagogues; while as
for the people, if left to themselves, they would
never act from reason alone. The rich would take
advantage of their passions, and the result would
be either a violent aristocracy, or a more violent
despotism. — The speech containing these extraordinary sentiments, which do no particular credit
to either Morris's head or heart, is given in substance by Madison in the " Debates." Madison's
report is undoubtedly correct, for, after writing it,
he showed it to the speaker himself, who made but
one or two verbal alterations.

Morris applied an old theory in a new way when
he proposed to make " taxation proportional to
representation " throughout the Union. He considered the preservation of property as being the
distinguishing object of civilization, as liberty was
sufficiently guaranteed even by savagery; and
therefore he held that the representation in the
Senate should be according to property as well as
numbers. But when this proposition was defeated,
he declined to support one making property quali-

fications for congressmen, remarking that such
were proper for the electors rather than the
elected.

His views as to the power and functions of the
national executive were in the main sound, and he
succeeded in having most of them embodied in the
Constitution.   He wished to have the President
hold office during good behavior ; and, though this
was negatived, he succeeded in having him made
reëligible to the position.   He was instrumental in
giving him a qualified veto over legislation, and
in providing for his impeachment for misconduct ;
and also in having him made commander-in-chief
of the forces of the republic, and in allowing him
the appointment of governmental officers.   The
especial service he rendered, however, was his
successful opposition to the plan whereby the
President was to be elected by the legislature.
This proposition he combated with all his strength,
showing that it would take away greatly from the
dignity of the executive, and would render his
election a matter of cabal and faction, "like the
election of the pope by a conclave of cardinals."
He contended that the President should be chosen
by the people at large, by the citizens of the United
States, acting through electors whom they had
picked out.   He showed the probability that in such
a case the people would unite upon a man of continental reputation, as the influence of designing
demagogues and tricksters is generally powerful in
proportion as the limits within which they work

are narrow; and the importance of the stake
would make all men inform themselves thoroughly
as to the characters and capacities of those who
were contending for it; and he flatly denied the
statements, that were made in evident good faith,
to the effect that in a general election each State
would cast its vote for its own favorite citizen.
He inclined to regard the President in the light of
a tribune chosen by the people to watch over the
legislature; and giving him the appointing power,
he believed, would force him to make good use of
it, owing to his sense of responsibility to the people at large, who would be directly affected by its
exercise, and who could and would hold him ac-
countable for its abuse.

On the judiciary his views were also sound. He
upheld the power of the judges, and maintained
that they should have absolute decision as to the
constitutionality of any law. By this means he
hoped to provide against the encroachments of the
popular branch of the government, the one from
which danger was to be feared, as "virtuous citizens will often act as legislators in a way of which
they would, as private individuals, afterwards be
ashamed." He wisely disapproved of low salaries
for the judges, showing that the amounts must be
fixed from time to time in accordance with the
manner and style of living in the country; and that
good work on the bench, where it was especially
needful, like good work everywhere else, could only
be insured by a high rate of recompense. On the

other hand, he approved of introducing into the
national Constitution the foolish New York state
inventions of a Council of Revision and an Executive Council.

His ideas of the duties and powers of Congress
were likewise very proper on the whole. Most
citizens of the present day will agree with him that
"the excess rather than the deficiency of laws is
what we have to dread." He opposed the hurtful
provision which requires that each congressman
should be a resident of his own district, urging that
congressmen represented the people at large, as
well as their own small localities; and he also
objected to making officers of the army and navy
ineligible. He laid much stress on the propriety
of passing navigation acts to encourage American
bottoms and seamen, as a navy was essential to our
security, and the shipping business was always one
that stood in peculiar need of public patronage.
Also, like Hamilton and most other Federalists, he
favored a policy of encouraging domestic manufac-
tures. Incidentally he approved of Congress having
power to lay an embargo, although he has elsewhere
recorded his views as to the general futility of such
kinds of "commercial warfare." He believed in
having a uniform bankruptcy law; approved of
abolishing all religious tests as qualifications for
office, and was utterly opposed to the "rotation in
office" theory.

One curious incident in the convention was the
sudden outcropping, even thus early, of a "Native

American " movement against all foreigners, which was headed by Butler of South Carolina, who himself was of Irish parentage. He strenuously insisted that no foreigners whomsoever should be admitted to our councils, — a rather odd proposition, considering that it would have excluded quite a number of the eminent men he was then addressing. Pennsylvania in particular — whose array of native talent has always been far from imposing — had a number of foreigners among her delegates, and loudly opposed the proposition, as did New York. These States wished that there should be no discrimination whatever between native and foreign born citizens; but finally a compromise was agreed to, by which the latter were excluded only from the presidency, but were admitted to all other rights after a seven years' residence, — a period that was certainly none too long.

A much more serious struggle took place over the matter of slavery, quite as important then as ever, for at that time the negroes were a fifth of our population, instead of, as now, an eighth. The question, as it came before the convention, had several sides to it; the especial difficulty arising over the representation of the slave States in Congress, and the importation of additional slaves from Africa. No one proposed to abolish slavery offhand; but an influential though small number of delegates, headed by Morris, recognized it as a terrible evil, and were very loath either to allow the South additional representation for the slaves, or to permit the foreign trade in them to go on. When the Southern members banded together on the issue, and made it evident that it was the one which they regarded as almost the most important of all, Morris attacked them in a telling speech, stating with his usual boldness facts that most Northerners only dared hint at, and summing up with the remark that, if he was driven to the dilemma of doing injustice to the Southern States or to human nature, he would have to do it to the former; certainly he would not encourage the slave trade by allowing representation for negroes. Afterwards he characterized the proportional representation of the blacks even more strongly, as being "a bribe for the importation of slaves."

In advocating the proposal, first made by Hamilton, that the representation should in all cases be proportioned to the number of free inhabitants, Morris showed the utter lack of logic in the Virginian proposition, which was that the slave States should have additional representation to the extent of three fifths of their negroes. If negroes were to be considered as inhabitants, then they ought to be added in their entire number; if they were to be considered as property, then they ought to be counted only if all other wealth was likewise included. The position of the Southerners was ridiculous: he tore their arguments to shreds; but he was powerless to alter the fact that they were doggedly determined to carry their point, while most of the Northern members cared comparatively little about it.

In another speech he painted in the blackest colors the unspeakable misery and wrong wrought by slavery, and showed the blight it brought upon the land. " It was the curse of Heaven on the States where it prevailed." He contrasted the prosperity and happiness of the Northern States with the misery and poverty which overspread the barren wastes of those where slaves were numerous. " Every step you take through the great region of slavery presents a desert widening with the increasing number of these wretched beings." He indignantly protested against the Northern States being bound to march their militia for the defense of the Southern States against the very slaves of whose existence the Northern men complained. " He would sooner submit himself to a tax for paying for all the negroes in the United States than saddle posterity with such a Constitution."

Some of the high-minded Virginian statesmen were quite as vigorous as he was in their denunciation of the system. One of them, George Mason, portrayed the effect of slavery upon the people at large with bitter emphasis, and denounced the slave traffic as " infernal," and slavery as a national sin that would be punished by a national calamity, — stating therein the exact and terrible truth. In shameful contrast, many of the Northerners championed the institution; in particular, Oliver Ellsworth of Connecticut, whose name should be branded with infamy because of the words he then uttered. He actually advocated the

free importation of negroes into the south Atlantic States, because the slaves " died so fast in the
sickly rice swamps " that it was necessary ever to
bring fresh ones to labor and perish in the places
of their predecessors; and, with a brutal cynicism,
peculiarly revolting from its mercantile baseness,
he brushed aside the question of morality as irrelevant, asking his hearers to pay heed only to the
fact that "what enriches the part enriches the
whole."

The Virginians were opposed to the slave trade;
but South Carolina and Georgia made it a condition of their coming into the Union. It was accordingly agreed that it should be allowed for a
limited time, — twelve years; and this was afterwards extended to twenty by a bargain made by
Maryland and the three south Atlantic States
with the New England States, the latter getting in
return the help of the former to alter certain provisions respecting commerce. One of the main
industries of the New England of that day was
the manufacture of rum; and its citizens cared
more for their distilleries than for all the slaves
held in bondage throughout Christendom. The
rum was made from molasses which they imported
from the West Indies, and they carried there in
return the fish taken by their great fishing fleets;
they also carried the slaves into the Southern
ports. Their commerce was what they especially
relied on; and to gain support for it they were
perfectly willing to make terms with even such a

black Mammon of unrighteousness as the Southern slaveholding system. Throughout the contest, Morris and a few other stout anti-slavery men are the only ones who appear to advantage; the Virginians, who were honorably anxious to minimize the evils of slavery, come next; then the other Southerners who allowed pressing self-interest to overcome their scruples; and, last of all, the New Englanders whom a comparatively trivial self-interest made the willing allies of the extreme slaveholders. These last were the only Northerners who yielded anything to the Southern slaveholders that was not absolutely necessary; and yet they were the forefathers of the most determined and effective foes that slavery ever had.

As already said, the Southerners stood firm on the slave question: it was the one which perhaps more than any other offered the most serious obstacle to a settlement. Madison pointed out "that the real difference lay, not between the small States and the large, but between the Northern and the Southern States. The institution of slavery and its consequences formed the real line of discrimination." To talk of this kind Morris at first answered hotly enough: "He saw that the Southern gentlemen would not be satisfied unless they saw the way open to their gaining a majority in the public councils. . . . If [the distinction they set up between the North and South] was real, instead of attempting to blend incompatible things, let them at once take a friendly leave of each other." He afterwards went back from this position, and agreed to the compromise by which the slaves were to add, by three fifths of their number, to the representation of their masters, and the slave trade was to be allowed for a certain number of years, and prohibited forever after. He showed his usual straightforward willingness to call things by their right names in desiring to see " slavery " named outright in the Constitution, instead of being characterized with cowardly circumlocution, as was actually done.

In finally yielding and assenting to a compromise, he was perfectly right. The crazy talk about the iniquity of consenting to any recognition of slavery whatever in the Constitution is quite beside the mark; and it is equally irrelevant to assert that the so-called " compromises " were not properly compromises at all, because there were no mutual concessions, and the Southern States had " no shadow of right " to what they demanded and only in part gave up. It was all-important that there should be a Union, but it had to result from the voluntary action of all the States; and each State had a perfect " right " to demand just whatever it chose. The really wise and high-minded statesmen demanded for themselves nothing save justice; but they had to accomplish their purpose by yielding somewhat to the prejudices of their more foolish and less disinterested colleagues. It was better to limit the duration of the slave trade to twenty years than to allow it to be continued indefinitely,

as would have been the case had the South Atlantic
States remained by themselves. The three fifths
representation of the slaves was an evil anomaly,
but it was no worse than allowing the small States
equal representation in the Senate; indeed, bal-
ancing the two concessions against each other, it
must be admitted that Virginia and North Carolina surrendered to New Hampshire and Rhode
Island more than they got in return.

No man who supported slavery can ever have a
clear and flawless title to our regard; and those
who opposed it merit, in so far, the highest honor;
but the opposition to it sometimes took forms that
can be considered only as the vagaries of lunacy.
The only hope of abolishing it lay, first in the
establishment and then in the preservation of the
Union; and if we had at the outset dissolved into
a knot of struggling anarchies, it would have entailed an amount of evil both on our race and on
all North America, compared to which the endur-
ance of slavery for a century or two would have
been as nothing. If we had even split up into
only two republics, a Northern and a Southern, the
West would probably have gone with the latter,
and to this day slavery would have existed throughout the Mississippi valley; much of what is now
our territory would have been held by European
powers, scornfully heedless of our divided might,
while in not a few States the form of government
would have been a military dictatorship; and indeed our whole history would have been as con-

temptible as was that of Germany for some centuries prior to the rise of the house of Hohenzollern.

The fierceness of the opposition to the adoption
of the Constitution, and the narrowness of the
majority by which Virginia and New York decided in its favor, while North Carolina and Rhode
Island did not come in at all until absolutely
forced, showed that the refusal to compromise on
any one of the points at issue would have jeopar-
dized everything.   Had the slavery interest been
in the least dissatisfied, or had the plan of government been a shade less democratic, or had the
smaller States not been propitiated, the Constitution would have been rejected off-hand; and the
country would have had before it decades, perhaps
centuries, of misrule, violence, and disorder.

Madison paid a very just compliment to some
of Morris's best points when he wrote, anent his
services in the convention: "To the brilliancy of
his genius he added, what is too rare, a candid surrender of his opinions when the light of discussion
satisfied him that they had been too hastily formed,
and a readiness to aid in making the best of measures in which he had been overruled."   Although
so many of his own theories had been rejected, he
was one of the warmest advocates of the Constitution; and it was he who finally drew up the document and put the finish to its style and arrangement, so that, as it now stands, it comes from his
pen.

Hamilton, who more than any other man bore

the brunt of the fight for its adoption, asked Morris to help him in writing the "Federalist," but the latter was for some reason unable to do so; and Hamilton was assisted only by Madison, and to a very slight extent by Jay. Pennsylvania, the State from which Morris had been sent as a delegate, early declared in favor of the new experiment; although, as Morris wrote Washington, there had been cause to "dread the cold and sour temper of the back counties, and still more the wicked industry of those who have long habituated themselves to live on the public, and cannot bear the idea of being removed from the power and profit of state government, which has been and still is the means of supporting themselves, their families, and dependents, and (which perhaps is equally grateful) of depressing and humbling their political adversaries." In his own native State of New York the influences he thus describes were still more powerful, and it needed all Hamilton's wonderful genius to force a ratification of the Constitution in spite of the stupid selfishness of the Clintonian faction; as it was, he was only barely successful, although backed by all the best and ablest leaders in the community, — Jay, Livingston, Schuyler, Stephen Van Rensselaer, Isaac Roosevelt, James Duane, and a host of others.

About this time Morris came back to New York to live, having purchased the family estate at Morrisania from his elder brother, Staats Long Morris, the British general. He had for some time been engaged in various successful commercial ventures with his friend Robert Morris, including an East India voyage on a large scale, shipments of tobacco to France, and a share in iron works on the Delaware River, and had become quite a rich man. As soon as the war was ended, he had done what he could do to have the loyalists pardoned and reinstated in their fortunes; thereby risking his popularity not a little, as the general feeling against the Tories was bitter and malevolent in the highest degree, in curious contrast to the good-will that so rapidly sprang up between the Unionists and ex-Confederates after the civil war.

He also kept an eye on foreign politics, and one of his letters to Jay curiously foreshadows the good-will generally felt by Americans of the present day towards Russia, running: "If her ladyship (the Czarina) would drive the Turk out of Europe, and demolish the Algerines and other piratical gentry, she will have done us much good for her own sake; . . . but it is hardly possible the other powers will permit Russia to possess so wide a door into the Mediterranean. I may be deceived, but I think England herself would oppose it. As an American, it is my hearty wish that she may effect her schemes."

Shortly after this it became necessary for him to sail for Europe on business.

CHAPTER VII

FIRST STAY IN FRANCE

AFTER a hard winter passage of forty days' length Morris reached France, and arrived in Paris on February 3, 1789. He remained there a year on his private business; but his prominence in America, and his intimate friendship with many distinguished Frenchmen, at once admitted him to the highest social and political circles, where his brilliant talents secured him immediate importance.

The next nine years of his life were spent in Europe, and it was during this time that he unknowingly rendered his especial and peculiar service to the public. As an American statesman he has many rivals, and not a few superiors; but as a penetrating observer and recorder of contemporary events, he stands alone among the men of his time. He kept a full diary during his stay abroad, and was a most voluminous correspondent; and his capacity for keen, shrewd observation, his truthfulness, his wonderful insight into character, his sense of humor, and his power of graphic description, all combine to make his comments on the chief men and events of the day a unique record of the inside history of Western Europe during the tremendous convulsions of the French Revolution. He is always an entertaining and in all matters of fact a trustworthy writer. His letters and diary together form a real mine of wealth for the student either of the social life of the upper classes in France just before the outbreak, or of the events of the revolution itself.

In the first place, it must be premised that from the outset Morris was hostile to the spirit of the French Revolution, and his hostility grew in proportion to its excesses until at last it completely swallowed up his original antipathy to England, and made him regard France as normally our enemy, not our ally. This was perfectly natural, and indeed inevitable : in all really free countries, the best friends of freedom regarded the revolutionists, when they had fairly begun their bloody career, with horror and anger. It was only to oppressed, debased, and priest-ridden peoples that the French Revolution could come as the embodiment of liberty. Compared to the freedom already enjoyed by Americans, it was sheer tyranny of the most dreadful kind.

Morris saw clearly that the popular party in France, composed in part of amiable visionaries, theoretic philanthropists, and closet constitution-mongers, and in part of a brutal, sodden populace, maddened by the grinding wrongs of ages, knew not whither its own steps tended ; and he also saw that the then existing generation of Frenchmen were not, and never would be, fitted to use liberty aright. It is small matter for wonder that he could not see as clearly the good which lay behind the movement; that he could not as readily foretell the real and great improvement it was finally to bring about, though only after a generation of hideous convulsions. Even as it was, he discerned what was happening, and what was about to happen, more distinctly than did any one else. The wild friends of the French Revolution, especially in America, supported it blindly, with but a very slight notion of what it really signified. Keen though Morris's intellectual vision was, it was impossible for him to see what future lay beyond the quarter of a century of impending tumult. It did not lie within his powers to applaud the fiendish atrocities of the Red Terror for the sake of the problematical good that would come to the next generation. To do so he would have needed the granite heart of a zealot, as well as the prophetic vision of a seer.

The French Revolution was in its essence a struggle for the abolition of privilege, and for equality in civil rights. This Morris perceived, almost alone among the statesmen of his day; and he also perceived that most Frenchmen were willing to submit to any kind of government that would secure them the things for which they strove. As he wrote to Jefferson, when the republic was well under weigh: "The great mass of the French nation is less solicitous to preserve the present order of things than to prevent the return of the ancient

oppression, and of course would more readily submit
to a pure despotism than to that kind of monarchy
whose only limits were found in those noble, legal,
and clerical corps by which the people were alternately oppressed and insulted." To the down-
trodden masses of continental Europe, the gift of
civil rights and the removal of the tyranny of the
privileged classes, even though accompanied by the
rule of a directory, a consul, or an emperor, represented an immense political advance; but to the
free people of England, and to the freer people of
America, the change would have been wholly for
the worse.

Such being the case, Morris's attitude was natural and proper. There is no reason to question
the sincerity of his statement in another letter,
that " I do, from the bottom of my heart, wish well
to this country [France]." Had the French people
shown the least moderation or wisdom, he would
have unhesitatingly sided with them against their
oppressors. It must be kept in mind that he was
not influenced in the least in his course by the
views of the upper classes with whom he mingled.
On the contrary, when he first came to Europe, he
distinctly lost popularity in some of the social
circles in which he moved, because he was so much
more conservative than his aristocratic friends,
among whom the closet republicanism of the philosophers was for the moment all the rage. He
had no love for the French nobility, whose folly
and ferocity caused the revolution, and whose

craven cowardice could not check it even before it had gathered headway. Long afterwards he wrote of some of the *emigrés*: "The conversation of these gentlemen, who have the virtue and good fortune of their grandfathers to recommend them, leads me almost to forget the crimes of the French Revolution; and often the unforgiving temper and sanguinary wishes which they exhibit make me almost believe that the assertion of their enemies is true, namely, that it is success alone which has determined on whose side should be the crimes, and on whose the miseries." The truth of the last sentence was strikingly verified by the White Terror, even meaner, if less bloody, than the Red. Bourbon princes and Bourbon nobles were alike, and Morris only erred in not seeing that their destruction was the condition precedent upon all progress.

There was never another great struggle, in the end productive of good to mankind, where the tools and methods by which that end was won were so wholly vile as in the French Revolution. Alone among movements of the kind, it brought forth no leaders entitled to our respect; none who were both great and good; none even who were very great, save, at its beginning, strange, strong, crooked Mirabeau, and at its close the towering world-genius who sprang to power by its means, wielded it for his own selfish purposes, and dazzled all nations over the wide earth by the glory of his strength and splendor.

We can hardly blame Morris for not appreci-
ating a revolution whose immediate outcome was
to be Napoleon's despotism, even though he failed
to see all the good that would remotely spring
therefrom. He considered, as he once wrote a
friend, that " the true object of a great statesman
is to give to any particular nation the kind of laws
which is suitable to them, and the best constitution
which they are capable of." There can be no
sounder rule of statesmanship ; and none was more
flagrantly broken by the amiable but incompetent
political doctrinaires of 1789. Thus the American,
as a far-sighted statesman, despised the theorists
who began the revolution, and, as a humane and
honorable man, abhorred the black-hearted wretches
who carried it on. His view of the people among
whom he found himself, as well as his statement
of his own position, he himself has recorded : " To
fit people for a republic, as for any other form
of government, a previous education is necessary.
. . . In despotic governments the people, habituated to beholding everything bending beneath the
weight of power, never possess that power for a
moment without abusing it. Slaves, driven to despair, take arms, execute vast vengeance, and then
sink back to their former condition of slaves. In
such societies the patriot, the melancholy patriot,
sides with the despot, because anything is better
than a wild and bloody confusion."

So much for an outline of his views. His writings preserve them for us in detail on almost every

important question that came up during his stay
in Europe ; couched, moreover, in telling, piquant
sentences that leave room for hardly a dull line in
either letters or diary.

No sooner had he arrived in Paris than he
sought out Jefferson, then the American minister,
and Lafayette. They engaged him to dine on the
two following nights. He presented his various
letters of introduction, and in a very few weeks,
by his wit, tact, and ability, had made himself
completely at home in what was by far the most
brilliant and attractive — although also the most
hopelessly unsound — fashionable society of any
European capital. He got on equally well with
fine ladies, philosophers, and statesmen ; was as
much at his ease in the salons of the one as at the
dinner-tables of the other ; and all the time observed and noted down, with the same humorous
zest, the social peculiarities of his new friends as
well as the tremendous march of political events.
Indeed, it is difficult to know whether to set the
higher value on his penetrating observations concerning public affairs, or on his witty, light, half-
satirical sketches of the men and women of the
world with whom he was thrown in contact, told
in his usual charming and effective style. No
other American of note has left us writings half so
humorous and amusing, filled, too, with information
of the greatest value.

Although his relations with Jefferson were at
this time very friendly, yet his ideas on most sub-

jects were completely at variance with those of the
latter. He visited him very often ; and, after one
of these occasions, jots down his opinion of his
friend in his usual amusing vein: " Call on Mr.
Jefferson, and sit a good while. General conversation on character and politics. I think he does
not form very just estimates of character, but
rather assigns too many to the humble rank of
fools ; whereas in life the gradations are infinite,
and each individual has his peculiarities of fort
and feeble : " not a bad protest against the dangers of sweeping generalization. Another time he
records his judgment of Jefferson's ideas on public
matters as follows : " He and I differ in our systems of politics. He, with all the leaders of liberty here, is desirous of annihilating distinctions
of order. How far such views may be right respecting mankind in general is, I think, extremely
problematical. But with respect to this nation I
am sure they are wrong, and cannot eventuate
well."

As soon as he began to go out in Parisian society, he was struck by the closet republicanism
which it had become the fashion to affect. After
his first visit to Lafayette, who received him with
that warmth and frank, open-handed hospitality
which he always extended to Americans, Morris
writes : " Lafayette is full of politics ; he appears
to be too republican for the genius of his country."
And again, when Lafayette showed him the draft
of the celebrated Declaration of Rights, he notes :

"I gave him my opinions, and suggested several
amendments tending to soften the high-colored expressions of freedom. It is not by sounding words
that revolutions are produced." Elsewhere he
writes that "the young nobility have brought
themselves to an active faith in the natural equality of mankind, and spurn at everything which
looks like restraint." Some of their number, however, he considered to be actuated by considera-
tions more tangible than mere sentiment. He
chronicles a dinner with some members of the
National Assembly, where "one, a noble represent-
ing the *Tiers*, is so vociferous against his own order, that I am convinced he means to rise by his
eloquence, and finally will, I expect, vote with the
opinion of the court, let that be what it may."
The sentimental humanitarians — who always form
a most pernicious body, with an influence for bad
hardly surpassed by that of the professionally
criminal class — of course throve vigorously in an
atmosphere where theories of mawkish benevolence
went hand in hand with the habitual practice of
vices too gross to name. Morris, in one of his
letters, narrates an instance in point; at the same
time showing how this excess of watery philan-
thropy was, like all the other movements of the
French Revolution, but a violent and misguided
reaction against former abuses of the opposite sort.
The incident took place in Madame de Staël's
salon. "The Count de Clermont Tonnerre, one of
their best orators, read to us a very pathetic ora-

tion ; and the object was to show that no penalties
are the legal compensations for crimes or injuries :
the man who is hanged, having by that event
paid his debt to society, ought not to be held in
dishonor ; and in like manner he who has been
condemned for seven years to be flogged in the
galley should, when he has served out his appren-
ticeship, be received again into good company, as
if nothing had happened. You smile ; but observe
the extreme to which the matter was carried the
other way. Dishonoring thousands for the guilt
of one has so shocked the public sentiment as to
render this extreme fashionable. The oration was
very fine, very sentimental, very pathetic, and the
style harmonious. Shouts of applause and full
approbation. When this was pretty well over, I
told him that his speech was extremely eloquent,
but that his principles were not very solid. Universal surprise ! "

At times he became rather weary of the constant
discussion of politics, which had become the chief
drawing-room topic. Among the capacities of his
lively and erratic nature was the power of being
intensely bored by anything dull or monotonous.
He remarked testily that " republicanism was
absolutely a moral influenza, from which neither
titles, places, nor even the diadem can guard the
possessor." In a letter to a friend on a different
subject he writes : " Apropos, — a term which my
Lord Chesterfield well observes we generally use
to bring in what is not at all to the purpose, —

apropos, then, I have here the strangest employment imaginable. A republican, and just as it
were emerged from that assembly which has formed
one of the most republican of all republican constitutions, I preach incessantly respect for the
prince, attention to the rights of the nobles, and
above all moderation, not only in the object, but
also in the pursuit of it. All this you will say is
none of my business; but I consider France as the
natural ally of my country, and, of course, that we
are interested in her prosperity; besides, to say
the truth, I love France."

His hostility to the fashionable cult offended
some of his best friends. The Lafayettes openly
disapproved his sentiments. The marquis told him
that he was injuring the cause, because his sentiments were being continually quoted against "the
good party." Morris answered that he was opposed
to democracy from a regard to liberty; that the
popular party were going straight to destruction,
and he would fain stop them if he could; for their
views respecting the nation were totally inconsistent with the materials of which it was composed,
and the worst thing that could happen to them
would be to have their wishes granted. Lafayette
half admitted that this was true: "He tells me that
he is sensible his party are mad, and tells them so,
but is not the less determined to die with them. I
tell him that I think it would be quite as well to
bring them to their senses and live with them," —
the last sentence showing the impatience with which

the shrewd, fearless, practical American at times
regarded the dreamy inefficiency of his French associates. Madame de Lafayette was even more
hostile than her husband to Morris's ideas. In
commenting on her beliefs he says: "She is a very
sensible woman, but has formed her ideas of government in a manner not suited, I think, either to
the situation, the circumstances, or the disposition
of France."

He was considered too much of an aristocrat in
the salon of the Comtesse de Tessé, the resort of
"republicans of the first feather;" and at first was
sometimes rather coldly received there. He felt,
however, a most sincere friendship and regard for
the comtesse, and thoroughly respected the earnestness with which she had for twenty years done
what lay in her power to give her country greater
liberty. She was a genuine enthusiast, and, when
the National Assembly met, was filled with exultant
hope for the future. The ferocious outbreaks of
the mob, and the crazy lust for blood shown by the
people at large, startled her out of her faith, and
shocked her into the sad belief that her lifelong
and painful labors had been wasted in the aid of a
bad cause. Later in the year Morris writes : " I
find Madame de Tessé is become a convert to my
principles. We have a gay conversation of some
minutes on their affairs, in which I mingle sound
maxims of government with that piquant *légèreté*
which this nation delights in. She insists that I
dine with her at Versailles the next time I am

there. We are vastly gracious, and all at once, in a serious tone, 'Mais attendez, madame, est-ce que je suis trop aristocrat?' To which she answers, with a smile of gentle humility, 'Oh, mon Dieu, non!'"

It is curious to notice how rapidly Morris's brilliant talents gave him a commanding position, stranger and guest though he was, among the most noted statesmen of France; how often he was consulted, and how widely his opinions were quoted. Moreover, his incisive truthfulness makes his writings more valuable to the historian of his time than are those of any of his contemporaries, French, English, or American. Taine, in his great work on the revolution, ranks him high among the small number of observers who have recorded clear and sound judgments of those years of confused, formless tumult and horror.

All his views on French politics are very striking. As soon as he reached Paris, he was impressed by the unrest and desire for change prevailing everywhere, and wrote home: " I find on this side of the Atlantic a resemblance to what I left on the other, — a nation which exists in hopes, prospects, and expectations; the reverence for ancient establishments gone; existing forms shaken to the very foundation; and a new order of things about to take place, in which, perhaps, even the very names of all former institutions will be disregarded." And again: " This country presents an astonishing spectacle to one who has collected his ideas from

books and information half a dozen years old.
Everything is *à l'Anglaise*, and a desire to imitate
the English prevails alike in the cut of a coat and
the form of a constitution.   Like the English, too,
all are engaged in parliamenteering ; and when we
consider how novel this last business must be, I
assure you the progress is far from contemptible,"
— a reference to Lafayette's electioneering trip to
Auvergne.   The rapidity with which, in America,
order had come out of chaos, while in France the
reverse process had been going on, impressed him
deeply; as he says: " If any new lesson were wanting to impress on our hearts a deep sense of the
mutability of human affairs, the double contrast
between France and America two years ago and at
the present would surely furnish it."

He saw at once that the revolutionists had it in
their power to do about as they chose.   " If there
be any real vigor in the nation the prevailing party
in the States-General may, if they please, overturn
the monarchy itself, should the king commit his
authority to a contest with them.   The court is extremely feeble, and the manners are so extremely
corrupt that they cannot succeed if there be any
consistent opposition, unless the whole nation be
equally depraved."

He did not believe that the people would be able
to profit by the revolution, or to use their oppor-
tunities aright.   For the numerous class of patriots
who felt a vague, though fervent, enthusiasm for
liberty in the abstract, and who, without the slight-

est practical knowledge, were yet intent on having
all their own pet theories put into practice, he felt
profound scorn and contempt; while he distrusted
and despised the mass of Frenchmen, because of
their frivolity and viciousness. He knew well that
a pure theorist may often do as much damage to a
country as the most corrupt traitor; and very properly considered that in politics the fool is quite
as obnoxious as the knave. He also realized that
levity and the inability to look life seriously in the
face, or to attend to the things worth doing, may
render a man just as incompetent to fulfill the
duties of citizenship as would actual viciousness.

To the crazy theories of the constitution-makers
and closet republicans generally, he often alludes
in his diary, and in his letters home. In one place
he notes: "The literary people here, observing the
abuses of the monarchical form, imagine that everything must go the better in proportion as it recedes
from the present establishment, and in their closets
they make men exactly suited to their systems;
but unluckily they are such men as exist nowhere
else, and least of all in France." And he writes
almost the same thing to Washington: "The middle party, who mean well, have unfortunately acquired their ideas of government from books, and
are admirable fellows upon paper : but as it hap-
pens, somewhat unfortunately, that the men who
live in the world are very different from those who
dwell in the heads of philosophers, it is not to be
wondered at if the systems taken out of books are

fit for nothing but to be put back into books again."
And once more: "They have all that romantic
spirit, and all those romantic ideas of government,
which, happily for America, we were cured of before it was too late." He shows how they had
never had the chance to gain wisdom through experience. "As they have hitherto felt severely the
authority exercised in the name of their princes,
every limitation of that power seems to them desirable. Never having felt the evils of too weak an
executive, the disorders to be apprehended from
anarchy make as yet no impression." Elsewhere
he comments on their folly in trying to apply to
their own necessities systems of government suited
to totally different conditions; and mentions his
own attitude in the matter: "I have steadily combated the violence and excess of those persons who,
either inspired with an enthusiastic love of freedom,
or prompted by sinister designs, are disposed to
drive everything to extremity. Our American example has done them good; but, like all novelties,
liberty runs away with their discretion, if they have
any. They want an American constitution with
the exception of a king instead of a president,
without reflecting that they have not American
citizens to support that constitution. . . . Whoever
desires to apply in the practical science of government those rules and forms which prevail and succeed in a foreign country, must fall into the same
pedantry with our young scholars, just fresh from
the university, who would fain bring everything to

the Roman standard. . . . The scientific tailor who should cut after Grecian or Chinese models would not have many customers, either in London or Paris; and those who look to America for their political forms are not unlike the tailors in Laputa, who, as Gulliver tells us, always take measures with a quadrant."

He shows again and again his abiding distrust and fear of the French character, as it was at that time, volatile, debauched, ferocious, and incapable of self-restraint. To Lafayette he insisted that the "extreme licentiousness" of the people rendered it indispensable that they should be kept under authority; and on another occasion told him "that the nation was used to being governed, and would have to be governed; and that if he expected to lead them by their affections, he would himself be the dupe." In writing to Washington he painted the outlook in colors that, though black indeed, were not a shade too dark. "The materials for a revolution in this country are very indifferent. Everybody agrees that there is an utter prostration of morals; but this general proposition can never convey to an American mind the degree of depravity. It is not by any figure of rhetoric or force of language that the idea can be communicated. A hundred anecdotes and a hundred thousand examples are required to show the extreme rottenness of every member. There are men and women who are greatly and eminently virtuous. I have the pleasure to number many in my own acquaintance;

but they stand forward from a background deeply
and darkly shaded.   It is however from such crum-
bling matter that the great edifice of freedom is to
be erected here.   Perhaps like the stratum of rock
which is spread under the whole surface of their
country, it may harden when exposed to the air;
but it seems quite as likely that it will fall and
crush the builders.   I own to you that I am not
without such apprehensions, for there is one fatal
principal which pervades all ranks.   It is a perfect
indifference to the violation of engagements.   In-
constancy is so mingled in the blood, marrow, and
very essence of this people, that when a man of
high rank and importance laughs to-day at what he
seriously asserted yesterday, it is considered as in
the natural order of things.   Consistency is a phe-
nomenon.   Judge, then, what would be the value
of an association should such a thing be proposed
and even adopted.   The great mass of the common
people have no religion but their priests, no law
but their superiors, no morals but their interest.   These are the creatures who, led by drunken
curates, are now on the high road *à la liberté.*"

Morris and Washington wrote very freely to
each other.   In one of his letters, the latter gave
an account of how well affairs were going in America (save in Rhode Island, the majority of whose
people " had long since bid adieu to every principle
of honor, common sense, and honesty "), and then
went on to discuss things in France.   He expressed
the opinion that, if the revolution went no farther

than it had already gone, France would become the most powerful and happy state in Europe; but he trembled lest, having triumphed in the first paroxysms, it might succumb to others still more violent that would be sure to follow. He feared equally the " licentiousness of the people " and the folly of the leaders, and doubted if they possessed the requisite temperance, firmness, and foresight; and if they did not, then he believed they would run from one extreme to another, and end with " a higher toned despotism than the one which existed before."

Morris answered him with his usual half-satiric humor: " Your sentiments on the revolution here I believe to be perfectly just, because they perfectly accord with my own, and that is, you know, the only standard which Heaven has given us by which to judge," and went on to describe how the parties in France stood. " The king is in effect a prisoner in Paris and obeys entirely the National Assembly. This Assembly may be divided into three parts: one, called the *aristocrats*, consists of the high clergy, the members of the law (note, these are not the lawyers) and such of the nobility as think they ought to form a separate order. Another, which has no name, but which consists of all sorts of people, really friends to a good free government. The third is composed of what is here called the *enragées*, that is, the madmen. These are the most numerous, and are of that class which in America is known by the name of pettifogging lawyers;

together with . . . those persons who in all revolutions throng to the standard of change because they are not well. This last party is in close alliance with the populace here, and they have already unhinged everything, and, according to custom on such occasions, the torrent rushes on irresistibly until it shall have wasted itself." The *literati* he pronounced to have no understanding whatever of the matters at issue, and as was natural to a shrewd observer educated in the intensely practical school of American political life, he felt utter contempt for the wordy futility and wild theories of the French legislators. "For the rest, they *discuss* nothing in their assembly. One large half of the time is spent in hallooing and bawling."

Washington and Morris were both so alarmed and indignant at the excesses committed by the revolutionists, and so frankly expressed their feelings, as to create an impression in some quarters that they were hostile to the revolution itself. The exact reverse was originally the case. They sympathized most warmly with the desire for freedom, and with the efforts made to attain it. Morris wrote to the President: "We have, I think, every reason to wish that the patriots may be successful. The generous wish that a free people must have to disseminate freedom, the grateful emotion which rejoices in the happiness of a benefactor, the interest we must feel as well in the liberty as in the power of this country, all conspire to make us far from indifferent spectators. I say that we have an

interest in the liberty of France. The leaders here
are our friends. Many of them have imbibed their
principles in America, and all have been fired by
our example. Their opponents are by no means
rejoiced at the success of our revolution, and many
of them are disposed to form connections of the
strictest kind with Great Britain." Both Washington and Morris would have been delighted to
see liberty established in France; but they had no
patience with the pursuit of the bloody chimera
which the revolutionists dignified with that title.
The one hoped for, and the other counseled, moderation among the friends of republican freedom,
not because they were opposed to it, but because
they saw that it could only be gained and kept by
self-restraint. They were, to say the least, perfectly
excusable for believing that at that time some form
of monarchy, whether under king, dictator, or emperor, was necessary to France. Every one agrees
that there are certain men wiser than their fellows;
the only question is as to how these men can be
best chosen out, and to this there can be no absolute answer. No mode will invariably give the
best results; and the one that will come nearest to
doing so under given conditions will not work at
all under others. Where the people are enlightened and moral they are themselves the ones to
choose their rulers; and such a form of government
is unquestionably the highest of any, and the only
one that a high-spirited and really free nation will
tolerate; but if they are corrupt and degraded,

they are unfit for republicanism, and need to be
under an entirely different system. The most genuine republican, if he has any common sense, does
not believe in a democratic government for every
race and in every age.

Morris was a true republican, and an American
to the core. He was alike free from truckling
subserviency to European opinion, — a degrading
remnant of colonialism that unfortunately still lin-
gers in certain limited social and literary circles, —
and from the uneasy self-assertion that springs
partly from sensitive vanity, and partly from a
smothered doubt as to one's real position. Like
most men of strong character, he had no taste for
the "cosmopolitanism" that so generally indicates
a weak moral and mental make-up. He enjoyed
his stay in Europe to the utmost, and was intimate
with the most influential men and charming women
of the time; but he was heartily glad to get back
to America, refused to leave it again, and always
insisted that it was the most pleasant of all places
in which to live. While abroad he was simply a
gentleman among gentlemen. He never intruded
his political views or national prejudices upon his
European friends; but he was not inclined to suffer
any imputation on his country. Any question about
America that was put in good faith, no matter how
much ignorance it displayed, he always answered
good-humoredly; and he gives in his diary some
amusing examples of such conversations. Once he
was cross-examined by an inquisitive French noble-

man, still in the stage of civilization which believes
that no man can be paid to render a service to
another, especially a small service, and yet retain
his self-respect and continue to regard himself as
the full political equal of his employer. One of
this gentleman's sagacious inquiries was as to how
a shoemaker could, in the pride of his freedom,
think himself equal to a king, and yet accept an
order to make shoes; to which Morris replied that
he would accept it as a matter of business, and be
glad of the chance to make them, since it lay in the
line of his duty; and that he would all the time
consider himself at full liberty to criticise his visitor, or the king, or any one else, who lapsed from
his own duty. After recording several queries of
the same nature, and some rather abrupt answers,
the diary for that day closes rather caustically
with the comment: " This manner of thinking and
speaking, however, is too masculine for the climate
I am now in."

In a letter to Washington Morris made one of
his usual happy guesses — if forecasting the future
by the aid of marvelous insight into human character can properly be called a guess — as to what
would happen to France: " It is very difficult to
guess whereabouts the flock will settle when it flies
so wild; but as far as it is possible to guess this
(late) kingdom will be cast into a congeries of little democracies, laid out, not according to rivers,
mountains, etc., but with the square and compass
according to latitude and longitude," and adds that

he thinks so much fermenting matter will soon give the nation " a kind of political colic."

He rendered some services to Washington that did not come in the line of his public duty. One of these was to get him a watch, Washington having written to have one purchased in Paris, of gold, " not a small, trifling, nor a finical ornamental one, but a watch well executed in point of workmanship, large and flat, with a plain, handsome key." Morris sent it to him by Jefferson, " with two copper keys and one golden one, and a box containing a spare spring and glasses." His next service to the great Virginian, or rather to his family, was of a different kind, and he records it with a smile at his own expense. " Go to M. Houdon's; he has been waiting for me a long time. I stand for his statue of General Washington, being the humble employment of a manikin. This is literally taking the advice of St. Paul, to be all things to all men."

He corresponded with many men of note; not the least among whom was the daring corsair, Paul Jones. The latter was very anxious to continue in the service of the people with whom he had cast in his lot, and in command of whose vessels he had reached fame. Morris was obliged to tell him that he did not believe an American navy would be created for some years to come, and advised him meanwhile to go into the service of the Russians, as he expected there would soon be warm work on the Baltic; and even gave him a hint as to what would probably be the best plan of campaign. Paul Jones wanted to come to Paris; but from this Morris dissuaded him. "A journey to this city can, I think, produce nothing but the expense attending it; for neither pleasure nor profit can be expected here, by one of your profession in particular; and, except that it is a more dangerous residence than many others, I know of nothing which may serve to you as an inducement."

CHAPTER VIII

LIFE IN PARIS

ALTHOUGH Morris entered into the social life of Paris with all the zest natural to his pleasure-loving character, yet he was far too clear-headed to permit it to cast any glamour over him. Indeed, it is rather remarkable that a young provincial gentleman, from a raw, new, far-off country, should not have had his head turned by being made somewhat of a lion in what was then the foremost city of the civilized world. Instead of this happening, his notes show that he took a perfectly cool view of his new surroundings, and appreciated the over-civilized, aristocratic society, in which he found himself, quite at its true worth. He enjoyed the life of the salon very much, but it did not in the least awe or impress him; and he was of too virile fibre, too essentially a man, to be long contented with it alone. He likewise appreciated the fashionable men, and especially the fashionable women, whom he met there; but his amusing comments on them, as shrewd as they are humorous, prove how little he respected their philosophy, and how completely indifferent he was to their claims to social preëminence.

Much has been written about the pleasure-loving, highly cultured society of eighteenth-century France; but to a man like Morris, of real ability and with an element of sturdiness in his make-up, both the culture and knowledge looked a little like veneering; the polish partook of effeminacy; the pleasure so eagerly sought after could be called pleasure only by people of ignoble ambition; and the life that was lived seemed narrow and petty, agreeable enough for a change, but dreary beyond measure if followed too long. The authors, philosophers, and statesmen of the salon were rarely, almost never, men of real greatness; their metal did not ring true; they were shams, and the life of which they were a part was a sham. Not only was the existence hollow, unwholesome, effeminate, but also in the end tedious: the silent, decorous dullness of life in the dreariest country town is not more insufferable than, after a time, become the endless chatter, the small witticisms, the mock enthusiasms, and vapid affectations of an aristocratic society as artificial and unsound as that of the Parisian drawing-rooms in the last century.

But all this was delightful for a time, especially to a man who had never seen any city larger than the overgrown villages of New York and Philadelphia. Morris thus sums up his first impressions in a letter to a friend: "A man in Paris lives in a sort of whirlwind, which turns him round so fast that he can see nothing. And as all men and things are in the same vertiginous condition, you

can neither fix yourself nor your object for regular
examination. Hence the people of this metropolis
are under the necessity of pronouncing their defini-
tive judgment from the first glance; and being
thus habituated to shoot flying, they have what
sportsmen call a quick sight. *Ex pede Herculem.*
They know a wit by his snuff-box, a man of taste
by his bow, and a statesman by the cut of his coat.
It is true that, like other sportsmen, they sometimes miss; but then, like other sportsmen too,
they have a thousand excuses besides the want of
skill: the fault, you know, may be in the dog, or
the bird, or the powder, or the flint, or even the
gun, without mentioning the gunner."

Among the most famous of the salons where he
was fairly constant in his attendance was that of
Madame de Staël. There was not a little contempt mixed with his regard for the renowned
daughter of Necker. She amused him, however,
and he thought well of her capacity, though in his
diary he says that he never in his life saw "such
exuberant vanity" as she displayed about her
father, Necker, — a very ordinary personage, whom
the convulsions of the time had for a moment
thrown forward as the most prominent man in
France. By way of instance he mentions a couple
of her remarks, one to the effect that a speech of
Talleyrand on the church property was "excellent,
admirable, in short that there were two pages in
it which were worthy of M. Necker;" and another
wherein she said that wisdom was a very rare

quality, and that she knew of no one who possessed
it in a superlative degree except her father.

The first time he met her was after an exciting
discussion in the Assembly over the finances, which
he describes at some length. Necker had introduced an absurd scheme for a loan. Mirabeau,
who hated Necker, saw the futility of his plan, but
was also aware that popular opinion was blindly in
his favor, and that to oppose him would be ruinous; so in a speech of " fine irony " he advocated
passing Necker's proposed bill without change or
discussion, avowing that his object was to have
the responsibility and glory thrown entirely on the
proposer of the measure. He thus yielded to the
popular view, while at the same time he shouldered
on Necker all the responsibility for a deed which
it was evident would in the end ruin him. It was
a not very patriotic move, although a good example of selfish political tactics, and Morris sneered
bitterly at its adoption by the representatives of a
people who prided themselves on being " the modern Athenians."   To his surprise, however, even
Madame de Staël took Mirabeau's action seriously;
she,went into raptures over the wisdom of the Assembly in doing just what Necker said, for " the
only thing they could do was to comply with her
father's wish, and there could be no doubt as to
the success of her father's plans !   Bravo! "

With Morris she soon passed from politics to
other subjects. " Presented to Madame de Staël
as *un homme d'esprit*," he writes, " she singles me

out and makes *a talk;* asks if I have not written
a book on the American Constitution. 'Non madame, j'ai fait mon devoir en assistant à la formation de cette constitution.' 'Mais, monsieur, votre
conversation doit être très intéressante, car je vous
entends cité de toute parti.' 'Ah, madame, je ne
suis pas digne de cette éloge.' How I lost my leg?
It was unfortunately not in the military service of
my country. 'Monsieur, vous avez l'air très im-
posant,' and this is accompanied with that look
which, without being what Sir John Falstaff calls
the 'leer of invitation,' amounts to the same thing.
. . . This leads us on, but in the midst of the chat
arrive letters, one of which is from her lover, Narbonne, now with his regiment. It brings her to a
little recollection, which a little time will, I think,
again banish, and a few interviews would stimulate
her to try the experiment of her fascinations even
on the native of a new world who has left one of
his legs behind him."

An entry in Morris's diary previous to this conversation shows that he had no very high opinion
of this same Monsieur de Narbonne: "He considers a civil war inevitable, and is about to join
his regiment, being, as he says, in a conflict between the dictates of his duty and his conscience.
I tell him that I know of no duty but that which
conscience dictates. I presume that his conscience
will dictate to join the strongest side."

Morris's surmises as to his fair friend's happy
forgetfulness of her absent lover proved true : she

soon became bent on a flirtation with the good-
looking American stranger, and when he failed
to make any advances she promptly made them
herself ; told him that she " rather invited than
repelled those who were inclined to be attentive,"
and capped this exhibition of modest feminine
reserve by suggesting that " perhaps he might become an admirer." Morris dryly responded that
it was not impossible, but that, as a previous condition, she must agree not to repel him, — which
she instantly promised. Afterwards, at dinner,
" we become engaged in an animated conversation,
and she desires me to speak English, which her
husband does not understand. In looking round
the room, I observe in him very much emotion,
and I tell her that he loves her distractedly, which
she says she knows, and that it renders her miserable. . . . I condole with her a little on her widow-
hood, the Chevalier de Narbonne being absent in
Franche Comté. . . . She asks me if I continue to
think she has a preference for Monsieur de Tonnerre. I reply only by observing that each of
them has wit enough for one couple, and therefore
I think they had better separate, and take each a
partner who is *un peu bête*. After dinner I seek a
conversation with the husband, which relieves him.
He inveighs bitterly [poor, honest Swede] against
the manners of the country, and the cruelty of
alienating a wife's affection. I regret with him on
general grounds that prostitution of morals which
unfits them for good government, and convince

him, I think, I shall not contribute to making
him any more uncomfortable than he already is."
Certainly, according to Morris's evidence, Madame
de Staël's sensitive delicacy could only be truthfully
portrayed by the unfettered pen of a Smollett.

He was an especial *habitué* of the salon of
Madame de Flahaut, the friend of Talleyrand and
Montesquieu. She was a perfectly characteristic
type; a clever, accomplished little woman, fond of
writing romances, and a thorough-paced *intriguante*.
She had innumerable enthusiasms, with perhaps a
certain amount of sincerity in each, and was a more
infatuated political schemer than any of her male
friends. She was thoroughly conversant with the
politics of both court and Assembly; her "preci-
sion and justness of thought was very uncommon
in either sex," and, as time went on, made her a
willing and useful helper in some of Morris's
plans. Withal she was a mercenary, self-seeking
little personage, bent on increasing her own fortune by the aid of her political friends. Once,
when dining with Morris and Talleyrand, she told
them in perfect good faith that, if the latter was
made minister, "they must be sure to make a million for her."

She was much flattered by the deference that
Morris showed for her judgment, and in return
let him into not a few state secrets. She and he
together drew up a translation of the outline for
a constitution for France, which he had prepared,
and through her it was forwarded to the king.

Together with her two other intimates, Talleyrand
and Montesquieu, they made just a party of four,
often dining at her house; and when her husband
was sent to Spain, the dinners became more numerous than ever, sometimes merely *parties carrées*,
sometimes very large entertainments. Morris records that, small or large, they were invariably
"excellent dinners, where the conversation was
always extremely gay."

Once they planned out a ministry together, and
it must be kept in mind that it was quite on the
cards that their plan would be adopted. After
disposing suitably of all the notabilities, some in
stations at home, others in stations abroad, the
scheming little lady turned to Morris: "'Enfin,'
she says, 'mon ami, vous et moi nous gouvernerons
la France.' It is an odd combination, but the kingdom is actually in much worse hands."

This conversation occurred one morning when
he had called to find madame at her toilet, with
her dentist in attendance. It was a coarse age,
for all the gilding; and the coarseness was in-
grained in the fibre even of the most ultra sentimental. At first Morris felt perhaps a little
surprised at the easy familiarity with which the
various ladies whose friends he was admitted him
to the privacy of boudoir and bedroom, and chronicles with some amusement the graceful indifference
with which one of them would say to him: "Monsieur Morris me permettra de faire ma toilette?"
But he was far from being a strait-laced man, — in

fact, he was altogether too much the reverse, —
and he soon grew habituated to these as well as to
much worse customs.   However, he notes that the
different operations of the toilet " were carried on
with an entire and astounding regard to modesty."

Madame de Flahaut was a very charming member of the class who, neither toiling nor spinning,
were supported in luxury by those who did both,
and who died from want while so doing.   At this
very time, while France was rapidly drifting into
bankruptcy, the fraudulent pensions given to a
horde of courtiers, titled placemen, well-born har-
lots and their offspring, reached the astounding
total of two hundred and seventy odd millions of
livres.   The Assembly passed a decree cutting
away these pensions right and left, and thereby
worked sad havoc in the gay society that nothing
could render serious but immediate and pressing
poverty, — not even the loom of the terror ahead,
growing darker moment by moment.   Calling on
his fascinating little friend immediately after the
decree was published, Morris finds her " *au déses-
poir*, and she intends to cry very loud, she says.
. . . She has been in tears all day.   Her pensions
from Monsieur and the Comte d'Artois are stopped.
On that from the king she receives but three thousand francs, — and must therefore quit Paris.   I
try to console her, but it is impossible.   Indeed,
the stroke is severe ; for, with youth, beauty,
wit, and every loveliness, she must quit all she
loves, and pass her life with what she abhors."   In

the time of adversity Morris stood loyally by the
friends who had treated him so kindly when the
world was a merry one and things went well with
them. He helped them in every way possible ; his
time and his purse were always at their service ;
and he performed the difficult feat of giving pecu-
niary assistance with a tact and considerate delicacy that prevented the most sensitive from taking
offense.

He early became acquainted with the Duchess
of Orleans, wife of Philippe Egalité, the vicious
voluptuary of liberal leanings and clouded character. He met her at the house of an old friend,
Madame de Chastellux. At first he did not fancy
her, and rather held himself aloof, being uncertain
" how he would get on with royalty." The duchess,
however, was attracted by him, asked after him repeatedly, made their mutual friends throw them
together, and finally so managed that he became
one of her constant visitors and attendants. This
naturally flattered him, and he remained sincerely
loyal to her always afterwards. She was particularly anxious that he should be interested in her
son, then a boy, afterwards destined to become the
citizen king, — not a bad man, but a mean one,
and rather an unkingly king even for the nineteenth century, fertile though it has been in ignoble royalty. Morris's further dealings with this
precious youth will have to be considered hereafter.

After his first interview he notes that the duchess was " handsome enough to punish the duke for

his irregularities." He also mentioned that she
still seemed in love with her husband. However,
the lady was not averse to seeking a little sentimental consolation from her new friend, to whom
she confided, in their after intimacy, that she was
weary at heart and not happy, and — a thoroughly
French touch — that she had the " besoin d'être
aimée." On the day they first met, while he is
talking to her, " the widow of the late Duke of Orleans comes in, and at going away, according to
custom, kisses the duchess. I observe that the
ladies of Paris are very fond of each other; which
gives rise to some observations from her royal
highness on the person who has just quitted the
room, which show that the kiss does not always be-
token great affection. In going away she is pleased
to say that she is glad to have met me, and I
believe her. The reason is that I dropped some
expressions and sentiments a little rough, which
were agreeable because they contrasted with the
palling polish she meets with everywhere. Hence
I conclude that the less I have the honor of such
good company the better; for when the novelty
ceases all is over, and I shall probably be worse
than insipid."

Nevertheless, the " good company" was determined he should make one of their number. He
was not very loath himself, when he found he was
in no danger of being patronized, — for anything
like patronage was always particularly galling to
his pride, which was of the kind that resents a

tone of condescension more fiercely than an overt
insult, — and he became a fast friend of the house
of Orleans. The duchess made him her confidant;
unfolded to him her woes about the duke; and
once, when he was dining with her, complained to
him bitterly of the duke's conduct in not paying her
allowance regularly. She was in financial straits
at the time; for, though she was allowed four
hundred and fifty thousand livres a year, yet three
hundred and fifty thousand were appropriated for
the house-servants, table, etc., — an item wherein
her American friend, albeit not over-frugal, thought
a very little economy would result in a great saving.

His description of one of the days he spent at
Raincy with the duchess and her friends gives us
not only a glimpse of the life of the great ladies
and fine gentlemen of the day, but also a clear
insight into the reasons why these same highly
polished ladies and gentlemen had utterly lost their
hold over the people whose God-given rulers they
deemed themselves to be.

Déjeuner à la fourchette was not served till noon,
— Morris congratulating himself that he had taken
a light breakfast earlier. " After breakfast we go
to mass in the chapel. In the tribune above we
have a bishop, an abbé, the duchess, her maids
and some of their friends. Madame de Chastellux
is below on her knees. We are amused above by
a number of little tricks played off by Monsieur de
Ségur and Monsieur de Cabières with a candle,
which is put into the pockets of different gentle-

men, the bishop among the rest, and lighted, while
they are otherwise engaged (for there is a fire in
the tribune), to the great merriment of the spectators.   Immoderate laughter is the consequence.
The duchess preserves as much gravity as she can.
This scene must be very edifying to the domestics
who are opposite to us, and the villagers who worship below." The afternoon's amusements were not
to his taste.   They all walked, which he found very
hot; then they got into bateaux, and the gentlemen
rowed the ladies, which was still hotter; and then
there came more walking, so he was glad to get
back to the château.   The formal dinner was served
after five; the conversation thereat varied between
the vicious and the frivolous.   There was much
bantering, well-bred in manner and excessively
under-bred in matter, between the different guests
of both sexes, about the dubious episodes in their
past careers, and the numerous shady spots in their
respective characters.   Epigrams and "epitaphs"
were bandied about freely, some in verse, some not;
probably very amusing then, but their lustre sadly
tarnished in the eyes of those who read them now.
While they were dining, "a number of persons
surround the windows, doubtless from a high idea
of the company, to whom they are obliged to look
up at an awful distance.   Oh, did they but know
how trivial the conversation, how very trivial the
characters, their respect would soon be changed to
an emotion entirely different!"

This was but a month before the Bastille fell;

and yet, on the threshold of their hideous doom, the people who had most at stake were incapable not only of intelligent action to ward off their fate, but even of serious thought as to what their fate would be. The men — the nobles, the clerical dignitaries, and the princes of the blood — chose the church as a place wherein to cut antics that would have better befitted a pack of monkeys; while the women, their wives and mistresses, exchanged with them impure jests at their own expense, relished because of the truth on which they rested. Brutes might still have held sway at least for a time; but these were merely vicious triflers. They did not believe in their religion; they did not believe in themselves; they did not believe in anything. They had no earnestness, no seriousness; their sensibilities and enthusiasms were alike affectations. There was still plenty of fire and purpose and furious energy in the hearts of the French people; but these and all the other virile virtues lay not among the noblesse, but among the ranks of the common herd beneath them, down-trodden, bloody in their wayward ferocity, but still capable of fierce, heroic devotion to an ideal in which they believed, and for which they would spill the blood of others, or pour out their own, with the proud waste of utter recklessness.

Many of Morris's accounts of the literary life of the salon read as if they were explanatory notes to "Les Précieuses Ridicules." There was a certain pretentiousness about it that made it a bit of a sham at the best; and the feebler variety of salon, built on such a foundation, thus became that most despicable of things, an imitation of a pretense. At one of the dinners which Morris describes, the company was of a kind that would have done no discredit to an entertainment of the great social and literary light of Eatanswill. " Set off in great haste to dine with the Comtesse de R., on an invitation of a week's standing. Arrive at about a quarter past three, and find in the drawing-room some dirty linen and no fire. While a waiting-woman takes away one, a valet lights up the other. Three small sticks in a deep bed of ashes give no great expectation of heat. By the smoke, however, all doubts are removed respecting the existence of fire. To expel the smoke, a window is opened, and, the day being cold, I have the benefit of as fresh air as can reasonably be expected in so large a city.

" Towards four o'clock the guests begin to assemble, and I begin to expect that, as madame is a poetess, I shall have the honor to dine with that exalted part of the species who devote themselves to the muses. In effect, the gentlemen begin to compliment their respective works ; and, as regular hours cannot be expected in a house where the mistress is occupied more with the intellectual than the material world, I have a delightful prospect of a continuance of the scene. Towards five, madame steps in to announce dinner, and the hungry poets advance to the charge. As they bring

good appetites, they have certainly reason to praise
the feast. And I console myself with the persua-
sion that for this day at least I shall escape an
indigestion. A very narrow escape, too, for some
rancid butter, of which the cook had been liberal,
puts me in bodily fear. If the repast is not abun-
dant, we have at least the consolation that there is
no lack of conversation. Not being perfectly master of the language, most of the jests escaped me.
As for the rest of the company, each being employed either in saying a good thing, or else in
studying one to say, it is no wonder if he cannot
find time to applaud that of his neighbors. They
all agree that we live in an age alike deficient in
justice and in taste. Each finds in the fate of his
own works numerous instances to justify this censure. They tell me, to my great surprise, that the
public now condemn theatrical compositions before
they have heard the first recital. And, to remove
my doubts, the comtesse is so kind as to assure me
that this rash decision has been made on one of
her own pieces. In pitying modern degeneracy,
we rise from the table.

" I take my leave immediately after the coffee,
which by no means dishonors the precedent repast;
and madame informs me that on Tuesdays and
Thursdays she is always at home, and will always
be glad to see me. While I stammer out some
return to the compliment, my heart, convinced of
my unworthiness to partake of such attic entertainments, makes me promise never again to occupy

the place from which perhaps I had excluded a
worthier personage."

Among Morris's other qualities, he was the first
to develop that peculiarly American vein of humor
which is especially fond of gravely pretending to
believe without reserve some preposterously untrue
assertion, — as throughout the above quotation.

Though the society in which he was thrown
interested him, he always regarded it with half-
sarcastic amusement, and at times it bored him
greatly. Meditating on the conversation in " this
upper region of wits and graces," he concludes
that " the sententious style " is the one best fitted
for it, and that in it " observations with more of
justice than splendor cannot amuse," and sums up
by saying that " he could not please, because he
was not sufficiently pleased."

His comments upon the various distinguished
men he met are always interesting, on account of
the quick, accurate judgment of character which
they show. It was this insight into the feelings
and ideas alike of the leaders and of their followers
which made his political predictions often so accurate. His judgment of many of his contemporaries comes marvelously near the cooler estimate
of history.

He was originally prejudiced in favor of the
king, poor Louis XVI., and, believing him " to be
an honest and good man, he sincerely wished him
well," but he very soon began to despise him for
his weakness. This quality was the exact one that

under existing circumstances was absolutely fatal;
and Morris mentions it again and again, pronouncing the king "a well-meaning man, but extremely
weak, without genius or education to show the way
towards that good which he desires," and "a prince
so weak that he can influence very little either by
his presence or absence." Finally, in a letter to
Washington, he gives a biting sketch of the unfortunate monarch. "If the reigning prince were
not the small-beer character that he is, there can
be but little doubt that, watching events and making a tolerable use of them, he would regain his
authority; but what will you have from a creature
who, situated as he is, eats and drinks, sleeps well
and laughs, and is as merry a grig as lives? The
idea that they will give him some money, which he
can economize, and that he will have no trouble in
governing, contents him entirely. Poor man! He
little thinks how unstable is his situation. He is
beloved, but it is not with the sort of love which a
monarch should inspire. It is that kind of good-
natured pity which one feels for a led captive.
There is besides no possibility of serving him, for
at the slightest show of opposition he gives up
everything and every person." Morris had too
robust a mind to feel the least regard for mere
amiability and good intentions when unaccom-
panied by any of the ruder, manlier virtues.

The Count d'Artois had "neither sense to counsel himself, nor to choose counselors for himself,
much less to counsel others." This gentleman,

afterwards Charles X., stands as perhaps the most
shining example of the monumental ineptitude of
his royal house.   His fellow Bourbon, the amiable
Bomba of Naples, is his only equal for dull silli-
ness, crass immorality, and the lack of every manly
or kingly virtue.   Democracy has much to answer
for, but after all it would be hard to find, even
among the aldermen of New York and Chicago,
men whose moral and mental shortcomings would
put them lower than this royal couple.   To our
shame be it said, our system of popular government once let our greatest city fall under the control of Tweed; but it would be rank injustice to
that clever rogue to compare him with the two
vicious dullards whom the opposite system permitted to tyrannize at Paris and Naples.   Moreover, in the end, we of the democracy not only
overthrew the evil-doer who oppressed us, but also
put him in prison; and in the long run we have
usually meted out the same justice to our lesser
criminals.   Government by manhood suffrage shows
at its worst in large cities; and yet even in these
experience certainly does not show that a despotism works a whit better, or as well.

Morris described the Count de Montmorin pith-
ily, saying: "He has more understanding than
people in general imagine, and he means well, very
well, but he means it feebly."

When Morris came to France, Necker was the
most prominent man in the kingdom.   He was a
hard-working, well-meaning, conceited person, not

in the least fitted for public affairs, a banker but
not a financier, and affords a beautiful illustration
of the utter futility of the popular belief that a
good business man will necessarily be a good
statesman. Accident had made him the most conspicuous figure of the government, admired and
hated, but not looked down upon; yet Morris saw
through him at a glance. After their first meeting, he writes down in his diary: "He has the
look and manner of the counting-house, and, being
dressed in embroidered velvet, he contrasts strongly
with his habiliments. His bow, his address, say,
'I am the man.' . . . If he is really a very great
man, I am deceived; and yet this is a rash judgment. If he is not a laborious man, I am also
deceived." He soon saw that both the blame and
the praise bestowed on him were out of all proportion to his consequence, and he wrote: "In their
anguish [the nobles] curse Necker, who is in fact
less the cause than the instrument of their suffer-
ings. His popularity depends now more on the
opposition he meets with from one party than any
serious regard of the other. It is the attempt to
throw him down which saves him from falling;
. . . as it is, he must soon fall." To Washington
he gave a fuller analysis of his character. "As
to M. Necker, he is one of those people who has obtained a much greater reputation than he has any
right to. . . . In his public administration he has always been honest and disinterested; which proves
well, I think, for his former private conduct, or

else it proves that he has more vanity than cupid-
ity. Be that as it may, an unspotted integrity as
minister, and serving at his own expense in an
office which others seek for the purpose of enrich-
ing themselves, have acquired for him very deservedly much confidence. Add to this that his
writings on finance teem with that sort of sensibility which makes the fortune of modern romances,
and which is exactly suited to this lively nation,
who love to read but hate to think. Hence his
reputation. He . . . [has not] the talents of a
great minister. His education as a banker has
taught him to make tight bargains, and put him
upon his guard against projects. But though he
understands man as a covetous creature, he does
not understand mankind, — a defect which is
remediless. He is utterly ignorant of politics, by
which I mean politics in the great sense, or that
sublime science which embraces for its object the
happiness of mankind. Consequently he neither
knows what constitution to form, nor how to obtain the consent of others to such as he wishes.
From the moment of convening the States-General,
he has been afloat upon the wide ocean of inci-
dents. But what is most extraordinary is that M.
Necker is a very poor financier. This I know will
sound like heresy in the ears of most people, but
it is true. The plans he has proposed are feeble
and inept."

A far more famous man, Talleyrand, then Bishop
of Autun, he also gauged correctly from the start,

writing down that he appeared to be "a sly, cool, cunning, ambitious, and malicious man. I know not why conclusions so disadvantageous to him are formed in my mind, but so it is, and I cannot help it." He was afterwards obliged to work much in common with Talleyrand, for both took substantially the same view of public affairs in that crisis, and were working for a common end. Speaking of his new ally's plan respecting church property, he says: "He is bigoted to it, and the thing is well enough ; but the mode is not so well. He is attached to this *as an author*, which is not a good sign for a man of business." And again he criticises Talleyrand's management of certain schemes for the finances, as showing a willingness " to sacrifice great objects for the sake of small ones . . . an inverse ratio of moral proportion."

Morris was fond of Lafayette, and appreciated highly his courage and keen sense of honor; but he did not think much of his ability, and became at times very impatient with his vanity and his impractical theories. Besides, he deemed him a man who was carried away by the current, and could neither stem nor guide it. "I have known my friend Lafayette now for many years, and can estimate at the just value both his words and actions. He means ill to no one, but he is very much below the business he has undertaken; and if the sea runs high, he will be unable to hold the helm." And again, in writing to Washington: "Unluckily he has given in to measures . . . which he does not heartily approve, and he heartily approves many things which experience will demonstrate to be dangerous."

The misshapen but mighty genius of Mirabeau he found more difficulty in estimating; he probably never rated it quite high enough. He naturally scorned a man of such degraded debauchery, who, having been one of the great inciters to revolution, had now become a subsidized ally of the court. He considered him "one of the most unprincipled scoundrels that ever lived," although of "superior talents," and "so profligate that he would disgrace any administration," besides having so little principle as to make it unsafe to trust him. After his death he thus sums him up: "Vices both degrading and detestable marked this extraordinary being. Completely prostitute, he sacrificed everything to the whim of the moment; — *cupidus alieni prodigus sui;* venal, shameless; and yet greatly virtuous when pushed by a prevailing impulse, but never truly virtuous, because never under the steady control of reason, nor the firm authority of principle. I have seen this man, in the short space of two years, hissed, honored, hated, mourned. Enthusiasm has just now presented him gigantic. Time and reflection will sink this stature." Even granting this to be wholly true, as it undoubtedly is in the main, it was nevertheless the fact that in Mirabeau alone lay the last hope of salvation for the French nation; and Morris erred in strenuously opposing Lafayette's going into a ministry

with him. Indeed, he seems in this case to have
been blinded by prejudice, and certainly acted very
inconsistently; for his advice and the reasons he
gave for it were completely at variance with the
rules he himself laid down to Lafayette, with even
more cynicism than common sense, when the latter
once made some objections to certain proposed
coadjutors of his: "I state to him . . . that, as to
the objections he has made on the score of morals
in some, he must consider that men do not go into
an administration as the direct road to heaven;
that they are prompted by ambition or avarice,
and therefore that the only way to secure the
most virtuous is by making it their interest to act
rightly."

Morris thus despised the king, and distrusted the
chief political leaders; and, as he wrote Washington, he was soon convinced that there was an immense amount of corruption in the upper circles.
The people at large he disliked even more than he
did their advisers, and he had good grounds, too,
as the following extract from his journal shows:
"July 22. After dinner, walk a little under the
arcade of the Palais Royal, waiting for my carriage.
In this period the head and body of M. de Toulon
are introduced in triumph, the head on a pike, the
body dragged naked on the earth. Afterwards
this horrible exhibition is carried through the different streets. His crime is, to have accepted a
place in the ministry. This mutilated form of an
old man of seventy-five is shown to his son-in-law,

Berthier, the intendant of Paris; and afterwards
he also is put to death and cut to pieces, the populace carrying about the mangled fragments with
a savage joy. Gracious God, what a people!"

He describes at length, and most interestingly,
the famous opening of the States-General, "the
beginning of the revolution." He eyed this body
even at the beginning with great distrust; and he
never thought that any of the delegates showed
especial capacity for grappling with the terrible
dangers and difficulties by which they were en-
compassed. He comments on the extreme enthusiasm with which the king was greeted, and sym-
pathizes strongly with Marie Antoinette, who was
treated with studied and insulting coldness. "She
was exceedingly hurt. I cannot help feeling the
mortification which the poor queen meets with, for
I see only the woman; and it seems unmanly to
treat a woman with unkindness. . . . Not one
voice is heard to wish her well. I would certainly
raise mine if I were a Frenchman; but I have no
right to express a sentiment, and in vain solicit
those who are near me to do it." . . . At last "the
queen rises, and, to my great satisfaction, she hears,
for the first time in several months, the sound of
'Vive la reine!' She makes a low courtesy, and
this produces a louder acclamation, and that a
lower courtesy."

The sympathy was for the woman, not the queen,
the narrow minded, absolute sovereign, the intriguer
against popular government, whose policy was as

heavily fraught with bale for the nation as was
that of Robespierre himself. The king was more
than competent to act as his own evil genius ; had
he not been, Marie Antoinette would have amply
filled the place.

He characterized the carrying of " that diabol-
ical castle," the Bastille, as " among the most extraordinary things I have met with." The day it
took place he wrote in his journal, with an irony
very modern in its flavor : " Yesterday it was the
fashion at Versailles not to believe that there were
any disturbances at Paris. I presume that this
day's transactions will induce a conviction that all
is not perfectly quiet."

He used the Bastille as a text when, shortly afterwards, he read a brief lesson to a certain eminent
painter. The latter belonged to that class of artists
with pen or pencil (only too plentiful in America
at the present day) who always insist on devoting
their energies to depicting subjects worn thread-
bare by thousands of predecessors, instead of working in the new, broad fields, filled with picturesque
material, opened to them by their own country and
its history. " The painter shows us a piece he is
now about for the king, taken from the Æneid :
Venus restraining the arm which is raised in the
temple of the Vestals to shed the blood of Helen.
I tell him he had better paint the storm of the
Bastille."

CHAPTER IX

In March, 1790, Morris went to London, in obedience to a letter received from Washington appointing him private agent to the British government, and inclosing him the proper credentials.

Certain of the conditions of the treaty of peace between Great Britain and the United States, although entered into seven years before, were still unfulfilled. It had been stipulated that the British should give up the fortified frontier posts within our territory, and should pay for the negroes they had taken away from the Southern States during the war. They had done neither, and Morris was charged to find out what the intentions of the government were in the matter. He was also to find out whether there was a disposition to enter into a commercial treaty with the United States; and finally, he was to sound them as to their sending a minister to America.

On our part we had also failed to fulfill a portion of our treaty obligations, not having complied with the article which provided for the payment of debts due before the war to British merchants. Both sides had been to blame; each, of course,

blamed only the other. But now, when we were
ready to perform our part, the British refused to
perform theirs.

As a consequence, Morris, although he spent
most of the year in London, failed to accomplish
anything. The feeling in England was hostile to
America; to the king, in particular, the very name
was hateful. The English were still sore over their
defeat, and hated us because we had been victors;
and yet they despised us also, for they thought we
should be absolutely powerless except when we were
acting merely on the defensive. From the days of
the Revolution till the days of the civil war, the
ruling classes of England were bitterly antagonistic
to our nation; they always saw with glee any check
to our national well-being; they wished us ill, and
exulted in our misfortunes, while they sneered at
our successes. The results have been lasting, and
now work much more to their hurt than to ours.
The past conduct of England certainly offers much
excuse for, though it cannot in the least justify, the
unreasonable and virulent anti-English feeling —
that is, the feeling against Englishmen politically
and nationally, not socially or individually — which
is so strong in many parts of our country where the
native American blood is purest.

The English ministry in 1790 probably had the
general feeling of the nation behind them in their
determination to injure us as much as they could;
at any rate, their aim seemed to be, as far as lay
in them, to embitter our already existing hostility

to their empire. They not only refused to grant us any substantial justice, but they were inclined to inflict on us and on our representatives those petty insults which rankle longer than injuries.

When it came to this point, however, Morris was quite able to hold his own. He had a ready, biting tongue; and, excepting Pitt and Fox, was intellectually superior to any of the public men whom he met. In social position, even as they understood it, he was their equal; they could hardly look down on the brother of a British major-general, and a brother-in-law of the Duchess of Gordon. He was a man of rather fiery courage, and any attacks upon his country were not likely to be made twice in his presence. Besides, he never found the English congenial as friends or companions; he could not sympathize, or indeed get along well, with them. This distaste for their society he always retained, and though he afterwards grew to respect them, and to be their warm partisan politically, he was at this time much more friendly to France, and was even helping the French ministers concoct a scheme of warfare against their neighbor. To his bright, impatient temperament, the English awkwardness seemed to be an insuperable obstacle to bringing people together " as in other countries." He satirized the English drawing-rooms, " where the arrangement of the company was stiff and formal, the ladies all ranged in battalia on one side of the room ;" and remarked " that the French, having no liberty in their government, have compensated to

themselves that misfortune by bestowing a great
deal upon society.   But that, I fear, in England, is
all confined to the House of Commons." Years
afterwards he wrote to a friend abroad : " Have you
reflected that there is more of real society in one
week at [a continental watering-place] than in a
London year ? Recollect that a tedious morning, a
great dinner, a boozy afternoon, and dull evening
make the sum total of English life.   It is admirable for young men who shoot, hunt, drink, — but
for us ! How are we to dispose of ourselves ? No.
Were I to give you a rendezvous in Europe, it
should be on the Continent.   I respect, as you know,
the English nation highly, and love many individuals among them, but I do not love their manners."
Times have changed, and the manners of the is-
landers with them.   Exactly as the " rude Carin-
thian boor " has become the most polished of mor-
tals, so, after a like transformation, English society
is now perhaps the pleasantest and most interesting
in Europe.   Were Morris alive to-day, he would
probably respect the English as much as he ever
did, and like them a good deal more ; and, while he
might well have his preference for his own country
confirmed, yet, if he had to go abroad, it is hard to
believe that he would now pass by London in favor
of any continental capital or watering-place.

In acknowledging Washington's letter of appointment, Morris wrote that he did not expect much
difficulty, save from the king himself, who was very
obstinate, and bore a personal dislike to his former

subjects. But his interviews with the minister of foreign affairs, the Duke of Leeds, soon undeceived him. The duke met him with all the little tricks of delay and evasion known to old-fashioned diplomacy; tricks that are always greatly relished by men of moderate ability, and which are successful enough where the game is not very important, as in the present instance, but are nearly useless when the stakes are high and the adversary determined. The worthy nobleman was profuse in expressions of general good-will, and vague to a degree in his answers to every concrete question; affected to misunderstand what was asked of him, and, when he could not do this, " slumbered profoundly " for weeks before making his reply. Morris wrote that " his explanatory comments were more unintelligible than his texts," and was delighted when he heard that he might be replaced by Lord Hawksbury; for the latter, although strongly anti-American, " would at least be an efficient minister," whereas the former was " evidently afraid of committing himself by saying or doing anything positive." He soon concluded that Great Britain was so uncertain as to how matters were going in Europe that she wished to keep us in a similar state of suspense. She had recovered with marvelous rapidity from the effects of the great war; she was felt on all sides to hold a position of commanding power; this she knew well, and so felt like driving a very hard bargain with any nation, especially with a weak one that she hated. It was particularly

difficult to form a commercial treaty. There were
very many Englishmen who agreed with a Mr.
Irwin, " a mighty sour sort of creature," who assured Morris that he was utterly opposed to all
American trade in grain, and that he wished to
oblige the British people, by the force of starvation,
to raise enough corn for their own consumption.
Fox told Morris that he and Burke were about the
only two men left who believed that Americans
should be allowed to trade in their own bottoms to
the British islands ; and he also informed him that
Pitt was not hostile to America, but simply indifferent, being absorbed in European matters, and allowing his colleagues free hands.

Becoming impatient at the long-continued delay, Morris finally wrote, very courteously but very
firmly, demanding some sort of answer, and this
produced a momentary activity, and assurances that
he was under a misapprehension as to the delay,
etc. The subject of the impressment of American
sailors into British men-of-war, — a matter of
chronic complaint throughout our first forty years
of national life — now came up ; and he remarked
to the Duke of Leeds, with a pithy irony that
should have made the saying famous: "I believe,
my lord, that this is the only instance in which we
are not treated as aliens." He proposed a plan
which would have at least partially obviated the
difficulties in the way of a settlement of the matter, but the duke would do nothing. Neither
would he come to any agreement in reference to

the exchange of ministers between the two countries.

Then came an interview with Pitt, and Morris,
seeing how matters stood, now spoke out perfectly
clearly. In answer to the accusations about our
failure wholly to perform certain stipulations of the
treaty, after reciting the counter accusations of the
Americans, he brushed them all aside with the remark: "But, sir, what I have said tends to show
that these complaints and inquiries are excellent if
the parties mean to keep asunder; if they wish to
come together, all such matters should be kept out
of sight." He showed that the House of Representatives, in a friendly spirit, had recently decided
against laying extraordinary restrictions on British
vessels in our ports. "Mr. Pitt said that, instead
of restrictions, we ought to give them particular
privileges, in return for those we enjoy here. I
assured him that I knew of none except that of
being impressed, a privilege which of all others we
least wished to partake of. . . . Mr. Pitt said seriously that they had certainly evinced good-will to
us by what they had done respecting our commerce.
I replied therefore, with like seriousness, that their
regulations had been dictated with a view to their
own interests; and therefore, as we felt no favor,
we owed no obligation." Morris realized thoroughly that they were keeping matters in suspense
because their behavior would depend upon the con-
tingencies of war or peace with the neighboring
powers; he wished to show that, if they acted thus,

we would also bide our time till the moment came to strike a telling blow; and accordingly he ended by telling Pitt, with straightforward directness, a truth that was also a threat: " We do not think it worth while to go to war with you for the [frontier] forts; but we know our rights, and will avail ourselves of them when time and circumstances may suit."

After this conversation he became convinced that we should wait until England herself felt the necessity of a treaty before trying to negotiate one. He wrote Washington " that those who, pursuing the interests of Great Britain, wish to be on the best terms with America, are outnumbered by those whose sour prejudice and hot resentment render them averse to any intercourse except that which may immediately subserve a selfish policy. These men do not yet know America. Perhaps America does not yet know herself. . . . We are yet in but the seeding-time of national prosperity, and it will be well not to mortgage the crop before it is gathered. . . . England will not, I am persuaded, enter into a treaty with us unless we give for it more than it is worth now, and infinitely more than it will be worth hereafter. A present bargain would be that of a young heir with an old usurer. . . . But, should war break out [with a European power], the anti-American party here will agree to *any* terms; for it is more the taste of the medicine which they nauseate than the quantity of the dose."

Accordingly all negotiations were broken off. In America his enemies blamed Morris for this failure. They asserted that his haughty manners and proud bearing had made him unpopular with the ministers, and that his consorting with members of the opposition had still further damaged his cause. The last assertion was wholly untrue; for he had barely more than met Fox and his associates. But on a third point there was genuine reason for dissatisfaction. Morris had confided his purpose to the French minister at London, M. de la Luzerne, doing so because he trusted to the latter's honor, and did not wish to seem to take any steps unknown to our ally; and he was in all probability also influenced by his constant association and intimacy with the French leaders. Luzerne, however, promptly used the information for his own purposes, letting the English ministers know that he was acquainted with Morris's objects, and thus increasing the weight of France by making it appear that America acted only with her consent and advice. The affair curiously illustrates Jay's wisdom eight years before, when he insisted on keeping Luzerne's superior at that time, Vergennes, in the dark as to our course during the peace negotiations. However, it is not at all likely that Mr. Pitt or the Duke of Leeds were influenced in their course by anything Luzerne said.

Leaving London, Morris made a rapid trip through the Netherlands and up the Rhine. His journals, besides the usual comments on the inns,

the bads roads, poor horses, sulky postilions, and
the like, are filled with very interesting observations on the character of the country through
which he passed, its soil and inhabitants, and the
indications they afforded of the national resources.
He liked to associate with people of every kind,
and he was intensely fond of natural scenery; but,
what seems rather surprising in a man of his culture, he apparently cared very little for the great
cathedrals, the picture galleries, and the works of
art for which the old towns he visited were so
famous.

He reached Paris at the end of November, but
was almost immediately called to London again,
returning in January, 1791, and making three or
four similar trips in the course of the year. His
own business affairs took up a great deal of his
time. He was engaged in very many different
operations, out of which he made a great deal of
money, being a shrewd business man with a strong
dash of the speculator. He had to prosecute a suit
against the farmers-general of France for a large
quantity of tobacco shipped them by contract; and
he gives a very amusing description of the visits he
made to the judges before whom the case was to be
tried. Their occupations were certainly various,
being those of a farrier, a goldsmith, a grocer, a
currier, a woolen draper, and a bookseller respectively. As a sample of his efforts, take the following: " Return home and dine. At five resume
my visits to my judges, and first wait upon the

honorable M. Gillet, the grocer, who is in a little
cuddy adjoining his shop, at cards. He assures
me that the courts are impartial, and alike un-
influenced by farmers, receivers, and grand sei-
gneurs; that they are generally of the same opinion; that he will do everything in his power; and
the like. *De l'autre côté*, perfect confidence in
the ability and integrity of the court. Wish only
to bring the cause to such a point as that I may
have the honor to present a memorial. Am vastly
sorry to have been guilty of an intrusion upon the
amusements of his leisure hours. Hope he will
excuse the solicitude of a stranger, and patronize
a claim of such evident justice. The whole goes
off very well, though I with difficulty restrain my
risible faculties. . . . A disagreeable scene, the
ridicule of which is so strongly painted to my own
eyes that I cannot forbear laughing."

He also contracted to deliver Necker twenty
thousand barrels of flour for the relief of Paris;
wherein, by the way, he lost heavily. He took part
in sundry shipping operations. Perhaps the most
lucrative business in which he was engaged was in
negotiating the sale of wild lands in America. He
even made many efforts to buy the Virginian and
Pennsylvanian domains of the Fairfaxes and the
Penns. On behalf of a syndicate, he endeavored
to purchase the American debts to France and
Spain; these being purely speculative efforts, as it
was supposed that the debts could be obtained at
quite a low figure, while, under the new Constitu-

tion, the United States would certainly soon make
arrangements for paying them off.   These various
operations entailed a wonderful amount of downright hard work ; yet all the while he remained
not only a close observer of French politics, but,
to a certain extent, even an actor in them.

He called upon Lafayette as soon as he was
again established in Paris, after his mission to
London. He saw that affairs had advanced to
such a pitch in France that "it was no longer a
question of liberty, but simply who shall be master."   He had no patience with those who wished
the king to place himself, as they phrased it, at
the head of the revolution, remarking : " The
trade of a revolutionist appears to me a hard one
for a prince."   What with the folly of one side
and the madness of the other, things were going
to pieces very rapidly.   At one of his old haunts,
the club, the " sentiment aristocratique " had made
great headway : one of his friends, De Moustin,
now in favor with the king and queen, was " as
usual on the high ropes of royal prerogative."
Lafayette, however, was still wedded to his theories, and did not appear over-glad to see his American friend, all whose ideas and habits of thought
were so opposed to his own ; while madame was
still cooler in her reception.   Morris, nothing
daunted, talked to his friend very frankly and
seriously.   He told him that the time had come
when all good citizens would be obliged, simply
from lack of choice, to cling to the throne ; that

the executive must be strengthened, and good and able men put into the council. He pronounced the "thing called a constitution" good for nothing, and showed that the National Assembly was rapidly falling into contempt. He pointed out, for the hundredth time, that each country needed to have its own form of government; that an American constitution would not do for France, for the latter required an even higher-toned system than that of England; and that, above all things, France needed stability. He gave the reasons for his advice clearly and forcibly; but poor Lafayette flinched from it, and could not be persuaded to take any effectual step.

It is impossible to read Morris's shrewd comments on the events of the day, and his plans in reference to them, without wondering that France herself should at the crisis have failed to produce any statesmen to be compared with him for force, insight, and readiness to do what was practically best under the circumstances; but her past history for generations had been such as to make it out of the question for her to bring forth such men as the founders of our own government. Warriors, lawgivers, and diplomats she had in abundance. Statesmen who would be both hard-headed and true-hearted, who would be wise and yet unselfish, who would enact laws for a free people that would make that people freer still, and yet hinder them from doing wrong to their neighbors, — statesmen of this order she neither had nor could have had.

Indeed, had there been such, it may well be doubted if they could have served France. With a people who made up in fickle ferocity what they lacked in self-restraint, and a king too timid and short-sighted to turn any crisis to advantage, the French statesmen, even had they been as wise as they were foolish, would hardly have been able to arrest or alter the march of events. Morris said bitterly that France was the country where everything was talked of, and where hardly anything was understood.

He told Lafayette that he thought the only hope of the kingdom lay in a foreign war; it is possible that the idea may have been suggested to him by Lafayette's naïve remark that he believed his troops would readily follow him into action, but that they would not mount guard when it rained. Morris not only constantly urged the French ministers to make war, but actually drew up a plan of campaign for them. He believed it would turn the popular ardor, now constantly inflamed against the aristocrats, into a new channel, and that "there was no word perhaps in the dictionary which would take the place of *aristocrat* so readily as *Anglais*." In proof of the wisdom of his propositions he stated, with absolute truthfulness: "If Britain had declared war in 1774 against the house of Bourbon, the now United States would have bled freely in her cause." He was disgusted with the littleness of the men who, appalled at their own surroundings, and unable to make shift even for

the moment, found themselves thrown by chance
to the helm, and face to face with the wildest
storm that had ever shaken a civilized government.
Speaking of one of the new ministers, he remarked :
" They say he is a good kind of man, which is saying very little ; " and again, " You want just now
great men, to pursue great measures." Another
time, in advising a war, — a war of men, not of
money, — and speaking of the efforts made by the
neighboring powers against the revolutionists in
Flanders, he told his French friends that they must
either suffer for or with their allies ; and that the
latter was at once the noblest and the safest course.

In a letter to Washington he drew a picture of
the chaos as it really was, and at the same time,
with wonderful clear-sightedness, showed the great
good which the change was eventually to bring to
the mass of the people. Remembering how bitter
Morris's feelings were against the revolutionists, it
is extraordinary that they did not blind him to the
good that would in the long run result from their
movement. Not another statesman would have
been able to set forth so clearly and temperately
the benefits that would finally come from the convulsions he saw around him, although he rightly
believed that these benefits would be even greater
could the hideous excesses of the revolutionists be
forthwith stopped and punished.

His letter runs : " This unhappy country, bewil-
dered in the pursuit of metaphysical whimsies, presents to our moral view a mighty ruin. . . . The

sovereign, humbled to the level of a beggar without
pity, without resources, without authority, without
a friend. The Assembly, at once a master and a
slave, new in power, wild in theory, raw in practice. It engrosses all functions, though incapable
of exercising any, and has taken from this fierce,
ferocious people every restraint of religion and of
respect." Where this would all end, or what sum
of misery would be necessary to change the popular
will and awaken the popular heart, he could not
say. A glorious opportunity had been lost, and for
the time being the revolution had failed. Yet,
he went on to say, in the consequences flowing
from it he was confident he could see the foundation of future prosperity. For among these consequences were, — 1. The abolition of the different
rights and privileges which had formerly kept the
various provinces asunder; 2. The abolition of
feudal tyranny, by which the tenure of real property would be simplified, and the rent no longer
be dependent upon idle vanity, capricious taste, or
sullen pride; 3. The throwing into the circle of
industry those vast possessions formerly held by
the clergy in mortmain, wealth conferred upon
them as wages for their idleness; 4. The destruction of the system of venal jurisprudence which
had established the pride and privileges of the few
on the misery and degradation of the general mass;
5. Above all, the establishment of the principles
of true liberty, which would remain as solid facts
after the superstructure of metaphysical froth and

vapor should have been blown away. Finally,
"from the chaos of opinion and the conflict of its
jarring elements a new order will at length arise,
which, though in some degree the child of chance,
may not be less productive of human happiness
than the forethought provisions of human speculation." Not one other contemporary statesman
could have begun to give so just an estimate of the
good the revolution would accomplish; no other
could have seen so deeply into its ultimate results,
while also keenly conscious of the dreadful evil
through which these results were being worked
out.

The social life of Paris still went on, though
with ever less of gayety, as the gloom gathered
round about. Going with Madame de Chastellux
to dine with the Duchess of Orleans, Morris was
told by her royal highness that she was "ruined,"
that is, that her income was reduced from four
hundred and fifty thousand to two hundred thousand livres a year, so that she could no longer give
him good dinners; but if he would come and fast
with her, she would be glad to see him. The poor
lady was yet to learn by bitter experience that real
ruin was something very different from the loss of
half of an enormous income.

On another occasion he breakfasted with the
duchess, and was introduced to her father, with
whom he agreed to dine. After breakfast she
went out walking with him till nearly dinner-time,
and gave him the full history of her breach with

her husband, Egalité, showing the letters that had passed between them, complaining of his numerous misdeeds, and assuring Morris that what the world had attributed to fondness for her worthless spouse was merely discretion; that she had hoped to bring him to a decent and orderly behavior, but had finally made up her mind that he could only be governed by fear.

Now and then he indulges in a quiet laugh at the absurd pretensions and exaggerated estimates of each other still affected by some of the frequenters of the various salons. " Dine with Madame de Staël. The Abbé Sieyès is here, and descants with much self-sufficiency on government, despising all that has been said or sung on that subject before him; and madame says that his writings and opinions will form in politics a new era, like those of Newton in physics."

After dining with Marmontel, he notes in his diary that his host " thinks soundly," — rare praise for him to bestow on any of the French statesmen of the time. He records a *bon mot* of Talleyrand's. When the Assembly had declared war on the emperor conditionally upon the latter's failing to beg pardon before a certain date, the little bishop remarked that " the nation was *une parvenue*, and of course insolent." At the British ambassador's he met the famous Colonel Tarleton, who did not know his nationality, and amused him greatly by descanting at length on the American war.

He was very fond of the theatre, especially of

the Comédie Française, where Préville, whom he
greatly admired, was acting in Molière's "Am-
phitryon." Many of the plays, whose plots presented in any way analogies to what was actually
happening in the political world, raised great
excitement among the spectators. Going to see
"Brutus" acted, he records that the noise and
altercations were tremendous, but that finally the
democrats in the parterre got the upper hand by
sheer lusty roaring, which they kept up for a quarter of an hour at a time, and, at the conclusion of
the piece, insisted upon the bust of Voltaire being
crowned and placed on the stage. Soon afterwards
a tragedy called "Charles Neuf," founded on the
massacre of St. Bartholomew, was put on the stage,
to help the Assembly in their crusade against the
clergy; he deemed it a very extraordinary piece to
be represented in a Catholic country, and thought
that it would give a fatal blow to the Catholic
religion.

The priesthood, high and low, he disliked more
than any other set of men; all his comments on
them show his contempt. The high prelates he
especially objected to. The Bishop of Orleans he
considered to be a luxurious old gentleman, "of
the kind whose sincerest prayer is for the fruit of
good living, one who evidently thought it more
important to *speak* than to speak the *truth*." The
leader of the great church dignitaries, in their fight
for their rich benefices, was the Abbé Maury, who,
Morris writes, "is a man who looks like a down-

right ecclesiastical scoundrel." He met him in Madame de Nadaillac's salon, where were "a party of fierce aristocrats. They have the word 'valet' written on their foreheads in large characters. Maury is formed to govern such men, and they are formed to obey him or any one else. But Maury seems to have too much vanity for a great man." To tell the bare truth is sometimes to make the most venomous comment possible, and this he evidently felt when he wrote of his meeting with the Cardinal de Rohan: "We talk among other things about religion, for the cardinal is very devout. He was once the lover of Madame de Flahaut's sister."

But as the tremendous changes went on about him, Morris had continually less and less time to spend in mere social pleasures; graver and weightier matters called for his attention, and his diary deals with the shifts and stratagems of the French politicians, and pays little heed to the sayings and manners of nobles, bishops, and ladies of rank.

The talented, self-confident, fearless American, admittedly out of sympathy with what he called "this abominable populace," was now well known; and in their terrible tangle of dangers and perplexities, court and ministry alike turned to him for help. Perhaps there has hardly been another instance where, in such a crisis, the rulers have clutched in their despair at the advice of a mere private stranger sojourning in the land on his own business. The king and his ministers, as well as the queen, kept in constant communication with him. With Montmorin he dined continually, and was consulted at every stage. But he could not prevail on them to adopt the bold, vigorous measures he deemed necessary; his plain speaking startled them, and they feared it would not suit the temper of the people. He drafted numerous papers for them, among others a royal speech, which the king liked, but which his ministers prevented him from using. In fact, it had grown to be hopeless to try to help the court; for the latter pursued each course by fits and starts, now governed by advice from Coblentz, now by advice from Brussels, and then for a brief spasm going its own gait. All the while the people at large knew their own minds no better than poor Louis knew his, and cheered him with fervent ecstasy one day, only to howl at him with malignant fury the next. With such a monarch and such subjects it is not probable that any plan would have worked well; but Morris's was the ablest as well as the boldest and best defined of the many that were offered to the wretched, halting king; and had his proposed policy been pursued, things might have come out better, and they could not possibly have come out worse.

All through these engrossing affairs, he kept up the liveliest interest in what was going on in his own country, writing home shrewd observations on every step taken. One of his remarks deserves to be kept in mind. In speaking of the desire of

European nations to legislate against the introduction of our produce, he says that this effort has
after all its bright side ; because it will force us
" to make great and rapid progress in useful manu-
factures. This alone is wanting to complete our
independence. We shall then be, as it were, a
world by ourselves."

CHAPTER X

MINISTER TO FRANCE

In the spring of 1792, Morris received his credentials as minister to France. There had been determined opposition in the Senate to the confirmation of his appointment, which was finally carried only by a vote of sixteen to eleven, mainly through the exertions of Rufus King. His opponents urged the failure of the British negotiations, the evidences repeatedly given of his proud, impatient spirit, and above all his hostility to the French Revolution, as reasons why he should not be made minister. Washington, however, as well as Hamilton, King, and the other Federalists, shared most of Morris's views with regard to the revolution, and insisted upon his appointment.

But the President, as good and wise a friend as Morris had, thought it best to send him a word of warning, coupling with the statement of his own unfaltering trust and regard the reasons why the new diplomat should observe more circumspection than his enemies thought him capable of showing. For his opponents asserted that his brilliant, lively imagination always inclined him to act so promptly as to leave no time for cool judgment, and was,

wrote Washington, "the primary cause of those
sallies which too often offend, and of that ridicule
of character which begets enmity not easy to be
forgotten, but which might easily be avoided if it
were under the control of caution and prudence.
. . . By reciting [their objections] I give you a
proof of my friendship, if I give none of my
policy."

Morris took his friend's advice in good part, and
profited by it as far as lay in his nature. He knew
that he had a task of stupendous difficulty before
him; as it would be almost impossible for a minister to steer clear of the quarrels springing from the
ferocious hatred borne to each other by the royalists
and the various republican factions. To stand *well*
with all parties he knew was impossible: but he
thought it possible, and merely so, to stand well
with the best people in each, without greatly offending the others; and, in order to do this, he had to
make up his mind to mingle with the worst as well
as the best, to listen unmoved to falsehoods so foul
and calumnies so senseless as to seem the ravings
of insanity; and meanwhile to wear a front so firm
and yet so courteous as to ward off insult from his
country and injury from himself during the days
when the whole people went crazy with the blood-
lust, when his friends were butchered by scores
around him, and when the rulers had fulfilled Mirabeau's terrible prophecy, and had "paved the
streets with their bodies."

But when he began his duties, he was already entangled in a most dangerous intrigue, one of whose very existence he should not, as a foreign minister, have known, still less have entered into. He got enmeshed in it while still a private citizen, and could not honorably withdraw, for it dealt with nothing less than the escape of the king and queen from Paris. His chivalrous sympathy for the two hemmed-in, hunted creatures, threatened by madmen and counseled by fools, joined with his characteristic impulsiveness and fearlessness to incline him to make an effort to save them from their impending doom. A number of plans had been made to get the king out of Paris ; and as the managers of each were of necessity ignorant of all the rest, they clashed with and thwarted one another. Morris's scheme was made in concert with a M. de Monciel, one of the royal ministers, and some other French gentlemen; and their measures were so well taken that they would doubtless have succeeded had not the king's nerve invariably failed him at the critical moment, and brought delay after delay. The Swiss guards, faithful to their salt, were always ready to cover his flight, and Lafayette would have helped them.

Louis preferred Morris's plan to any of the others offered, and gave a most striking proof of his preference by sending to the latter, towards the end of July, to say how much he regretted that his advice had not been followed, and to ask him if he would not take charge of the royal papers and money. Morris was unwilling to take the papers, but finally

consented to receive the money, amounting in all to
nearly seven hundred and fifty thousand livres,
which was to be paid out in hiring and bribing the
men who stood in the way of the escape ; for most
of the revolutionists were as venal as they were
bloodthirsty. Still the king lingered ; then came
the 10th of August; the Swiss guards were slaugh-
tered, and the whole scheme was at an end. Some
of the men engaged in the plot were suspected ; one,
D'Angrémont, was seized and condemned, but he
went to his death without betraying his fellows.
The others, by the liberal use of the money in Morris's possession, were saved, the authorities being
bribed to wink at their escape or concealment. Out
of the money that was left advances were made to
Monciel and others ; finally, in 1796, Morris gave
an accurate account of the expenditures to the dead
king's daughter, the Duchesse d'Angoulême, then
at the Austrian court, and turned over to her the
remainder, consisting of a hundred and forty-seven
pounds.

Of course all this was work in which no minister
had the least right to share; but the whole crisis
was one so completely without precedent that it is
impossible to blame Morris for what he did. The
extraordinary trust reposed in him, and the feeling
that his own exertions were all that lay between the
two unfortunate sovereigns and their fate roused
his gallantry and blinded him to the risk he himself ran, as well as to the hazard to which he put
his country's interests. He was under no illusion

as to the character of the people whom he was trying to serve. He utterly disapproved the queen's
conduct, and he despised the king, noting the latter's feebleness and embarrassment, even on the
occasion of his presentation at court; he saw in
them " a lack of mettle which would ever prevent
them from being truly royal;" but when in their
mortal agony they held out their hands to him for
aid, his generous nature forbade him to refuse it,
nor could he look on unmoved as they went help-
lessly down to destruction.

The rest of his two years' history as minister
forms one of the most brilliant chapters in our diplomatic annals. His boldness, and the frankness
with which he expressed his opinions, though they
at times irritated beyond measure the factions of
the revolutionists who successively grasped a brief
but tremendous power, yet awed them, in spite of
themselves. He soon learned to combine courage
and caution, and his readiness, wit, and dash always
gave him a certain hold over the fiery nation to
which he was accredited. He was firm and dignified in insisting on proper respect being shown our
flag, while he did all he could to hasten the payment
of our obligations to France. A very large share of
his time, also, was taken up with protesting against
the French decrees aimed at neutral — which meant
American — commerce, and with interfering to save
American shipmasters, who had got into trouble
by unwittingly violating them. Like his successor,
Mr. Washburne, in the time of the commune, Mor-

ris was the only foreign minister who remained in Paris during the terror. He stayed at the risk of his life ; and yet, while fully aware of his danger, he carried himself as coolly as if in a time of profound peace, and never flinched for a moment when he was obliged for his country's sake to call to account the rulers of France for the time being, — men whose power was as absolute as it was ephemeral and bloody, who had indulged their desire for slaughter with the unchecked ferocity of madmen, and who could by a word have had him slain as thousands had been slain before him. Few foreign ministers have faced such difficulties, and not one has ever come near to facing such dangers as Morris did during his two years' term of service. His feat stands by itself in diplomatic history ; and, as a minor incident, the letters and dispatches he sent home give a very striking view of the French Revolution.

As soon as he was appointed he went to see the French minister of foreign affairs ; and, in answer to an observation of the latter, stated with his customary straightforwardness that it was true that, while a mere private individual, sincerely friendly to France, and desirous of helping her, and whose own nation could not be compromised by his acts, he had freely taken part in passing events, had criticised the Constitution, and advised the king and his ministers ; but he added that, now that he was a public man, he would no longer meddle with their affairs. To this resolution he kept, save that,

as already described, sheer humanity induced him
to make an effort to save the king's life. He had
predicted what would ensue as the result of the
exaggerated decentralization into which the opponents of absolutism had rushed; when they had
split the state up into more than forty thousand
sovereignties, each district the sole executor of the
law, and the only judge of its propriety, and therefore obedient to it only so long as it listed, and
until rendered hostile by the ignorant whim or
ferocious impulse of the moment; and now he was
to see his predictions come true. In that brilliant
and able state paper, the address he had drawn
up for Louis to deliver when in 1791 the latter
accepted the Constitution, the keynote of the situation was struck in the opening words : " It is no
longer a king who addresses you, Louis XVI. is
a private individual ; " and he had then scored off,
point by point, the faults in a document that created an unwieldy assembly of men unaccustomed
to govern, that destroyed the principle of authority,
though no other could appeal to a people helpless
in their new-born liberty, and that created out of
one whole a jarring multitude of fractional sovereignties. Now he was to see one of these same
sovereignties rise up in successful rebellion against
the government that represented the whole, destroy
it and usurp its power, and establish over all
France the rule of an anarchic despotism which,
by what seems to a free American a gross misno-
mer, they called a democracy.

All through June, at the beginning of which
month Morris had been formally presented at
court, the excitement and tumult kept increasing.
When, on the 20th, the mob forced the gates of
the château, and made the king put on the red cap,
Morris wrote in his diary that the Constitution
had given its last groan. A few days afterwards
he told Lafayette that in six weeks everything
would be over, and tried to persuade him that his
only chance was to make up his mind instantly to
fight either for a good constitution or for the
wretched piece of paper which bore the name.
Just six weeks to a day from the date of this prediction came the 10th of August to verify it.

Throughout July the fevered pulses of the people beat with always greater heat. Looking at the
maddened mob, the American minister thanked
God from his heart that in his own country there
was no such populace, and prayed with unwonted
earnestness that our education and morality should
forever stave off such an evil. At court even the
most purblind dimly saw their doom. Calling
there one morning, he chronicles with a matter of
fact brevity, impressive from its very baldness,
that nothing of note had occurred except that they
had stayed up all night expecting to be murdered.
He wrote home that he could not tell " whether the
king would live through the storm; for it blew
hard."

His horror of the base mob, composed of people
whose kind was absolutely unknown in America,

increased continually, as he saw them going on
from crimes that were great to crimes that were
greater, incited by the demagogues who flattered
them and roused their passions and appetites, and
blindly raging because they were of necessity disappointed in the golden prospects held out to
them. He scorned the folly of the enthusiasts and
doctrinaires who had made a constitution all sail
and no ballast, that overset at the first gust; who
had freed from all restraint a mass of men as savage and licentious as they were wayward; who had
put the executive in the power of the legislature,
and this latter at the mercy of the leaders who
could most strongly influence and inflame the mob.
But his contempt for the victims almost exceeded
his anger at their assailants. The king, who could
suffer with firmness, and who could act either not
at all, or else with the worst possible effect, had
the head and heart that might have suited the
monkish idea of a female saint, but which were
hopelessly out of place in any rational being supposed to be fitted for doing good in the world.
Morris wrote home that he knew his friend Hamilton had no particular aversion to kings, and would
not believe them to be tigers, but that if Hamilton came to Europe to see for himself, he would
surely believe them to be monkeys; the Empress
of Russia was the only reigning sovereign whose
talents were not "considerably below par." At
the moment of the final shock, the court was involved in a set of paltry intrigues " unworthy of

anything above the rank of a footman or a cham-
bermaid.   Every one had his or her little project,
and every little project had some abettors. Strong,
manly counsels frightened the weak, alarmed the
envious, and wounded the enervated minds of the
lazy and luxurious."   The few such counsels that
appeared were always approved, rarely adopted,
and never followed out.

Then, in the sweltering heat of August, the end
came. A raving, furious horde stormed the château, and murdered, one by one, the brave moun-
taineers who gave their lives for a sovereign too
weak to be worthy of such gallant bloodshed. King
and queen fled to the National Assembly, and the
monarchy was over. Immediately after the awful
catastrophe Morris wrote to a friend : " The vo-
racity of the court, the haughtiness of the nobles,
the sensuality of the church, have met their punishment in the road of their transgressions. The
oppressor has been squeezed by the hands of the
oppressed ; but there remains yet to be acted an
awful scene in this great tragedy, played on the
theatre of the universe for the instruction of mankind."

Not the less did he dare everything, and jeop-
ardize his own life in trying to save some at least
among the innocent who had been overthrown in
the crash of the common ruin. When on the 10th
of August the whole city lay abject at the mercy
of the mob, hunted men and women, bereft of all
they had, and fleeing from a terrible death, with

no hiding-place, no friend who could shield them, turned in their terror-struck despair to the one man in whose fearlessness and generous gallantry they could trust. The shelter of Morris's house and flag was sought from early morning till past midnight by people who had nowhere else to go, and who felt that within his walls they were sure of at least a brief safety from the maddened savages in the streets. As far as possible they were sent off to places of greater security ; but some had to stay with him till the storm lulled for a moment. An American gentleman who was in Paris on that memorable day, after viewing the sack of the Tuileries, thought it right to go to the house of the American minister. He found him surrounded by a score of people, of both sexes, among them the old Count d'Estaing, and other men of note, who had fought side by side with us in our war for independence, and whom now our flag protected in their hour of direst need. Silence reigned, only broken occasionally by the weeping of the women and children. As his visitor was leaving, Morris took him to one side, and told him that he had no doubt there were persons on the watch who would find fault with his conduct as a minister in receiving and protecting these people ; that they had come of their own accord, uninvited. "Whether my house will be a protection to them or to me, God only knows ; but I will not turn them out of it, let what will happen to me ; you see, sir, they are all persons to whom our country is more or less indebted, and, had they no such claim upon me, it would be inhuman to force them into the hands of the assassins." No one of Morris's countrymen can read his words even now without feeling a throb of pride in the dead statesman who, a century ago, held up so high the honor of his nation's name in the times when the souls of all but the very bravest were tried and found wanting.

Soon after this he ceased writing in his diary, for fear it might fall into the hands of men who would use it to incriminate his friends; and for the same reason he had also to be rather wary in what he wrote home, as his letters frequently bore marks of being opened, thanks to what he laughingly called "patriotic curiosity." He was, however, perfectly fearless as regards any ill that might befall himself; his circumspection was only exercised on behalf of others, and his own opinions were given as frankly as ever.

He pictured the French as huddled together, in an unreasoning panic, like cattle before a thunderstorm. Their every act increased his distrust of their capacity for self-government. They were for the time agog with their republic, and ready to adopt any form of government with a huzza; but that they would adopt a good form, or, having adopted it, keep it, he did not believe; and he saw that the great mass of the population were already veering round, under the pressure of accumulating horrors, until they would soon be ready to welcome as a blessing even a despotism, if so they could gain security to life and property. They had made the common mistake of believing that to enjoy liberty they had only to abolish authority; and the equally common consequence was that they were now, through anarchy, on the high road to absolutism. Said Morris: " Since I have been in this country I have seen the worship of many idols, and but little of the true God. I have seen many of these idols broken, and some of them beaten to the dust. I have seen the late constitution in one short year admired as a stupendous monument of human wisdom, and ridiculed as an egregious production of folly and vice. I wish much, very much, the happiness of this inconstant people. I love them, I feel grateful for their efforts in our cause, and I consider the establishment of a good constitution here as the principal means, under Divine Providence, of extending the blessings of freedom to the many millions of my fellow men who groan in bondage on the continent of Europe. But I do not greatly indulge the flattering illusions of hope, because I do not yet perceive that reformation of morals without which liberty is but an empty sound." These words are such as could only come from a genuine friend of France, and champion of freedom; from a strong, earnest man, saddened by the follies of dreamers, and roused to stern anger by the licentious wickedness of scoundrels who used the name of liberty to cloak the worst abuses of its substance.

His stay in Paris was now melancholy indeed. The city was shrouded in a gloom only relieved by the frenzied tumults that grew steadily more numerous. The ferocious craving once roused could not be sated; the thirst grew ever stronger as the draughts were deeper. The danger to Morris's own person merely quickened his pulses, and roused his strong, brave nature; he liked excitement, and the strain that would have been too tense for weaker nerves keyed his own up to a fierce, half-exultant thrilling. But the woes that befell those who had befriended him caused him the keenest grief. It was almost unbearable to be seated quietly at dinner, and hear by accident "that a friend was on his way to the place of execution," and to have to sit still and wonder which of the guests dining with him would be the next to go to the scaffold. The vilest criminals swarmed in the streets, and amused themselves by tearing the earrings from women's ears, and snatching away their watches. When the priests shut up in the *carnes* and the prisoners in the *abbaie* were murdered, the slaughter went on all day, and eight hundred men were engaged in it.

He wrote home that, to give a true picture of France, he would have to paint it like an Indian warrior, black and red. The scenes that passed were literally beyond the imagination of the American mind. The most hideous and nameless atrocities were so common as to be only alluded to incidentally, and to be recited in the most matter-

of-fact way in connection with other events. For
instance, a man applied to the Convention for a
recompense for damage done to his quarry, a pit
dug deep through the surface of the earth into the
stone bed beneath: the damage consisted in such
a number of dead bodies having been thrown into
the pit as to choke it up so that he could no longer
get men to work it. Hundreds, who had been the
first in the land, were thus destroyed without form
or trial, and their bodies thrown like dead dogs
into the first hole that offered. Two hundred
priests were killed for no other crime than having
been conscientiously scrupulous about taking the
prescribed oath. The guillotine went smartly on,
watched with a devilish merriment by the fiends
who were themselves to perish by the instrument
their own hands had wrought. "Heaven only
knew who was next to drink of the dreadful cup;
as far as man could tell, there was to be no lack of
liquor for some time to come."

Among the new men who, one after another,
sprang into the light, to maintain their unsteady
footing as leaders for but a brief time before top-
pling into the dark abyss of death or oblivion that
waited for each and all, Dumouriez was for the
moment the most prominent. He stood towards
the Gironde much as Lafayette had stood towards
the Constitutionalists of 1789: he led the army, as
Lafayette once had led it; and as the constitutional
monarchists had fallen before his fellow republicans, so both he and they were to go down before

the even wilder extremists of the "Mountain."
For the factions in Paris, face to face with the
banded might of the European monarchies, and
grappling in a grim death - struggle with the
counter-revolutionists of the provinces, yet fought
one another with the same ferocity they showed
towards the common foe. Nevertheless, success
was theirs; for against opponents only less wicked
than themselves they moved with an infinitely
superior fire and enthusiasm. Reeking with the
blood of the guiltless, steeped in it to the lips,
branded with fresh memories of crimes and in-
famies without number, and yet feeling in their
very marrow that they were avenging centuries of
grinding and intolerable thralldom, and that the
cause for which they fought was just and right-
eous; with shameless cruelty and corruption eat-
ing into their hearts' core, yet with their foreheads
kindled by the light of a glorious morning, — they
moved with a ruthless energy that paralyzed their
opponents, the worn-out, tottering, crazy despot-
isms, rotten with vice, despicable in their ludicrous
pride of caste, moribund in their military pedantry
and foredoomed to perish in the conflict they had
courted. The days of Danton and Robespierre
are not days to which a French patriot cares to
look back; but at any rate he can regard them
without the shame he must feel when he thinks of
the times of Louiz Quinze. Danton and his like,
at least, were men, and stood far, far above the
palsied coward — a eunuch in his lack of all virile

virtues — who misruled France for half a century; who, with his followers, indulged in every crime and selfish vice known, save only such as needed a particle of strength, or the least courage, in the committing.

Morris first met Dumouriez when the latter was minister of foreign affairs, shortly before the poor king was driven from the Tuileries. He dined with him, and afterwards noted down that the society was noisy and in bad style ; for the grace and charm of French social life were gone, and the raw republicans were ill at ease in the drawing-room. At this time Morris commented often on the change in the look of Paris : all his gay friends gone ; the city sombre and uneasy. When he walked through the streets, in the stifling air of a summer hot beyond precedent, as if the elements sympathized with the passions of men, he met, instead of the brilliant company of former days, only the few peaceable citizens left, hurrying on their ways with frightened watchfulness ; or else groups of lolling ruffians, with sinister eyes and brutalized faces ; or he saw in the Champs de Mars squalid ragamuffins signing the petition for the *déchéance*.

Morris wrote Washington that Dumouriez was a bold, determined man, bitterly hostile to the Jacobins and all the extreme revolutionary clubs, and, once he was in power, willing to risk his own life in the effort to put them down. However, the hour of the Jacobins had not yet struck, and the

revolution had now been permitted to gather such
headway that it could be stopped only by a master
genius; and Dumouriez was none such.

Still he was an able man, and, as Morris wrote
home, in his military operations he combined the
bravery of a skilled soldier and the arts of an as-
tute politician.   To be sure, his victories were not
in themselves very noteworthy; the artillery skir-
mish at Valmy was decided by the reluctance of
the Germans to come on, not by the ability of the
French to withstand them; and at Jemappes the
imperialists were hopelessly outnumbered. Still
the results were most important, and Dumouriez
overran Flanders in the face of hostile Europe.
He at once proceeded to revolutionize the government of his conquest in the most approved French
fashion, which was that all the neighbors of France
should receive liberty whether or no, and should
moreover pay the expense of having it thrust upon
them ; accordingly he issued a proclamation to his
new fellow citizens, "which might be summed up
in a few words as being an order to them to be free
forthwith, according to his ideas of freedom, on
pain of military execution."

He had things all his own way for the moment,
but after a while he was defeated by the Germans ;
then, while the Gironde tottered to its fall, he fled
to the very foes he had been fighting, as the only
way of escaping death from the men whose favorite
he had been. Morris laughed bitterly at the fickle
people. One anecdote he gives is worth preserv-

ing: "It is a year ago that a person who mixed in tumults to see what was doing, told me of a *sans culottes* who, bellowing against poor Lafayette, when Petion appeared, changed at once his note to ' *Vive Petion !* ' and then, turning round to one of his companions, 'Vois tu! C'est notre ami, n'est ce pas? Eh bien, il passera comme les autres.' And, lo! the prophecy is fulfilled; and I this instant learn that Petion, confined to his room as a traitor or conspirator, has fled, on the 24th of June, 1793, from those whom he sent, on the 20th of June, 1792, to assault the king in the Tuileries. In short you will find, in the list of those who were ordered by their brethren to be arrested, the names of those who have proclaimed themselves to be the prime movers of the revolution of the 10th of August, and the fathers of the republic."

About the time the *sans culottes* had thus bellowed against Lafayette, the latter met Morris, for the first time since he was presented at court as minister, and at once spoke to him in his tone of ancient familiarity. The Frenchman had been brought at last to realize the truth of his American friend's theories and predictions. It was much too late to save himself, however. After the 10th of August he was proclaimed by the Assembly, found his troops falling away from him, and fled over the frontier; only to be thrown into prison by the allied monarchs, who acted with their usual folly and baseness. Morris, contemptuously impatient of the part he had played, wrote of him:

"Thus his circle is completed. He has spent his
fortune on a revolution, and is now crushed by
the wheel which he put in motion. He lasted longer
than I expected." But this momentary indignation soon gave way to a generous sympathy for the
man who had served America so well, and who,
if without the great abilities necessary to grapple
with the tumult of French affairs, had yet always
acted with such unselfish purity of motive. Lafayette, as soon as he was imprisoned, wrote to the
American minister in Holland, alleging that he
had surrendered his position as a French subject
and was now an American citizen, and requesting
the American representatives in Europe to procure
his release. His claim was of course untenable;
and, though the American government did all it
could on his behalf through its foreign ministers,
and though Washington himself wrote a strong
letter of appeal to the Austrian emperor, he remained in prison until the peace, several years
later.

All Lafayette's fortune was gone, and while in
prison he was reduced to want. As soon as Morris heard this, he had the sum of ten thousand
florins forwarded to the prisoner by the United
States bankers at Amsterdam; pledging his own
security for the amount, which was, however, finally
allowed by the government under the name of
compensation for Lafayette's military services in
America. Morris was even more active in befriend-
ing Madame de Lafayette and her children. To

the former he lent from his own private funds a hundred thousand livres, enabling her to pay her debts to the many poor people who had rendered services to her family. To the proud, sensitive lady the relief was great, much though it hurt her to be under any obligation : she wrote to her friend that he had broken the chains that loaded her down, and had done it in a way that made her feel the consolation, rather than the weight, of the obligation. But he was to do still more for her ; for, when she was cast into prison by the savage Parisian mob, his active influence on her behalf saved her from death. In a letter to him, written some time later, she says, after speaking of the money she had borrowed : " This is a slight obligation, it is true, compared with that of my life, but allow me to remember both while life lasts, with a sentiment of gratitude which it is precious to feel."

There were others whose fortunes turned with the wheel of fate, for whom Morris felt no such sympathy as for the Lafayettes. Among the number was the Duke of Orleans, now transformed into *citoyen Egalité*. Morris credited this graceless debauchee with criminal ambitions which he probably did not possess, saying that he doubted the public virtue of a profligate, and could not help distrusting such a man's pretensions ; nor is it likely that he regretted much the fate of the man who died under the same guillotine which, with his assent, had fallen on the neck of the king, his cousin.

It needed no small amount of hardihood for a man of Morris's prominence and avowed sentiments to stay in Paris when Death was mowing round him with a swath at once so broad and so irregular. The power was passing rapidly from hand to hand, through a succession of men fairly crazy in their indifference to bloodshed. Not a single other minister of a neutral nation dared stay. In fact, the foreign representatives were preparing to go away even before the final stroke was given to the monarchy, and soon after the 10th of August the entire *corps diplomatique* left Paris as rapidly as the various members could get their passports. These the new republican government was at first very reluctant to grant; indeed, when the Venetian ambassador started off he was very ignominiously treated and brought back. Morris went to the British ambassador's to take leave, having received much kindness from him, and having been very intimate in his house. He found Lord Gower in a tearing passion because he could not get passports; he had burned his papers, and strongly advised his guest to do likewise. On this advice the latter refused to act, nor would he take the broad hints given him to the effect that honor required him to quit the country. Morris could not help showing his amusement at the fear and anger exhibited at the ambassador's, "which exhibition of spirits his lordship could hardly bear." Talleyrand, who was getting his own passport, also did all in his power to persuade the American minister

to leave, but without avail. Morris was not a man
to be easily shaken in any determination he had
taken after careful thought. He wrote back to
Jefferson that his opinion was directly opposed to
the views of such people as had tried to persuade
him that his own honor, and that of America,
required him to leave France; and that he was
inclined to attribute such counsel mainly to fear.
It was true that the position was not without danger; but he presumed that, when the President
named him to the embassy, it was not for his own
personal pleasure or safety, but for the interests of
the country; and these he could certainly serve
best by staying.

He was able to hold his own only by a mixture
of tact and firmness. Any signs of flinching would
have ruined him outright. He would submit to
no insolence. The minister of foreign affairs was,
with his colleagues, engaged in certain schemes in
reference to the American debt, which were designed to further their own private interests; he
tried to bully Morris into acquiescence, and, on
the latter's point-blank refusal, sent him a most
insulting letter. Morris promptly retorted by demanding his passports. France, however, was very
desirous not to break with the United States, the
only friend she had left in the world; and the
offending minister sent a sullen letter of apology,
asking him to reconsider his intention to leave,
and offering entire satisfaction for every point of
which he complained. Accordingly Morris stayed.

He was, however, continually exposed to insults and worries, which were always apologized for by the government for the time being, on the ground, no doubt true, that in such a period of convulsions it was impossible to control their subordinate agents. Indeed, the changes from one form of anarchy to another went on so rapidly that the laws of nations had small chance of observance.

One evening a number of people, headed by a commissary of the section, entered his house, and demanded to search it for arms said to be hidden therein. Morris took a high tone, and was very peremptory with them; told them that they should not examine his house, that it held no arms, and moreover that, if he had possessed any, they should not touch one of them; he also demanded the name of "the blockhead or rascal" who had informed against him, announcing his intention to bring him to punishment. Finally he got them out of the house, and the next morning the commissary called with many apologies, which were accepted.

Another time he was arrested in the street for not having a *carté de citoyen*, but he was released as soon as it was found out who he was. Again he was arrested while traveling in the country, on the pretense that his passport was out of date; an insult for which the government at once made what amends they could. His house was also visited another time by armed men, whom, as before, he persuaded to go away. Once or twice, in the popular tumults, even his life was in danger; on one

occasion it is said that it was only saved by the
fact of his having a wooden leg, which made him
known to the mob as "a cripple of the American
war for freedom." Rumors even got abroad in
England and America that he had been assas-
sinated.

Morris's duties were manifold, and as harassing
to himself as they were beneficial to his country.
Sometimes he would interfere on behalf of America
as a whole, and endeavor to get obnoxious decrees
of the Assembly repealed; and again he would try
to save some private citizen of the United States
who had got himself into difficulties. Reports of
the French minister of foreign affairs, as well as
reports of the *comité de salut public*, alike bear
testimony to the success of his endeavors, whenever success was possible, and unconsciously show
the value of the services he rendered to his country. Of course it was often impossible to obtain
complete redress, because, as Morris wrote home,
the government, while all-powerful in certain cases,
was in others not merely feeble, but enslaved, and
was often obliged to commit acts the consequences
of which the nominal leaders both saw and la-
mented. Morris also, while doing all he could for
his fellow citizens, was often obliged to choose between their interests and those of the nation at
large ; and he, of course, decided in favor of the
latter, though well aware of the clamor that was
certain to be raised against him in consequence by
those who, as he caustically remarked, found it the

easiest thing in the world to get anything they wanted from the French government *until they had tried.*

One of his most important transactions was in reference to paying off the debt due by America for amounts loaned her during the war for independence. The interest and a part of the principal had already been paid. At the time Morris was made minister, the United States had a large sum of money, destined for the payment of the public debt, lying idle in the hands of the bankers at Amsterdam; and this sum both Morris and the American minister to Holland, Mr. Short, thought could be well applied to the payment of part of our remaining obligation to France. The French government was consulted, and agreed to receive the sum; but hardly was the agreement entered into before the monarchy was overturned. The question at once arose as to whether the money could be rightfully paid over to the men who had put themselves at the head of affairs, and who, a month hence, might themselves be ousted by others who would not acknowledge the validity of a payment made to them. Short thought the payment should be stopped, and, as it afterwards turned out, the home authorities agreed with him. But Morris thought otherwise, and paid over the amount. Events fully justified his course, for France never made any difficulty in the matter, and even had she done so, as Morris remarked, America had the staff in her own hands, and could walk which way she pleased, for she owed more money, and in the final adjustment could insist on the amount paid being allowed on account of the debt.

The French executive council owed Morris gratitude for his course in this matter; but they became intensely irritated with him shortly afterwards because he refused to fall in with certain proposals they made to him as to the manner of applying part of the debt to the purchase of provisions and munitions for San Domingo. Morris had good reason to believe that there was a private speculation at the bottom of this proposal, and declined to accede to it. The urgency with which it was made, and the wrath which his course excited, confirmed his suspicions, and he persisted in his refusal although it almost brought about a break with the men then carrying on the government. Afterwards, when these men fell with the Gironde, he wrote home: " I mentioned to you the plan of a speculation on drafts to have been made on the United States, could my concurrence have been procured. Events have shown that this speculation would have been a good one to the parties, who would have gained (and the French nation of course have lost) about fifty thousand pounds sterling in eighty thousand. I was informed at that time that the disappointed parties would attempt to have me recalled, and some more tractable character sent, who would have the good sense to look after his own interest. Well, sir, nine months have elapsed, and now, if I were capable of such things, I think it would be no difficult matter to have some of them hanged; indeed it is highly probable that they will experience a fate of that sort."

Much of his time was also taken up in remonstrating against the attacks of French privateers on American shipping. These, however, went steadily on until, half a dozen years afterwards, we took the matter into our own hands, and in the West Indies inflicted a smart drubbing, not only on the privateers of France, but on her regular men-of-war as well. He also did what he could for the French officers who had served in America during the war for independence, most of whom were forced to flee from France after the outbreak of the revolution.

His letters home, even after his regular duties had begun to be engrossing, contained a running commentary on the events that were passing around him. His forecasts of events within France were remarkably shrewd, and he displayed a wonderful insight into the motives and characters of the various leaders; but at first he was all at sea in his estimate of the military situation, being much more at home among statesmen than soldiers. He had expected the allied sovereigns to make short work of the raw Republican armies, and was amazed at the success of the latter. But he very soon realized how the situation stood; that whereas the Austrian and Prussian troops simply came on in well-drilled, reluctant obedience to their commanding officers, the soldiers of France, on the contrary, were actuated by a fiery spirit the like of which had hardly been seen since the crusades. The bitterness of the contest was appalling, and so was the way in which the ranks of the contestants were thinned out. The extreme republicans believed in their creed with a furious faith; and they were joined by their fellow citizens with an almost equal zeal, when once it had become evident that the invaders were hostile not only to the Republic but to France itself, and very possibly meditated its dismemberment.

When the royal and imperial forces invaded France in 1792, they threatened such ferocious vengeance as to excite the most desperate resistance, and yet they backed up their high sounding words by deeds so faulty, weak, and slow as to make themselves objects of contempt rather than dread. The Duke of Brunswick in particular, as a prelude to some very harmless military manœuvres, issued a singularly lurid and foolish manifesto, announcing that he would deliver up Paris to utter destruction and would give over all the soldiers he captured to military execution. Morris said that his address was in substance, " Be all against me, for I am opposed to you all, and make a good resistance, for there is no longer any hope; " and added that it would have been wiser to have begun with some great success and then to have carried the danger near those whom it was desired to intimidate. As it was, the duke's campaign failed ignominiously, and all the invaders were

driven back, for France rose as one man, her warriors overflowed on every side, and bore down all
her foes by sheer weight of numbers and impetu-
ous enthusiasm. Her government was a despotism
as well as an anarchy; it was as totally free from
the drawbacks as from the advantages of the democratic system that it professed to embody. Nothing could exceed the merciless energy of the
measures adopted. Half way wickedness might
have failed; but a wholesale murder of the disaf-
fected, together with a confiscation of all the goods
of the rich, and a vigorous conscription of the poor
for soldiers, secured success, at least for the time
being. The French made it a war of men; so that
the price of labor rose enormously at once, and the
condition of the working classes forthwith changed
greatly for the better — one good result of the
revolution, at any rate.

Morris wrote home very soon after the 10th of
August that the then triumphant revolutionists,
the Girondists or party of Brissot, who had sup-
planted the moderate party of Lafayette exactly
as the latter had succeeded the aristocracy, would
soon in their turn be overthrown by men even
more extreme and even more bloodthirsty; and
that thus it would go on, wave after wave, until
at last the wizard arose who could still them. By
the end of the year the storm had brewed long
enough to be near the bursting point. One of the
promoters of the last outbreak, now himself marked
as a victim, told Morris that he personally would

die hard, but that most of his colleagues, though like him doomed to destruction, and though so fierce in dealing with the moderate men, now showed neither the nerve nor hardihood that alone could stave off the catastrophe.

Meanwhile the king, as Morris wrote home, showed in his death a better spirit than his life had promised; for he died in a manner becoming his dignity, with calm courage, praying that his foes might be forgiven and his deluded people be benefited by his death, — his words from the scaffold being drowned by the drums of Santerre. As a whole, the Gironde had opposed putting the king to death, and thus capping the structure whose foundations they had laid; they held back all too late. The fabric of their system was erected on a quagmire, and it now settled down and crushed the men who had built it. "All people of morality and intelligence had long agreed that as yet republican virtues were not of Gallic growth;" and so the power slipped naturally into the grasp of the lowest and most violent, of those who were loudest to claim the possession of republican principles, while in practice showing that they had not even the dimmest idea of what such principles meant.

The leaders were quite at the mercy of the gusts of fierce passion that swayed the breasts of their brutal followers. Morris wrote home that the nominal rulers, or rather the few by whom these rulers were directed, had finally gained very just ideas of the value of popular opinion; but that they were not in a condition to act according to their knowledge; and that if they were able to reach harbor there would be quite as much of good luck as of good management about it, and, at any rate, a part of the crew would have to be thrown overboard.

Then the Mountain rose under Danton and Marat, and the party of the Gironde was entirely put down. The leaders were cast into prison, with the certainty before their eyes that the first great misfortune to France would call them from their dungeons to act as expiatory victims. The Jacobins ruled supreme, and under them the government became a despotism in principle as well as in practice. Part of the Convention arrested the rest; and the revolutionary tribunals ruled red-handed, with a whimsical and ferocious tyranny. Said Morris: " It is an emphatical phrase among the patriots that *terror is the order of the day ;* some years have elapsed since Montesquieu wrote that the principle of arbitrary governments is *fear.*" The prisons were choked with *suspects*, and blood flowed more freely than ever. Terror had reached its highest point. Danton was soon to fall before Robespierre. Among a host of other victims the queen died, with a brave dignity that made people half forget her manifold faults; and Philippe Egalité, the dissolute and unprincipled scoundrel, after a life than which none could be meaner and more unworthy, now at the end went to his death with calm and unflinching courage.

One man had a very narrow escape. This was Thomas Paine, the Englishman, who had at one period rendered such a striking service to the cause of American independence, while the rest of his life had been as ignoble as it was varied. He had been elected to the Convention, and, having sided with the Gironde, was thrown into prison by the Jacobins. He at once asked Morris to demand him as an American citizen; a title to which he of course had no claim. Morris refused to interfere too actively, judging rightly that Paine would be saved by his own insignificance and would serve his own interests best by keeping still. So the filthy little atheist had to stay in prison, " where he amused himself with publishing a pamphlet against Jesus Christ." There are infidels and infidels; Paine belonged to the variety — whereof America possesses at present one or two shining examples — that apparently esteems a bladder of dirty water as the proper weapon with which to assail Christianity. It is not a type that appeals to the sympathy of an onlooker, be said onlooker religious or otherwise.

Morris never paid so much heed to the military events as to the progress of opinion in France, believing " that such a great country must depend more upon interior sentiment than exterior operations." He took a half melancholy, half sardonic interest in the overthrow of the Catholic religion by the revolutionists; who had assailed it with the true French weapon, ridicule, but ridicule of a very grim and unpleasant kind. The people who five years before had fallen down in the dirt as the consecrated matter passed by, now danced the carmagnole in holy vestments, and took part in some other mummeries a great deal more blasphemous. At the famous Feast of Reason, which Morris described as a kind of opera performed in Nôtre Dame, the president of the Convention, and other public characters, adored on bended knees a girl who stood in the place *ci-devant* most holy to personate Reason herself. This girl, Saunier by name, followed the trades of an opera dancer and harlot; she was " very beautiful and next door to an idiot as to her intellectual gifts." Among her feats was having appeared in a ballet in a dress especially designed, by the painter David, at her bidding, to be more indecent than nakedness. Altogether she was admirably fitted, both morally and mentally, to personify the kind of reason shown and admired by the French revolutionists.

Writing to a friend who was especially hostile to Romanism, Morris once remarked, with the humor that tinged even his most serious thoughts, " Every day of my life gives me reason to question my own infallibility; and of course leads me farther from confiding in that of the pope. But I have lived to see a new religion arise. It consists in a denial of all religion, and its votaries have the superstition of not being superstitious. They have this with as much zeal as any other sect, and are as ready to lay waste the world in order to make proselytes." An-

other time, speaking of his country place at Sain-
port, to which he had retired from Paris, he wrote:
"We are so scorched by a long drought that in
spite of all philosophic notions we are beginning
our procession to obtain the favor of the *bon dieu*.
Were it proper for *un homme public et protestant*
to interfere, I should be tempted to tell them that
mercy is before sacrifice." Those individuals of
arrested mental development who now make pil-
grimages to our Lady of Lourdes had plenty of
prototypes, even in the atheistical France of the
revolution.

In his letters home Morris occasionally made
clear-headed comments on American affairs. He
considered that "we should be unwise in the extreme to involve ourselves in the contests of European nations, where our weight could be but small,
though the loss to ourselves would be certain. We
ought to be extremely watchful of foreign affairs,
but there is a broad line between vigilance and
activity." Both France and England had violated
their treaties with us; but the latter "had behaved
worst, and with deliberate intention." He especially laid stress upon the need of our having a
navy; "with twenty ships of the line at sea no
nation on earth will dare to insult us;" even aside
from individual losses, five years of war would involve more national expense than the support of
a navy for twenty years, and until we rendered
ourselves respectable, we should continue to be insulted. He never showed greater wisdom than in

his views about our navy; and his party, the federalists, started to give us one; but it had hardly
been begun before the Jeffersonians came into
power, and, with singular foolishness, stopped the
work.

Washington heartily sympathized with Morris's
views as to the French Revolution; he wrote him
that events had more than made good his gloomiest
predictions.   Jefferson, however, was utterly opposed to his theories, and was much annoyed at
the forcible way in which he painted things as they
were; characteristically enough, he only showed his
annoyance by indirect methods, — leaving Morris's
letters unanswered, keeping him in the dark as to
events at home, etc.   Morris understood all this
perfectly, and was extremely relieved when Randolph became secretary of state in Jefferson's
stead.   Almost immediately afterwards, however,
he was himself recalled.   The United States, having requested the French government to withdraw
Genet, a harlequin rather than a diplomat, it was
done at once, and in return a request was forwarded that the United States would reciprocate
by relieving Morris, which of course had to be
done also.   The revolutionary authorities both
feared and disliked Morris; he could neither be
flattered nor bullied, and he was known to disapprove of their excesses.   They also took umbrage
at his haughtiness; an unfortunate expression he
used in one of his official letters to them, "ma
cour," gave great offense, as being unrepublican —

precisely as they had previously objected to Washington's using the phrase " your people " in writing to the king.

Washington wrote him a letter warmly approving of his past conduct. Nevertheless Morris was not over-pleased at being recalled. He thought that, as things then were in France, any minister who gave satisfaction to its government would prove forgetful of the interests of America. He was probably right; at any rate, what he feared was just what happened under his successor, Monroe — a very amiable gentleman, but distinctly one who comes in the category of those whose greatness is thrust upon them. However, under the circumstances, it was probably impossible for our government to avoid recalling Morris.

He could say truthfully: " I have the consolation to have made no sacrifice either of personal or national dignity, and I believe I should have obtained everything if the American government had refused to recall me." His services had been invaluable to us; he had kept our national reputation at a high point, by the scrupulous heed with which he saw that all our obligations were fulfilled, as well as by the firm courage with which he insisted on our rights being granted us. He believed " that all our treaties, however onerous, must be strictly fulfilled according to their true intent and meaning. The honest nation is that which, like the honest man, ' hath to its plighted faith and vow forever firmly stood, and though it promise to

its loss, yet makes that promise good;'" and in
return he demanded that others should mete to us
the same justice we meted to them.   He met each
difficulty the instant it arose, ever on the alert to
protect his country and his countrymen; and what
an ordinary diplomat could barely have done in
time of peace, he succeeded in doing amid the
wild, shifting tumult of the revolution, when almost every step he made was at his own personal
hazard. He took precisely the right stand; had he
taken too hostile a position, he would have been
driven from the country, whereas had he been a
sympathizer, he would have more or less compromised America, as his successor afterwards did.
We have never had a foreign minister who deserved more honor than Morris.

One of the noteworthy features in his letters
home was the accuracy with which he foretold the
course of events in the political world.   Luzerne
once said to him, " Vous dites toujours les chôses
extraordinaires qui se realisent; " and many other
men, after some given event had taken place, were
obliged to confess their wonder at the way in
which Morris's predictions concerning it had been
verified.   A notable instance was his writing to
Washington: " Whatever may be the lot of France
in remote futurity . . . it seems evident that she
must soon be governed by a single despot. Whether
she will pass to that point through the medium of
a triumvirate or other small body of men, seems
as yet undetermined.   I think it most probable

that she will." This was certainly a remarkably
accurate forecast as to the precise stages by which
the already existing despotism was to be concen-
trated in a single individual. He always insisted
that, though it was difficult to foretell how a single
man would act, yet it was easy with regard to a
mass of men, for their peculiarities neutralized
each other, and it was necessary only to pay heed
to the instincts of the average animal. He also
gave wonderfully clear-cut sketches of the more
prominent actors in affairs; although one of his
maxims was that " in examining historical facts
we are too apt to ascribe to individuals the events
which are produced by general causes." Danton,
for instance, he described as always believing, and,
what was worse for himself, maintaining, that a
popular system of government was absurd in
France; that the people were too ignorant, too
inconstant, too corrupt, and felt too much the need
of a master; in short, that they had reached the
point where Cato was a madman, and Cæsar a
necessary evil. He acted on these principles; but
he was too voluptuous for his ambition, too indo-
lent to acquire supreme power, and he cared for
great wealth rather than great fame; so he " fell
at the feet of Robespierre." Similarly, said Morris, there passed away all the men of the 10th of
August, all the men of the 2d of September; the
same mob that hounded them on with wild applause when they grasped the blood-stained reins
of power, a few months later hooted at them

with ferocious derision as they went their way to
the guillotine.   Paris ruled France, and the *sans
culottes* ruled Paris; factions continually arose,
waging inexplicable war, each in turn acquiring
a momentary influence which was founded on fear
alone, and all alike unable to build up any stable
or lasting government.

Each new stroke of the guillotine weakened the
force of liberal sentiment, and diminished the
chances of a free system.   Morris wondered only
that, in a country ripe for a tyrant's rule, four
years of convulsions among twenty-four millions of
people had brought forth neither a soldier nor yet
a statesman, whose head was fitted to wear the cap
that fortune had woven.   Despising the mob as
utterly as did Oliver Cromwell himself, and realiz-
ing the supine indifference with which the French
people were willing to accept a master, he yet did
full justice to the pride with which they resented
outside attack, and the enthusiasm with which they
faced their foes.   He saw the immense resources
possessed by a nation to whom war abroad was a
necessity for the preservation of peace at home,
and with whom bankruptcy was but a starting-
point for fresh efforts.   The whole energy and
power lay in the hands of the revolutionists; the
men of the old regime had fled, leaving only that
"waxen substance," the propertied class, "who in
foreign wars count so much, and in civil wars so
little."   He had no patience with those despicable
beings, the traders and merchants who have for-

gotten how to fight, the rich who are too timid to
guard their wealth, the men of property, large or
small, who need peace, and yet have not the sense
and courage to be always prepared to conquer it.

In his whole attitude towards the revolution,
Morris represents better than any other man the
clear-headed, practical statesman, who is genuinely
devoted to the cause of constitutional freedom. He
was utterly opposed to the old system of privilege
on the one hand, and to the wild excesses of the
fanatics on the other. The few liberals of the
revolution were the only men in it who deserve
our true respect. The republicans who champion
the deeds of the Jacobins are traitors to their own
principles; for the spirit of Jacobinism, instead of
being identical with, is diametrically opposed to
the spirit of true liberty. Jacobinism, socialism,
communism, nihilism, and anarchism, — these are
the real foes of a democratic republic, for each
one, if it obtains control, obtains it only as the sure
forerunner of a despotic tyranny and of some form
of the one-man power.

Morris, an American, took a clearer and truer
view of the French Revolution than did any of the
contemporary European observers. Yet while with
them it was the all-absorbing event of the age, with
him, as is evident by his writings, it was merely
an important episode; for to him it was dwarfed
by the American Revolution of a decade or two
back. To the Europeans of the present day, as
yet hardly awake to the fact that already the

change has begun that will make Europe but a
fragment, instead of the whole, of the civilized
world, the French Revolution is the great historical
event of our times. But in reality it affected only
the people of western and central Europe; not the
Russians, not the English-speaking nations, not the
Spaniards who dwelt across the Atlantic. America
and Australia had their destinies moulded by the
crisis of 1776, not by the crisis of 1789. What
the French Revolution was to the states within
Europe, that the American Revolution was to the
continents without.

CHAPTER XI

MONROE, as Morris's successor, entered upon his new duties with an immense flourish, and rapidly gave a succession of startling proofs that he was a minister altogether too much to the taste of the frenzied Jacobinical republicans to whom he was accredited. Indeed, his capers were almost as extraordinary as their own, and seem rather like the antics of some of the early French commanders in Canada, in their efforts to ingratiate themselves with their Indian allies, than like the performance we should expect from a sober Virginian gentleman on a mission to a civilized nation. He stayed long enough to get our affairs into a snarl, and was then recalled by Washington, receiving from the latter more than one scathing rebuke.

However, the fault was really less with him than with his party and with those who sent him. Monroe was an honorable man with a very un-original mind, and he simply reflected the wild, foolish views held by all his fellows of the Jeffersonian democratic-republican school concerning France — for our politics were still French and English, but not yet American. His appointment was an

excellent example of the folly of trying to carry on
a government on a "non-partisan" basis. Washington was only gradually weaned from this theory
by bitter experience; both Jefferson and Monroe
helped to teach him the lesson. It goes without
saying that in a well-ordered government the great
bulk of the employees in the civil service, the men
whose functions are merely to execute faithfully
routine departmental work, should hold office during good behavior, and should be appointed without
reference to their politics; but if the higher public
servants, such as the heads of departments and the
foreign ministers, are not in complete accord with
their chief, the only result can be to introduce
halting indecision and vacillation into the counsels
of the nation, without gaining a single compen-
sating advantage, and without abating by one iota
the virulence of party passion. To appoint Monroe, an extreme Democrat, to France, while at the
same time appointing Jay, a strong Federalist, to
England, was not only an absurdity which did
nothing towards reconciling the Federalists and
Democrats, but, bearing in mind how these parties
stood respectively towards England and France, it
was also an actual wrong, for it made our foreign
policy seem double-faced and deceitful. While
one minister was formally embracing such of the
Parisian statesmen as had hitherto escaped the
guillotine, and was going through various other
theatrical performances that do not appeal to any
but a Gallic mind, his fellow was engaged in nego-

tiating a treaty in England that was so obnoxious
to France as almost to bring us to a rupture with
her. The Jay treaty was not altogether a good
one, and a better might perhaps have been secured;
still, it was better than nothing, and Washington
was right in urging its adoption, even while admit-
ting that it was not entirely satisfactory. But
certainly, if we intended to enter into such engagements with Great Britain, it was rank injustice to
both Monroe and France to send such a man as
the former to such a country as the latter.

Meanwhile Morris, instead of returning to
America, was forced by his business affairs to
prolong his stay abroad for several years. During
this time he journeyed at intervals through England, the Netherlands, Germany, Prussia, and
Austria. His European reputation was well established, and he was everywhere received gladly
into the most distinguished society of the time.
What made him especially welcome was his having now definitely taken sides with the anti-revolu-
tionists in the great conflict of arms and opinions
then raging through Europe; and his brilliancy,
the boldness with which he had behaved as minister during the terror, and the reputation given
him by the French *emigrés*, all joined to cause
him to be hailed with pleasure by the aristocratic
party. It is really curious to see the consideration
with which he was everywhere treated, although
again a mere private individual, and the terms of
intimacy on which he was admitted into the most

exclusive social and diplomatic circles at the various courts. He thus became an intimate friend of many of the foremost people of the period. His political observation, however, became less trustworthy than heretofore; for he was undoubtedly soured by his removal, and the excesses of the revolutionists had excited such horror in his mind as to make him no longer an impartial judge. His forecasts and judgments on the military situation in particular, although occasionally right, were usually very wild. He fully appreciated Napoleon's utter unscrupulousness and marvelous mendacity; but to the end of his life he remained unwilling to do justice to the emperor's still more remarkable warlike genius, going so far, after the final Russian campaign, as to speak of old Kutusoff as his equal. Indeed, in spite of one or two exceptions, — notably his predicting almost the exact date of the retreat from Moscow, — his criticisms on Napoleon's military operations do not usually stand much above the rather ludicrous level recently reached by Count Tolstoï.

Morris was relieved by Monroe in August, 1794, and left Paris for Switzerland in October. He stopped at Coppet and spent a day with Madame de Staël, where there was a little French society that lived at her expense and was as gay as circumstances would permit. He had never been particularly impressed with the much vaunted society of the salon, and this small survival thereof certainly had no overpowering attraction for him, if

we may judge by the entry in his diary: "The
road to her house is up-hill and execrable, and I
think I shall not again go thither." Mankind was
still blind to the grand beauty of the Alps, — it
must be remembered that the admiration of mountain scenery is, to the shame of our forefathers be
it said, almost a growth of the present century, —
and Morris took more interest in the Swiss population than in their surroundings. He wrote that
in Switzerland the spirit of commerce had brought
about a baseness of morals which nothing could
cure but the same spirit carried still farther:
"It teaches eventually fair dealing as the most
profitable dealing. The first lesson of trade is,
My son, get money. The second is, My son, get
money, honestly if you can, but get money. The
third is, My son, get money; but honestly, if you
would get much money."

He went to Great Britain in the following summer, and spent a year there. At one time he
visited the North, staying with the Dukes of Ar-
gyle, Atholl, and Montrose, and was very much
pleased with Scotland, where everything he saw
convinced him that the country was certain of a
rapid and vigorous growth. On his return he
stopped with the Bishop of Landaff, at Colgate
Park. The bishop announced that he was a
stanch opposition man, and a firm Whig; to which
statement Morris adds in his diary: "Let this be
as it will, he is certainly a good landlord and a
man of genius."

But Morris was now a favored guest in minis-
terial, even more than in opposition circles; he
was considered to belong to what the czar afterwards christened the "parti sain ' de l'Europe."
He saw a good deal of both Pitt and Grenville,
and was consulted by them not only about American, but also about European affairs; and a number of favors which he asked for some of his
friends among the *emigrés* were granted. All his
visits were not on business, however; as, for instance, on July 14: "Dine at Mr. Pitt's. We
sit down at six. Lords Grenville, Chatham, and
another come later. The rule is established for
six precisely, which is right, I think. The wines
are good and the conversation flippant." Morris
helped Grenville in a number of ways, at the Prussian court for instance; and was even induced by
him to write a letter to Washington, attempting
to put the English attitude toward us in a good
light. Washington, however, was no more to be
carried off his feet in favor of the English than
against them; and the facts he brought out in his
reply showed that Morris had rather lost his poise,
and had been hurried into an action that was ill
advised. He was quite often at court; and relates
a conversation with the king, wherein that monarch's language seems to have been much such as
tradition assigns him — short, abrupt sentences,
repetitions, and the frequent use of " what."

He also saw a good deal of the royalist refugees.
Some of them he liked and was intimate with; but

the majority disgusted him and made him utterly
impatient with their rancorous folly. He commented on the strange levity and wild negotiations
of the Count d'Artois, and prophesied that his
character was such as to make his projected attempt on La Vendée hopeless from the start.
Another day he was at the Marquis de Spinola's:
" The conversation here, where our company consists of aristocrats of the first feather, turns on
French affairs. They, at first, agree that union
among the French is necessary. But when they
come to particulars, they fly off and are mad.
Madame Spinola would send the Duke of Orleans
to Siberia. An abbé, a young man, talks much
and loud, to show his *esprit;* and to hear them
one would suppose they were quite at their ease in
a *petit souper de Paris.*" Of that ponderous
exile, the chief of the House of Bourbon, and
afterwards Louis XVIII. he said that, in his
opinion, he had nothing to do but to try to get
shot, thereby redeeming by valor the foregone
follies of his conduct.

In June, 1796, Morris returned to the Continent,
and started on another tour, in his own carriage;
having spent some time himself in breaking in his
young and restive horses to their task. He visited
all the different capitals, at one time or another;
among them, Berlin, where, as usual, he was very
well received. For all his horror of Jacobinism,
Morris was a thorough American, perfectly independent, without a particle of the snob in his dis-

position, and valuing his acquaintances for what they were, not for their titles. In his diary he puts down the Queen of England as "a well-bred, sensible woman," and the Empress of Austria as "a good sort of little woman," and contemptuously dismisses the Prussian king with a word, precisely as he does with any one else. One of the entries in his journal, while he was staying in Berlin, offers a case in point. "July 23, I dine, very much against my will, with Prince Ferdinand. I was engaged to a very agreeable party, but it seems the highnesses must never be denied, unless it be from indisposition. I had, however, written a note declining the intended honor; but the messenger, upon looking at it, for it was a letter patent, like the invitation, said he could not deliver it; that nobody ever refused; all of which I was informed of after he was gone. On consulting I found that I must go or give mortal offense, which last I have no inclination to do; so I write another note, and send out to hunt up the messenger. While I am abroad this untoward incident is arranged, and of course I am at Bellevue." While at court on one occasion he met, and took a great fancy to, the daughter of the famous Baroness Riedesel; having been born in the United States, she had been christened America.

In one of his conversations with the king, who was timid and hesitating, Morris told him that the Austrians would be all right if he would only lend them some Prussian generals — a remark upon

which Jena and Auerstadt later on offered a curious commentary. He became very impatient with
the king's inability to make up his mind; and
wrote to the Duchess of Cumberland that "the
guardian angel of the French Republic kept him
lingering on this side of the grave." He wrote to
Lord Grenville that Prussia was "seeking little
things by little means," and that the war with
Poland was popular " because the moral principles
of a Prussian go to the possession of whatever he
can acquire. And so little is he the slave of what
he calls vulgar prejudice, that, give him opportunity and means, and he will spare you the trouble of finding a pretext. This liberality of sentiment greatly facilitates negotiation, for it is not
necessary to clothe propositions in honest and decent forms." Morris was a most startling phe-
nomenon to the diplomatists of the day, trampling
with utter disregard on all their hereditary theories
of finesse and cautious duplicity. The timid for-
malists, and more especially those who considered
double-dealing as the legitimate, and in fact the
only legitimate, weapon of their trade, were displeased with him; but he was very highly thought
of by such as could see the strength and originality
of the views set forth in his frank, rather over-
bold language.

At Dresden he notes that he was late on the day
set down for his presentation at court, owing to
his valet having translated *halb zwölf* as half past
twelve. The Dresden picture galleries were the

first that drew from him any very strong expressions of admiration. In the city were numbers of the *emigrés*, fleeing from their countrymen, and only permitted to stop in Saxony for a few days; yet they were serene and gay, and spent their time in busy sight-seeing, examining everything curious which they could get at. Morris had become pretty well accustomed to the way in which they met fate; but such lively resignation surprised even him, and he remarked that so great a calamity had never lighted on shoulders so well fitted to bear it.

At Vienna he made a long stay, not leaving it until January, 1797. Here, as usual, he fraternized at once with the various diplomatists; the English ambassador, Sir Morton Eden, in particular, going out of his way to show him every attention. The Austrian prime minister, M. Thugut, was also very polite; and so were the foreign ministers of all the powers. He was soon at home in the upper social circles of this German Paris; but from the entries in his journal it is evident that he thought very little of Viennese society. He liked talking and the company of brilliant conversationalists, and he abominated gambling; but in Vienna every one was so devoted to play that there was no conversation at all. He considered a dumb circle round a card-table as the dullest society in the world, and in Vienna there was little else. Nor was he impressed with the ability of the statesmen he met. He thought the Austrian nobles to be on the decline; they stood for the dying feudal system. The great families had been squandering their riches with the most reckless extravagance, and were becoming broken and impoverished; and the imperial government was glad to see the humiliation of the haughty nobles, not perceiving that, if preserved, they would act as a buffer between it and the new power beginning to make itself felt throughout Europe, and would save the throne if not from total overthrow, at least from shocks so fierce as greatly to weaken it.

Morris considered Prince Esterhazy as an archtypical representative of the class. He was captain of the noble Hungarian Guard, a small body of tall, handsome men on fiery steeds, magnificently caparisoned. The prince, as its commander, wore a Hungarian dress, scarlet, with fur cape and cuffs, and yellow morocco boots; everything embroidered with pearls, four hundred and seventy large ones, and many thousand small, but all put on in good taste. He had a collar of large diamonds, a plume of diamonds in his cap; and his sword-hilt, scabbard, and spurs were inlaid with the same precious stones. His horse was equally bejeweled; steed and rider, with their trappings, "were estimated at a value of a quarter of a million dollars." Old Blücher would surely have considered the pair " very fine plunder."

The prince was reported to be nominally the richest subject in Europe, with a revenue that during the Turkish war went up to a million guilders annually; yet he was hopelessly in debt already,

and getting deeper every year. He lived in great
magnificence, but was by no means noted for lavish
hospitality; all his extravagance was reserved for
himself, especially for purposes of display. His
Vienna stable contained a hundred and fifty horses;
and during a six weeks' residence in Frankfort,
where he was ambassador at the time of an imperial
coronation, he spent eighty thousand pounds. Altogether, an outsider may be pardoned for not at
first seeing precisely what useful function such a
merely gorgeous being performed in the body politic; yet when summoned before the bar of the new
world-forces, Esterhazy and his kind showed that
birds of such fine feathers sometimes had beaks and
talons as well, and knew how to use them, the craven
flight of the French noblesse to the contrary notwithstanding.

Morris was often at court, where the constant
theme of conversation was naturally the struggle
with the French armies under Moreau and Bonaparte. After one of these mornings he mentions:
" The levee was oddly arranged, all the males being in one apartment, through which the emperor
passes in going to chapel, and returns the same way
with the empress and imperial family; after which
they go through their own rooms to the ladies as-
sembled on the other side."

The English members of the *corps diplomatique* in all the European capitals were especially
civil to him; and he liked them more than their
continental brethren. But for some of their young

tourist countrymen he cared less ; and it is curious to
see that the ridicule to which Americans have rightly
exposed themselves by their absurd fondness for
uniforms and for assuming military titles to which
they have no warrant, was no less deservedly earned
by the English at the end of the last century. One
of Morris's friends, Baron Groshlaer, being, like
the other Viennese, curious to know the object of
his stay, — they guessed aright that he wished to
get Lafayette liberated, — at last almost asked him
outright about it. " Finally I tell him that the
only difference between me and the young Englishmen, of whom there is a swarm here, is, that I seek
instruction with gray hairs and they with brown.
. . . At the archduchess's one of the little princes,
brother to the emperor, and who is truly an *arch-
duke*, asks me to explain to him the different uniforms worn by the young English, of whom there
are a great number here, all in regimentals. Some
of these belong to no corps at all, and the others to
yeomanry, fencibles and the like, all of which pur-
port to be raised for the defense of their country
in case she should be invaded ; but now, when the
invasion seems most imminent, they are abroad, and
cannot be made to feel the ridiculous indecency of
appearing in regimentals. Sir M. Eden and others
have given them the broadest hints without the
least effect. One of them told me that all the
world should not laugh him out of his regimentals.
I bowed. . . . I tell the prince that I really am
not able to answer his question, but that, in general,

their dresses I believe are worn for convenience in traveling. He smiles at this. . . . If I were an Englishman I should be hurt at these exhibitions, and as it is I am sorry for them. . . . I find that here they assume it as unquestionable that the young men of England have a right to adjust the ceremonial of Vienna. The political relations of the two countries induce the good company here to treat them with politeness; but nothing prevents their being laughed at, as I found the other evening at Madame de Groshlaer's, where the young women as well as the girls were very merry at the expense of these young men."

After leaving Vienna he again passed through Berlin, and in a conversation with the king he foreshadowed curiously the state of politics a century later, and showed that he thoroughly appreciated the cause that would in the end reconcile the traditional enmity of the Hohenzollerns and Hapsburgs. "After some trifling things I tell him that I have just seen his best friend. He asks who? and, to his great surprise, I reply, the emperor. He speaks of him well personally, and I observe that he is a very honest young man, to which his majesty replies by asking, "Mais, que pensez vous de Thugut." "Quant à cela, c'est une autre affaire, sire." I had stated the interest, which makes him and the emperor good friends, to be their mutual apprehensions from Russia. "But suppose we all three unite?" "Ce sera un diable de fricassée, sire, si vous vous mettez tous les trois à casser les œufs."

At Brunswick he was received with great hospitality, the duke, and particularly the duchess
dowager, the King of England's sister, treating
him very hospitably. He here saw General Riedesel, with whom he was most friendly; the general
in the course of conversation inveighed bitterly
against Burgoyne. He went to Munich also, where
he was received on a very intimate footing by
Count Rumford, then the great power in Bavaria,
who was busily engaged in doing all he could to
better the condition of his country. Morris was
much interested in his reforms. They were certainly needed; the count told his friend that on
assuming the reins of power the abuses to be remedied were beyond belief — for instance, there was
one regiment of cavalry that had five field officers
and only three horses. With some of the friends
that Morris made — such as the Duchess of Cumberland, the Princess de la Tour et Taxis and
others — he corresponded until the end of his life.

While at Vienna he again did all he could to
get Lafayette released from prison, where his wife
was confined with him; but in vain. Madame de
Lafayette's sister, the Marquise de Montagu, and
Madame de Staël, both wrote him the most urgent
appeals to do what he could for the prisoners; the
former writing, "My sister is in danger of losing
the life you saved in the prisons of Paris . . . has
not he whom Europe numbers among those citizens of whom North America ought to be most
proud, has not he the right to make himself heard

in favor of a citizen of the United States, and of a wife, whose life belongs to him, since he has preserved it?" Madame de Staël felt the most genuine grief for Lafayette, and very sincere respect for Morris; and in her letters to the latter she displayed both sentiments with a lavish exaggeration that hardly seems in good taste. If Morris had needed a spur the letters would have supplied it; but the task was an impossible one, and Lafayette was not released until the peace in 1797, when he was turned over to the American consul at Hamburg, in Morris's presence.

Morris was able to render more effectual help to an individual far less worthy of it than Lafayette. This was the then Duke of Orleans, afterwards King Louis Philippe, who had fled from France with Dumouriez. Morris's old friend, Madame de Flahaut, appealed to him almost hysterically on the duke's behalf; and he at once did even more than she requested, giving the duke money wherewith to go to America, and also furnishing him with unlimited credit at his own New York banker's, during his wanderings in the United States. This was done for the sake of the Duchess of Orleans, to whom Morris was devotedly attached, not for the sake of the duke himself. The latter knew this perfectly, writing: " Your kindness is a blessing I owe to my mother and to our friend " (Madame de Flahaut). The bourgeois king admirably represented the meanest, smallest side of the bourgeois character; he was not a bad man, but he was a very petty and contemptible one; had he been born in a different station of life, he would have been just the individual to take a prominent part in local temperance meetings, while he sanded the sugar he sold in his corner grocery. His treatment of Morris's loan was characteristic. When he came into his rights again, at the Restoration, he at first appeared to forget his debt entirely, and when his memory was jogged, he merely sent Morris the original sum, without a word of thanks; whereupon Morris, rather nettled, and as prompt to stand up for his rights against a man in prosperity as he had been to help him when in adversity, put the matter in the hands of his lawyer, through whom he notified Louis Philippe that if the affair was to be treated on a merely business basis, it should then be treated in a strictly business way, and the interest for the twenty years that had gone by should be forwarded also. This was accordingly done, although not until after Morris's death, the entire sum refunded being seventy thousand francs.

Morris brought his complicated business affairs in Europe to a close in 1798, and sailed from Hamburg on October 4 of that year, reaching New York after an exceedingly tedious and disagreeable voyage of eighty days.

CHAPTER XII

MORRIS was very warmly greeted on his return; and it was evident that the length of his stay abroad had in nowise made him lose ground with his friends at home. His natural affiliations were all with the Federalist party, which he immediately joined.

During the year 1799 he did not take much part in politics, as he was occupied in getting his business affairs in order and in putting to rights his estates at Morrisania. The old manor-house had become such a crazy, leaky affair that he tore it down and built a new one; a great, roomy building, not in the least showy, but solid, comfortable, and in perfect taste; having, across the tree-clad hills of Westchester, a superb view of the Sound, with its jagged coast and capes and islands.

Although it was so long since he had practiced law, he was shortly engaged in a very important case that was argued for eight days before the Court of Errors in Albany. Few trials in the State of New York have ever brought together such a number of men of remarkable legal ability; for among the lawyers engaged on one side or the

other were Morris, Hamilton, Burr, Robert Livingston, and Troup. There were some sharp passages
of arms: and the trial of wits between Morris and
Hamilton in particular were so keen as to cause a
passing coolness.

During the ten years that had gone by since
Morris sailed for Europe, the control of the national government had been in the hands of the
Federalists; when he returned, party bitterness
was at the highest pitch, for the Democrats were
preparing to make the final push for power which
should overthrow and ruin their antagonists. Four
fifths of the talent, ability, and good sense of the
country were to be found in the Federalist ranks;
for the Federalists had held their own so far, by
sheer force of courage and intellectual vigor, over
foes in reality more numerous. Their great prop
had been Washington. His colossal influence was
to the end decisive in party contests, and he had
in fact, although hardly in name, almost entirely
abandoned his early attempts at non-partisanship,
had grown to distrust Madison as he long before
had distrusted Jefferson, and had come into constantly closer relations with their enemies. His
death diminished greatly the chances of Federalist
success; there were two other causes at work that
destroyed them entirely.

One of these was the very presence in the domi-
nant party of so many men nearly equal in strong
will and great intellectual power; their ambitions
and theories clashed; even the loftiness of their

aims, and their disdain of everything small, made them poor politicians, and with Washington out of the way there was no one commander to overawe the rest and to keep down the fierce bickerings constantly arising among them; while in the other party there was a single leader, Jefferson, absolutely without a rival, but supported by a host of sharp political workers, most skillful in marshaling that unwieldy and hitherto disunited host of voters who were inferior in intelligence to their fellows.

The second cause lay deep in the nature of the Federalist organization: it was its distrust of the people. This was the fatally weak streak in Federalism. In a government such as ours it was a foregone conclusion that a party which did not believe in the people would sooner or later be thrown from power unless there was an armed break-up of the system. The distrust was felt, and of course excited corresponding and intense hostility. Had the Federalists been united, and had they freely trusted in the people, the latter would have shown that the trust was well founded; but there was no hope for leaders who suspected each other and feared their followers.

Morris landed just as the Federalist reaction, brought about by the conduct of France, had spent itself, — thanks partly to some inopportune pieces of insolence from England, in which country, as Morris once wrote to a foreign friend, "on a toujours le bon esprit de vouloir prendre les mouches avec du vinaigre." The famous Alien and Sedition

laws were exciting great disgust, and in Virginia
and Kentucky Jefferson was using them as handles
wherewith to guide seditious agitation — not that
he believed in sedition, but because he considered
it good party policy, for the moment, to excite it.
The parties hated each other with rancorous virulence; the newspapers teemed with the foulest
abuse of public men, accusations of financial dishonesty were rife, Washington himself not being
spared, and the most scurrilous personalities were
bandied about between the different editors.   The
Federalists were split into two factions, one following the President, Adams, in his efforts to keep
peace with France, if it could be done with honor,
while the others, under Hamilton's lead, wished
war at once.

Pennsylvanian politics were already very low.
The leaders who had taken control were men of
mean capacity and small morality, and the State
was not only becoming rapidly democratic but was
also drifting along in a disorganized, pseudo-jaco-
binical, half insurrectionary kind of way that would
have boded ill for its future had it not been fettered by the presence of healthier communities
round about it.   New England was the only part
of the community, excepting Delaware, where Federalism was on a perfectly sound footing; for in
that section there was no caste spirit, the leaders
and their followers were thoroughly in touch, and
all the citizens, shrewd, thrifty, independent, were
used to self-government, and fully awake to the

fact that honesty and order are the prerequisites of
liberty.   Yet even here Democracy had made some
inroads.

South of the Potomac the Federalists had lost
ground rapidly.   Virginia was still a battlefield;
as long as Washington lived, his tremendous personal influence acted as a brake on the democratic
advance, and the State's greatest orator, Patrick
Henry, had halted beside the grave to denounce
the seditious schemes of the disunion agitators with
the same burning, thrilling eloquence that, thirty
years before, had stirred to their depths the hearts
of his hearers when he bade defiance to the tyran-
nous might of the British king.   But when these
two men were dead, Marshall, — though destined,
as chief and controlling influence in the third division of our governmental system, to mould the
whole of that system on the lines of Federalist
thought, and to prove that a sound judiciary could
largely affect an unsound executive and legislature,
— even Marshall could not, single-handed, stem
the current that had gradually gathered head.
Virginia stands easily first among all our common-
wealths for the statesmen and warriors she has
brought forth; and it is noteworthy that during
the long contest between the nationalists and separatists, which forms the central fact in our history
for the first three quarters of a century of our
national life, she gave leaders to both sides at the
two great crises: Washington and Marshall to the
one, and Jefferson to the other, when the question

was one of opinion as to whether the Union should
be built up; and when the appeal to arms was
made to tear it down, Farragut and Thomas to the
north, Lee and Jackson to the south.

There was one eddy in the tide of democratic
success that flowed so strongly to the southward.
This was in South Carolina.   The fierce little Pal-
metto State has always been a free lance among
her Southern sisters; for instance, though usually
ultra-democratic, she was hostile to the two great
democratic chiefs, Jefferson and Jackson, though
both were from the South.   At the time that
Morris came home, the brilliant little group of
Federalist leaders within her bounds, headed by
men of national renown like Pinckney and Harper,
kept her true to Federalism by downright force of
intellect and integrity ; for they were among the
purest as well as the ablest statesmen of the day.

New York had been going through a series of
bitter party contests; any one examining a file of
papers of that day will come to the conclusion that
party spirit was even more violent and unreasonable then than now.   The two great Federalist
leaders, Hamilton and Jay, stood head and shoulders above all their democratic competitors, and
they were backed by the best men in the State,
like Rufus King, Schuyler, and others.   But, though
as orators and statesmen they had no rivals, they
were very deficient in the arts of political management.   Hamilton's imperious haughtiness had
alienated the powerful family of the Livingstons,

who had thrown in their lot with the Clintonians; and a still more valuable ally to the latter had arisen in that consummate master of "machine" politics, Aaron Burr. In 1792, Jay, then chief justice of the United States, had run for governor against Clinton, and had received the majority of the votes; but had been counted out by the returning board in spite of the protest of its four Federalist members — Gansevoort, Roosevelt, Jones, and Sands. The indignation was extreme, and only Jay's patriotism and good sense prevented an outbreak. However, the memory of the fraud remained fresh in the minds of the citizens, and at the next election for governor he was chosen by a heavy majority, having then just come back from his mission to England. Soon afterwards his treaty was published, and excited a whirlwind of indignation; it was only ratified in the Senate through Washington's great influence, backed by the magnificent oratory of Fisher Ames, whose speech on this occasion, when he was almost literally on his death-bed, ranks among the half dozen greatest of our country. The treaty was very objectionable in certain points, but it was most necessary to our well-being, and Jay was probably the only American who could have negotiated it. As with the Ashburton treaty many years later, extreme sections in England attacked it as fiercely as did the extreme sections here; and Lord Sheffield voiced their feelings when he hailed the war of 1812 as offering a chance to England to get back the

Rufus King

advantages out of which "Jay had duped Gren-ville."

But the· clash with France shortly afterwards swept away the recollection of the treaty, and Jay was reëlected in 1798. One of the arguments, by the way, which was used against him in the canvass was that he was an abolitionist. But, in spite of his reëlection, the New York Democrats were steadily gaining ground.

Such was the situation when Morris returned. He at once took high rank among the Federalists, and in April, 1800, just before the final wreck of their party, was chosen by them to fill an unexpired term of three years in the United States Senate. Before this he had made it evident that his sympathies lay with Hamilton and those who did not think highly of Adams. He did not deem it wise to renominate the latter for the presidency. He had even written to Washington, earnestly beseeching him to accept the nomination; but Washington died a day or two after the letter was sent. In spite of the jarring between the leaders, the Federalists nominated Adams and Pinckney. In the ensuing presidential election many of the party chiefs, notably Marshall of Virginia, already a strong Adams man, faithfully stood by the ticket in its entirety; but Hamilton, Morris, and many others at the North probably hoped in their hearts that, by the aid of· the curious electoral system which then existed, some chance would put the great Carolinian in the first place and make him president. Indeed, there is little question that this might have been done, had not Pinckney, one of the most high-minded and disinterested statesmen we have ever had, emphatically declined to profit in any way by the hurting of the grim old Puritan.

The house thus divided against itself naturally fell, and Jefferson was chosen president. It was in New York that the decisive struggle took place, for that was the pivotal State; and there the Democrats, under the lead of the Livingstons and Clintons, but above all by the masterly political manœuvres of Aaron Burr, gained a crushing victory. Hamilton, stung to madness by the defeat, and sincerely believing that the success of his opponents would be fatal to the republic, — for the two parties hated each other with a blind fury unknown to the organizations of the present day, — actually proposed to Jay, the governor, to nullify the action of the people by the aid of the old legislature, a Federalist body, which was still holding over, although the members of its successor had been chosen. Jay, as pure as he was brave, refused to sanction any such scheme of unworthy partisanship. It is worth noting that the victors in this election introduced for the first time the "spoils system," in all its rigor, into our state affairs; imitating the bad example of Pennsylvania a year or two previously.

When the Federalists in Congress, into which body the choice for president had been thrown, took up Burr, as a less objectionable alternative than Jefferson, Morris, much to his credit, openly and heartily disapproved of the movement, and was sincerely glad that it failed. For he thought Burr far the more dangerous man of the two, and, moreover, did not believe that the evident intention of the people should be thwarted. Both he and Hamilton, on this occasion, acted more wisely and more honestly than did most of their heated fellow partisans. Writing to the latter, the former remarked : " It is dangerous to be impartial in politics ; you, who are temperate in drinking, have never perhaps noticed the awkward situation of a man who continues sober after the company are drunk."

Morris joined the Senate at Philadelphia in May, 1800, but it almost immediately adjourned, to meet at Washington in November, when he was again present. Washington, as it then was, was a place whose straggling squalor has often been described. Morris wrote to the Princess de la Tour et Taxis, that it needed nothing " but houses, cellars, kitchens, well-informed men, amiable women, and other little trifles of the kind to make the city perfect ; " that it was " the very best city in the world for a future residence," but that as he was " not one of those good people whom we call posterity," he would meanwhile like to live somewhere else.

During his three years' term in the Senate he was one of the strong pillars of the Federalist party; but he was both too independent and too erratic to act always within strict party lines, and while he was an ultra-Federalist on some points, he openly abandoned his fellows on others. He despised Jefferson as a tricky and incapable theorist, skillful in getting votes, but in nothing else; a man who believed " in the wisdom of mobs, and the moderation of Jacobins," and who found himself " in the wretched plight of being forced to turn out good officers to make room for the unworthy."

After the election that turned them out of power, but just before their opponents took office, the Federalists in the Senate and House passed the famous judiciary bill, and Adams signed it. It provided for a number of new federal judges to act throughout the States, while the Supreme Court was retained as the ultimate court of decision. It was an excellent measure, inasmuch as it simplified the work of the judiciary, saved the highest branch from useless traveling, prevented the calendars from being choked with work, and supplied an upright federal judiciary to certain districts where the local judges could not be depended upon to act honestly. On the other hand, the Federalists employed it as a means to keep themselves partly in power, after the nation had decided that they should be turned out. Although the Democrats had bitterly opposed it, yet if, as was only right, the offices created by it had been left vacant until Jefferson came in, it would probably have

been allowed to stand. But Adams, most impro-
perly, spent the last hours of his administration in
putting in the new judges.

Morris, who heartily championed the measure,
wrote his reasons for so doing to Livingston; giving, with his usual frankness, those that were political and improper, as well as those based on
some public policy, but apparently not appreci-
ating the gravity of the charges he so lightly admitted. He said: " The new judiciary bill may
have, and doubtless has, many little faults, but it
answers the double purpose of bringing justice near
to men's doors, and of giving additional fibre to
the root of government. You must not, my friend,
judge of other States by your own. Depend on it,
that in some parts of this Union justice cannot
be readily obtained in the state courts." So far,
he was all right, and the truth of his statements,
and the soundness of his reasons, could not be
challenged as to the propriety of the law itself;
but he was much less happy in giving his views of
the way in which it would be carried out: " That
the leaders of the federal party may use this opportunity to provide for friends and adherents is, I
think, probable ; and if they were my enemies, I
should blame them for it. Whether I should do
the same thing myself is another question. . . .
They are about to experience a heavy gale of ad-
verse wind ; can they be blamed for casting many
anchors to hold their ship through the storm ? "
Most certainly they should be blamed for casting

this particular kind of anchor; it was a very gross
outrage for them to "provide for friends and adherents" in such a manner.

The folly of their action was seen at once; for
they had so maddened the Democrats that the latter repealed the act as soon as they came into
power. This also was of course all wrong, and
was a simple sacrifice of a measure of good government to partisan rage. Morris led the fight
against it, deeming the repeal not only in the highest degree unwise but also unconstitutional. After
the repeal was accomplished, the knowledge that
their greed to grasp office under the act was probably the cause of the loss of an excellent law must
have been rather a bitter cud for the Federalists to
chew. Morris always took an exaggerated view of
the repeal, regarding it as a death-blow to the Constitution. It was certainly a most unfortunate
affair throughout; and much of the blame attaches
to the Federalists, although still more to their antagonists.

The absolute terror with which even moderate
Federalists had viewed the victory of the Democrats was in a certain sense justifiable; for the
leaders who led the Democrats to triumph were the
very men who had fought tooth and nail against
every measure necessary to make us a free, orderly,
and powerful nation. But the safety of the nation
really lay in the very fact that the policy hitherto
advocated by the now victorious party had embodied principles so wholly absurd in practice that

it was out of the question to apply them at all to the actual running of the government. Jefferson could write or speak — and could feel too — the most high-sounding sentiments; but once it came to actions he was absolutely at sea, and on almost every matter — especially where he did well — he had to fall back on the Federalist theories. Almost the only important point on which he allowed himself free scope was that of the national defenses; and here, particularly as regards the navy, he worked very serious harm to the country. Otherwise he generally adopted and acted on the views of his predecessors; as Morris said, the Democrats "did more to strengthen the executive than Federalists dared think of, even in Washington's day." As a consequence, though the nation would certainly have been better off if men like Adams or Pinckney had been retained at the head of affairs, yet the change resulted in far less harm than it bade fair to.

On the other hand the Federalists cut a very sorry figure in opposition. We have never had another party so little able to stand adversity. They lost their temper first and they lost their principles next, and actually began to take up the heresies discarded by their adversaries. Morris himself, untrue to all his previous record, advanced various states'-rights doctrines; and the Federalists, the men who had created the Union, ended their days under the grave suspicion of having desired to break it up. Morris even opposed, and on a close vote temporarily defeated, the perfectly unobjectionable proposition to change the electoral system by designating the candidates for president and vice-president; the reason he gave was that he believed parties should be forced to nominate both of their best men, and that he regarded the Jefferson-Burr tie as a beautiful object-lesson for teaching this point!

On one most important question, however, he cut loose from his party, who were entirely in the wrong, and acted with the administration, who were behaving in strict accordance with Federalist precepts. This was in reference to the treaty by which we acquired Louisiana.

While in opposition, one of the most discreditable features of the Republican-Democratic party had been its servile truckling to France, which at times drove it into open disloyalty to America. Indeed this subservience to foreigners was a feature of our early party history; and the most confirmed pessimist must admit that, as regards patriotism and indignant intolerance of foreign control, the party organizations of to-day are immeasurably superior to those of eighty or ninety years back. But it was only while in opposition that either party was ready to throw itself into the arms of outsiders. Once the Democrats took the reins they immediately changed their attitude. The West demanded New Orleans and the valley of the Mississippi; and what it demanded it was determined to get. When we only had the decay-

ing weakness of Spain to deal with, there was no
cause for hurry ; but when Louisiana was ceded to
France, at the time when the empire of Napoleon
was a match for all the rest of the world put together, the country was up in arms at once.

The administration promptly began to negotiate
for the purchase of Louisiana. Morris backed
them up heartily, thus splitting off from the bulk
of the Federalists, and earnestly advocated far
stronger measures than had been taken. He believed that so soon as the French should establish
themselves in New Orleans we should have a war
with them ; he knew it would be impossible for the
haughty chiefs of a military despotism long to
avoid collisions with the reckless and warlike
backwoodsmen of the border. Nor would he have
been sorry had such a war taken place. He said
that it was a necessity to us, for we were dwin-
dling into a race of mere speculators and driveling
philosophers, whereas ten years of warfare would
bring forth a crop of heroes and statesmen, fit
timber out of which to hew an empire.

Almost his last act in the United States Senate
was to make a most powerful and telling speech in
favor of at once occupying the territory in dispute,
and bidding defiance to Napoleon. He showed
that we could not submit to having so dangerous
a neighbor as France, an ambitious and conquering nation, at whose head was the greatest warrior
of the age. With ringing emphasis he claimed
the western regions as peculiarly our heritage, as

the property of the fathers of America which they
held in trust for their children. It was true that
France was then enjoying the peace which she had
wrung from the gathered armies of all Europe;
yet he advised us to fling down the gauntlet fear-
lessly, not hampering ourselves by an attempt at
alliance with Great Britain or any other power,
but resting confident that, if America was heartily
in earnest, she would be able to hold her own in
any struggle. The cost of the conquest he brushed
contemptuously aside; he considered " that counting-house policy, which sees nothing but money,
a poor, short-sighted, half-witted, mean, and miserable thing, as far removed from wisdom as is a
monkey from a man." He wished for peace; but
he did not believe the emperor would yield us the
territory, and he knew that his fellow representatives, and practically all the American people,
were determined to fight for it if they could get
it in no other way; therefore he advised them to
begin at once, and gain forthwith what they
wanted, and perhaps their example would inspirit
Europe to rise against the tyrant.

It was bold advice, and if need had arisen it
would have been followed; for we were bound to
have Louisiana, if not by bargain and sale then by
fair shock of arms. But Napoleon yielded, and
gave us the land for fifteen millions, of which, said
Morris, " I am content to pay my share to deprive
foreigners of all pretext for entering our interior
country; if nothing else were gained by the treaty,
that alone would satisfy me."

Morris's term as senator expired on March 4, 1803, and he was not reëlected; for New York State had passed into the hands of the Democrats. But he still continued to play a prominent part in public affairs, for he was the leader in starting the project of the Erie Canal. It was to him that we owe the original idea of this great waterway, for he thought of it and planned it out long before any one else. He had publicly proposed it during the Revolutionary period; in 1803 he began the agitation in its favor that culminated in its realization, and he was chairman of the canal commissioners from the time of their appointment, in 1810, until within a few months of his death. The three first reports of the commission were all from his pen. As Stephen Van Rensselaer, himself one of the commissioners from the beginning, said, " Gouverneur Morris was the father of our great canal." He hoped ultimately to make it a ship canal. While a member of the commission, he not only discharged his duties as such with characteristic energy and painstaking, but he also did most effective outside work in advancing the enterprise, while he mastered the subject more thoroughly in all its details than did any other man.

He spent most of his time at Morrisania, but traveled for two or three months every summer, sometimes going out to the then " far West," along the shores of Lakes Erie and Ontario, and once descending the St. Lawrence. At home he spent his time tilling his farm, reading, receiving visits

from his friends, and carrying on a wide correspondence on business and politics. Jay's home was
within driving distance, and the two fine old fellows saw much of each other. On the 25th of De-
cember, 1809, Morris, then fifty-six years old, married Miss Anne Cary Randolph, a member of the
famous Virginia family; he was very happy with
her, and by her he had one son. Three weeks after
the marriage he wrote Jay a pressing request to
visit him: " I pray you will, with your daughters,
embark immediately in your sleigh, after a very
early breakfast, and push on so as to reach this
house in the evening. My wife sends her love,
and says she longs to receive her husband's friend;
that his sickness must be no excuse, for she will
nurse him. Come, then, and see your old friend
perform his part in an old-fashioned scene of domestic enjoyment." Jay was very simple in his way
of living; but Morris was rather formal. When
he visited his friend he always came with his valet,
was shown straight to his room without seeing any
one, dressed himself with scrupulous nicety, — being very particular about his powdered hair, — and
then came down to see his host.

Although his letters generally dealt with public
matters, he sometimes went into home details. He
thus wrote an amusing letter to a good friend of
his, a lady, who was desirous, following the custom
of the day, to send her boy to what was called a
" college " at an absurdly early age; he closed by
warning her that " these children of eleven, after a

four years' course, in which they may learn to smatter a little of everything, become bachelors of arts before they know how to button their clothes, and are the most troublesome and useless, sometimes the most pernicious, little animals that ever infested a commonwealth."

At one time he received as his guest Moreau, the exiled French general, then seeking service in the United States. Writing in his diary an account of the visit, he says : " In the course of our conversation, touching very gently the idea of his serving (in case of necessity) against France, he declares frankly that, when the occasion arrives, he shall feel no reluctance ; that France having cast him out, he is a citizen of the country where he lives, and has the same right to follow his trade here as any other man."

He took the keenest pleasure in his life, and always insisted that America was the pleasantest of all places in which to live. Writing to a friend abroad, and mentioning that he respected the people of Britain, but did not find them congenial, he added : " But were the manners of those countries as pleasant as the people are respectable, I should never be reconciled to their summers. Compare the uninterrupted warmth and splendor of America, from the first of May to the last of September, and her autumn, truly celestial, with your shivering June, your July and August sometimes warm but often wet, your uncertain September, your gloomy October, and your dismal November. Compare

these things, and then say how a man who prizes
the charm of Nature can think of making the exchange. If you were to pass one autumn with us,
you would not give it for the best six months to be
found in any other country. . . . There is a bril-
liance in our atmosphere of which you can have no
idea."

He thoroughly appreciated the marvelous future
that lay before the race on this continent. Writing in 1801, he says: " As yet we only crawl along
the outer shell of our country. The interior excels
the part we inhabit in soil, in climate, in everything. The proudest empire in Europe is but a
bauble compared to what America *will* be, *must*
be, in the course of two centuries, perhaps of
one! " And again, " With respect to this country,
calculation outruns fancy, and fact outruns calculation."

Until his hasty, impulsive temper became so
soured by partisanship as to warp his judgment,
Morris remained as well satisfied with the people
and the system of government as with the land
itself. In one of his first letters after his return
to America he wrote: "There is a fund of good
sense and calmness of character here, which will, I
think, avoid all dangerous excesses. We are free:
we know it: and we know how to continue free."
On another occasion, about the same time, he said:
" *Nil desperandum de republica* is a sound principle." Again, in the middle of Jefferson's first
term: " We have indeed a set of madmen in the

administration, and they will do many foolish things; but there is a vigorous vegetative principle at the root which will make our tree flourish, let the winds blow as they may."

He at first took an equally just view of our political system, saying that in adopting a republican form of government he "not only took it, as a man does his wife, for better or worse, but, what few men do with their wives, knowing all its bad qualities." He observed that there was always a counter current in human affairs, which opposed alike good and evil. "Thus the good we hope is seldom attained, and the evil we fear is rarely realized. The leaders of faction must for their own sakes avoid errors of enormous magnitude; so that, while the republican form lasts, we shall be fairly well governed." He thought this form the one best suited for us, and remarked that "every kind of government was liable to evil; that the best was that which had fewest faults; that the excellence even of that best depended more on its fitness for the nation where it was established than on intrinsic perfection." He denounced, with a fierce scorn that they richly merit, the despicable demagogues and witless fools who teach that in all cases the voice of the majority must be implicitly obeyed, and that public men have only to carry out its will, and thus "acknowledge themselves the willing instruments of folly and vice. They declare that in order to please the people they will, regardless alike of what conscience may dic-

tate or reason approve, make the profligate sacrifice of public right on the altar of private interest.
What more can be asked by the sternest tyrant of
the most despicable slave ? Creatures of this sort
are the tools which usurpers employ in building
despotism."

Sounder and truer maxims never were uttered;
but unfortunately the indignation naturally excited
by the utter weakness and folly of Jefferson's
second term, and the pitiable incompetence shown
both by him, by his successor, and by their party
associates in dealing with affairs, so inflamed and
exasperated Morris as to make him completely
lose his head, and hurried him into an opposition
so violent that his follies surpassed the worst of
the follies he condemned. He gradually lost faith
in our republican system, and in the Union itself.
His old jealousy of the West revived more strongly
than ever; he actually proposed that our enormous
masses of new territory, destined one day to hold
the bulk of our population, " should be governed
as provinces, and allowed no voice in our councils."
So hopelessly futile a scheme is beneath comment;
and it cannot possibly be reconciled with his previous utterances when he descanted on our future
greatness as a people, and claimed the West as the
heritage of our children. His conduct can only
be unqualifiedly condemned; and he has but the
poor palliation that, in our early history, many of
the leading men in New York, and an even larger
proportion in New England, felt the same narrow,

illiberal jealousy of the West which had formerly been felt by the English statesmen for America as a whole.

It is well indeed for our land that we of this generation have at last learned to think nationally, and, no matter in what State we live, to view our whole country with the pride of personal posses-sion.

CHAPTER XIII

IT is a painful thing to have to record that the closing act in a great statesman's career not only compares ill with what went before, but is actually to the last degree a discreditable and unworthy performance.

Morris's bitterness and anger against the government grew apace; and finally his hatred for the administration became such, that, to hurt it, he was willing also to do irreparable harm to the nation itself. He violently opposed the various embargo acts, and all the other governmental measures of the decade before the war; and worked himself up to such a pitch, when hostilities began, that, though one of the founders of the Constitution, though formerly one of the chief exponents of the national idea, and though once a main upholder of the Union, he abandoned every patriotic principle and became an ardent advocate of Northern secession.

To any reasoning student of American history it goes without saying that there was very good cause for his anger with the administration. From the

time the House of Virginia came into power, until
the beginning of Monroe's administration, there
was a distinctly anti-New England feeling at
Washington, and much of the legislation bore
especially heavily on the Northeast. Excepting
Jefferson, we have never produced an executive
more helpless than Madison, when it came to grappling with real dangers and difficulties. Like his
predecessor, he was only fit to be president in a
time of profound peace; he was utterly out of
place the instant matters grew turbulent, or difficult problems arose to be solved, and he was a
ridiculously incompetent leader for a war with
Great Britain. He was entirely too timid to have
embarked on such a venture of his own accord,
and was simply forced into it by the threat of losing his second term. The fiery young Democrats
of the South and West, and their brothers of the
Middle States, were the authors of the war; they
themselves, for all their bluster, were but one
shade less incompetent than their nominal chief,
when it came to actual work, and were shamefully
unable to make their words good by deeds.

The administration thus drifted into a war which
it had neither the wisdom to avoid, nor the forethought to prepare for. In view of the fact that
the war was their own, it is impossible to condemn
sufficiently strongly the incredible folly of the
Democrats in having all along refused to build a
navy or provide any other adequate means of defense. In accordance with their curiously foolish

theories, they persisted in relying on that weakest
of all weak reeds, the militia, who promptly ran
away every time they faced a foe in the open.
This applied to all, whether eastern, western, or
southern; the men of the Northern States in 1812
and 1813 did as badly as, and no worse than, the
Virginians in 1814. Indeed, one of the good results of the war was that it did away forever with
all reliance on the old-time militia, the most expensive and inefficient species of soldiery that could
be invented. During the first year the monotonous record of humiliations and defeats was only
relieved by the splendid victories of the navy
which the Federalists had created twelve years
previously, and which had been hurt rather than
benefited in the intervening time. Gradually,
however, the people themselves began to bring out
leaders : two, Jackson and Scott, were really good
generals, under whom our soldiers became able to
face even the English regulars, then the most formidable fighting troops in the world ; and it must
be remembered that Jackson won his fights absolutely unhelped by the administration. In fact,
the government at Washington does not deserve
one shred of credit for any of the victories we won,
although to it we directly owe the greater number
of our defeats.

Granting, however, all that can be said as to
the hopeless inefficiency of the administration, both
in making ready for and in waging the war, it yet
remains true that the war itself was eminently

justifiable, and was of the greatest service to the
nation. We had been bullied by England and
France until we had to fight to preserve our national self-respect; and we very properly singled
out our chief aggressor, though it would perhaps
have been better still to have acted on the proposition advanced in Congress, and to have declared
war on both. Although nominally the peace left
things as they had been, practically we gained our
point; and we certainly came out of the contest
with a greatly increased reputation abroad. In
spite of the ludicrous series of failures which began
with our first attempt to invade Canada, and culminated at Bladensburg, yet in a succession of
contests on the ocean and the lakes, we shattered
the charmed shield of British naval invincibility;
while on the northern frontier we developed under
Scott and Brown an infantry which, unlike any of
the armies of continental Europe, was able to meet
on equal terms the British infantry in pitched
battle in the open; and at New Orleans we did
what the best of Napoleon's marshals, backed by
the flower of the French soldiers, had been unable
to accomplish during five years of warfare in Spain,
and inflicted a defeat such as no English army had
suffered during a quarter of a century of unbroken
warfare. Above all, the contest gave an immense
impetus to our national feeling, and freed our politics forever from any dependence on those of a
foreign power.

The war was distinctly worth fighting, and re-

sulted in good to the country. The blame that
attaches to Madison and the elder Democratic-
Republican leaders, as well as to their younger
associates, Clay, Calhoun, and the rest, who fairly
flogged them into action, relates to their utter failure to make any preparations for the contest, to
their helpless inability to carry it on, and to the
extraordinary weakness and indecision of their policy throughout; and on all these points it is hardly
possible to visit them with too unsparing censure.

Yet, grave though these faults were, they were
mild compared to those committed by Morris and
the other ultra-Federalists of New York and New
England. Morris's opposition to the war led him
to the most extravagant lengths. In his hatred of
the opposite party he lost all loyalty to the nation.
He championed the British view of their right to
impress seamen from our ships; he approved of
peace on the terms they offered, which included a
curtailment of our western frontier, and the erec-
tion along it of independent Indian sovereignties
under British protection. He found space in his
letters to exult over the defeats of Bonaparte, but
could spare no word of praise for our own victories.

He actually advocated repudiating our war debt,[1]
on the ground that it was void, being founded on
a moral wrong; and he wished the Federalists to
make public profession of their purpose, so that
when they should come back to power, the holders
might have no reason to complain that there had

---

[1] As, for instance, in a letter to David R. Ogden, April 5, 1813.

been no warning of their intention. To Josiah Quincy, on May 15, he wrote: "Should it be objected, as it probably will to favor lenders and their associates, that public faith is pledged, it may be replied that a pledge wickedly given is not to be redeemed." He thus advanced the theory that in a government ruled by parties, which come into power alternately, any debt could be repudiated, at any time, if the party in power happened to disapprove of its originally being incurred. No greenback demagogue of the lowest type ever advocated a proposition more dishonest or more contemptible.

He wrote that he agreed with Pickering that it was impious to raise taxes for so unjust a war. He endeavored, fortunately in vain, to induce Rufus King in the Senate to advocate the refusal of supplies of every sort, whether of men or money, for carrying on the war; but King was far too honorable to turn traitor. Singularly forgetful of his speeches in the Senate ten years before, he declared that he wished that a foreign power might occupy and people the West, so as, by outside pressure, to stifle our feuds. He sneered at the words union and constitution, as being meaningless. He railed bitterly at the honest and loyal majority of his fellow Federalists in New York, who had professed their devotion to the Union; and in a letter of April 29, to Harrison Gray Otis, — who was almost as bad as himself, — he strongly advocated secession, writing among other things

that he wished the New York Federalists to declare
publicly that " the Union, being the means of freedom, should be prized as such, but that the end
should not be sacrificed to the means." By comparing this with Calhoun's famous toast at the
Jefferson birthday dinner in 1830, " The Union;
next to our liberty the most dear; may we all
remember that it can only be preserved by respecting the rights of the States and distributing equally
the benefit and the burden of the Union," it can
be seen how completely Morris's utterances went
on all fours with those of the great nullifier.

To Pickering he wrote, on October 17, 1814:
" I hear every day professions of attachment to
the Union, and declarations as to its importance.
I should be glad to meet with some one who could
tell me what has become of the Union, in what it
consists, and to what useful purpose it endures."
He regarded the dissolution of the Union to be so
nearly an accomplished fact that the only question
was whether the boundary should be " the Delaware, the Susquehanna, or the Potomac;" for he
thought that New York would have to go with
New England. He nourished great hopes of the
Hartford Convention, which he expected would
formally come out for secession; he wrote Otis
that the convention should declare that the Union
was already broken, and that all that remained to
do was to take action for the preservation of the
interests of the Northeast. He was much cha-
grined when the convention fell under the control

of Cabot and the moderates. As late as January 10, 1815, he wrote that the only proceeding from which the people of his section would gain practical benefit would be a " severance of the Union."

In fact, throughout the war of 1812 he appeared as the open champion of treason to the nation, of dishonesty to the nation's creditors, and of cringing subserviency to a foreign power. It is as impossible to reconcile his course with his previous career and teachings as it is to try to make it square with the rules of statesmanship and morality. His own conduct affords a conclusive condemnation of his theories as to the great inferiority of a government conducted by the multitude, to a government conducted by the few who should have riches and education. Undoubtedly he was one of these few; he was an exceptionally able man, and a wealthy one; but he went farther wrong at this period than the majority of our people — the " mob " as he would have contemptuously called them — have ever gone at any time; for though every State in turn, and almost every statesman, has been wrong upon some issue or another, yet in the long run the bulk of the people have always hitherto shown themselves true to the cause of right. Morris strenuously insisted upon the need of property being defended from the masses; yet he advocated repudiation of the national debt, which he should have known to be quite as dishonest as the repudiation of his individual liabilities, and he was certainly aware that the step is a short one between refusing to pay a man what *ought* to be his and taking away from him what actually *is* his.

There were many other Federalist leaders in the same position as himself, especially in the three southern New England States, where the whole Federalist party laid itself open to the gravest charges of disloyalty. Morris was not alone in his creed at this time. On the contrary, his position is interesting because it is typical of that assumed by a large section of his party throughout the North-east. In fact, the Federalists in this portion of the Union had split in three, although the lines of cleavage were not always well marked. Many of them remained heartily loyal to the national idea; the bulk hesitated as to whether they should go all lengths or not; while a large and influential minority, headed by Morris, Pickering, Quincy, Lowell, and others, were avowed disunionists. Had peace not come when it did, it is probable that the moderates would finally have fallen under the control of these ultras. The party developed an element of bitter unreason in defeat; it was a really sad sight to see a body of able, educated men, interested and skilled in the conduct of public affairs, all going angrily and stupidly wrong on the one question that was of vital concern to the nation.

It is idle to try to justify the proceedings of the Hartford Convention, or of the Massachusetts and Connecticut legislatures. The decision to keep the New England troops as an independent command was of itself sufficient ground for condemnation;

moreover, it was not warranted by any show of superior prowess on the part of the New Englanders, for a portion of Maine continued in possession of the British till the close of the war. The Hartford resolutions were so framed as to justify seceding or not seceding as events turned out; a man like Morris could extract comfort from them, while it was hoped they would not frighten those who were more loyal. The majority of the people in New England were beyond question loyal, exactly as in 1860 a majority of Southerners were opposed to secession; but the disloyal element was active and resolute, and hoped to force the remainder into its own way of thinking. It failed signally, and was buried beneath a load of disgrace; and New England was taught thus early and by heart the lesson that wrongs must be righted within, and not without the Union. It would have been well for her sister section of the South, so loyal in 1815, if forty-five years afterwards she had spared herself the necessity of learning the same lesson at an infinitely greater cost.

The truth is that it is nonsense to reproach any one section with being especially disloyal to the Union. At one time or another almost every State has shown strong particularistic leanings; Connecticut and Pennsylvania, for example, quite as much as Virginia or Kentucky. Fortunately the outbursts were never simultaneous in a majority. It is as impossible to question the fact that at one period or another of the past, many of the States in each section have been very shaky in their allegiance, as it is to doubt that they are now all heartily loyal. The secession movement of 1860 was pushed to extremities, instead of being merely planned and threatened, and the revolt was peculiarly abhorrent, because of the intention to make slavery the " corner-stone " of the new nation, and to reintroduce the slave trade, to the certain ultimate ruin of the Southern whites, but at least it was entirely free from the meanness of being made in the midst of a doubtful struggle with a foreign foe. Indeed, in this respect the ultra-Federalists of New York and New England in 1814 should be compared with the infamous Northern copperheads of the Vallandigham stripe rather than with the gallant Confederates who risked and lost all in fighting for the cause of their choice. Half a century before the " stars and bars " waved over Lee's last intrenchments, perfervid New England patriots were fond of flaunting " the flag with five stripes," and drinking to the health of the — fortunately stillborn — new nation. Later on, the disunion movement among the Northern abolitionists, headed by Garrison, was perhaps the most absolutely senseless of all, for its success meant the immediate abandonment of every hope of abolition.

In each one of these movements men of the highest character and capacity took part. Morris had by previous services rendered the whole nation his debtor; Garrison was one of the little band who, in the midst of general apathy, selfishness, and cowardice, dared to demand the cutting out of the hideous plague spot of our civilization; while Lee and Jackson were as remarkable for stainless purity and high-mindedness as they were for their consummate military skill. But the disunion movements in which they severally took part were wholly wrong. An Englishman of to-day may be equally proud of the valor of Cavalier and Roundhead; but, if competent to judge, he must admit that the Roundhead was right. So it is with us. The man who fought for secession warred for a cause as evil and as capable of working lasting harm as the doctrine of the divine right of kings itself. But we may feel an intense pride in his gallantry; and we may believe in his honesty as heartily as we believe in that of the only less foolish being who wishes to see our government strongly centralized, heedless of the self-evident fact that over such a vast land as ours the nation can exist only as a Federal Union; and that, exactly as the liberty of the individual and the rights of the States can only be preserved by upholding the strength of the nation, so this same localizing of power in all matters not essentially national is vital to the well being and durability of the government.

Besides the honorable men drawn into such movements, there have always been plenty who took part in or directed them for their own selfish ends, or whose minds were so warped and their sense of political morality so crooked as to make

them originate schemes that would have reduced
us to the impotent level of the Spanish-American
republics. These men were peculiar to neither
section. In 1803, Aaron Burr of New York was
undoubtedly anxious to bring about in the Northeast [1] what sixty years later Jefferson Davis of
Mississippi so nearly succeeded in doing in the
South; and the attempt in the South to make a
hero of the one is as foolish as it would be to make
a hero of the other in the North. If there are such
virtues as loyalty and patriotism, then there must
exist the corresponding crime of treason; if there
is any merit in practicing the first, then there must
be equal demerit in committing the last. Emascu-
lated sentimentalists may try to strike from the
national dictionary the word treason; but until
that is done, Jefferson Davis must be deemed
guilty thereof.

There are, however, very few of our statesmen
whose characters can be painted in simple, uniform
colors, like Washington and Lincoln on the one
hand, or Burr and Davis on the other. Nor is
Morris one of these few. His place is alongside
of men like Madison, Samuel Adams, and Patrick
Henry, who did the nation great service at times,
but each of whom, at some one or two critical
junctures, ranged himself with the forces of disorder.

After the peace Morris accommodated himself

---

[1] People sometimes forget that Burr was as willing to try sedition in the East as in the West.

to the altered condition with his usual buoyant
cheerfulness; he was too light-hearted, and, to say
the truth, had too good an opinion of himself, to
be cast down even by the signal failure of his
expectations and the memory of the by no means
creditable part he had played. Besides, he had
the great virtue of always good-humoredly yielding
to the inevitable. He heartily wished the country well, and kept up a constant correspondence
with men high in influence at Washington. He
disliked the tariff bill of 1816; he did not believe
in duties or imposts, favoring internal, although
not direct, taxation. He was sharp-sighted enough
to see that the Federal party had shot its bolt and
outlived its usefulness, and that it was time for it
to dissolve. To a number of Federalists at Philadelphia, who wished to continue the organization,
he wrote strongly advising them to give up the
idea, and adding some very sound and patriotic
counsel. "Let us forget party and think of our
country. That country embraces both parties.
We must endeavor, therefore, to save and benefit
both. This cannot be effected while political de-
lusions array good men against each other. If
you abandon the contest, the voice of reason, now
drowned in factious vociferation, will be listened
to and heard. The pressure of distress will accel-
erate the moment of reflection; and when it arrives
the people will look out for men of sense, experience, and integrity. Such men may, I trust, be
found in both parties; and if our country be de-

livered, what does it signify whether those who operate her salvation wear a Federal or Democratic cloak?" These words formed almost his last public utterance, for they were penned but a couple of months before his death; and he might well be content to let them stand as a fit closing to his public career.

He died November 6, 1816, when sixty-four years old, after a short illness. He had suffered at intervals for a long time from gout; but he had enjoyed general good health, as his erect, commanding, well-built figure showed; for he was a tall and handsome man. He was buried on his own estate at Morrisania.

There has never been an American statesman of keener intellect or more brilliant genius. Had he possessed but a little more steadiness and self-control he would have stood among the two or three very foremost. He was gallant and fearless. He was absolutely upright and truthful; the least suggestion of falsehood was abhorrent to him. His extreme, aggressive frankness, joined to a certain imperiousness of disposition, made it difficult for him to get along well with many of the men with whom he was thrown in contact. In politics he was too much of a free lance ever to stand very high as a leader. He was very generous and hospitable; he was witty and humorous, a charming companion, and extremely fond of good living. He had a proud, almost hasty temper, and was quick to resent an insult. He was strictly just; and he made open war on all traits that displeased him, especially meanness and hypocrisy. He was essentially a strong man, and he was an American through and through.

Perhaps his greatest interest for us lies in the fact that he was a shrewder, more far-seeing observer and recorder of contemporary men and events, both at home and abroad, than any other American or foreign statesman of his time. But aside from this he did much lasting work. He took a most prominent part in bringing about the independence of the colonies, and afterwards in welding them into a single powerful nation, whose greatness he both foresaw and foretold. He made the final draft of the United States Constitution; he first outlined our present system of national coinage; he originated and got under way the plan for the Erie Canal; as minister to France he successfully performed the most difficult task ever allotted to an American representative at a foreign capital. With all his faults, there are few men of his generation to whom the country owes more than to Gouverneur Morris.

INDEX

and adopts Constitution, 53, 54 ;
debate in, over executive power, 54,
55 ; over appointment and veto, 55,
56 ; establishes religious toleration,
56–58 ; rejects proposal to abolish
slavery, 58 ; appoints committees
to organize government, 58, 59 ; its
action described by Morris, 65 ;
elects Morris delegate to Congress,
66 ; refuses to reëlect him on ground
of his alleged neglect of state interests, 85.

Lincoln, Abraham, compared with
Washington, 44, 115 ; combines the
best of Federalist and Jeffersonian
principles, 119, 120.

Livingston family, member of landed
aristocracy, 12 ; also in merchant
class, 13 ; supported by Presbyterians and Calvinists, 19 ; in Provincial Congress, 29 ; alienated from
Federalists by Hamilton, 283 ; aids
Jefferson to carry New York, 286.

Livingston, Robert R., his mixed ancestry, 9 ; on committee to draft
plan of Constitution, 52 ; on committee to organize new government,
58 ; satirical comments of Morris
on, 65 ; letter of Jay to, on foreign
policy, 107 ; in suit with Morris,
279 ; quarrels with Hamilton and
joins Democrats, 284 ; letter of
Morris to, on judiciary act, 289.

Llandaff, Bishop of, entertains Morris, 265 ; Morris's high opinion of,
265.

Louis XV., his reign compared to
Revolution, 234, 235.

Louis XVI., Morris's opinion of, 187,
188, 194 ; calls upon Morris for advice, 217 ; his situation, 217 ; plan
of Morris to aid his escape, 221 ;
ruins it by his weakness, 221 ; asks
Morris to take charge of royal papers and money, 221 ; Morris's contempt for, 223, 227 ; address drawn
up by Morris for, 225 ; made by
mob to put on red cap, 226 ; flies to
National Assembly, 228 ; his death,
249.

Louis XVIII., contempt of Morris for,
267.

Louis Philippe, acquaintance of Mor-

ris with, 180 ; flies from France
with Dumouriez, 276 ; helped by
Morris with money and credit, 276 ;
subsequent mean conduct toward
Morris, 277.

Louisiana, negotiations for, 293 ; its
seizure advocated by Morris, 293,
294 ; sold by Napoleon, 294.

Lowell, John, disunionist in 1814, 310.

Luzerne, M. de la, confided in by
Morris, 205 ; betrays fact to English ministry, 205 ; does not influence it, 205 ; compliments Morris
on his ability to predict, 256.

MacDougall, General Alexander,
his ancestry, 9.

McClellan, Gen. George B., his conduct compared with that of Philip
Schuyler, 64.

Madison, James, in Constitutional
Convention, 115 ; does his best work
in it, 120 ; later overshadowed by
Jefferson, 120 ; his activity in Convention, 120 ; protests against Morris's cynical view of human nature,
121 ; wishes to give Congress a veto
on state legislation, 126 ; advocates
a freehold suffrage, 130 ; reports
Morris's speech on aristocracy in
Senate, 132 ; points out need of
compromise between free and slave
States, 140 ; praises Morris's genius
and candor, 143 ; connection with
" Federalist," 144 ; distrusted by
Washington, 279 ; his administration disgusts Morris, 300 ; his character and helplessness as president,
303 ; his advocacy of disunion compared with Morris's, 314.

Manorial system, in New York, 12,
13.

Marmontel, Jean François, praised by
Morris, 214.

Marie Antoinette, sympathy of Morris for, 195 ; asks Morris's counsel,
217 ; plan of Morris to aid her escape, 221 ; disapproved of by Morris, 223 ; her death, 250.

Marshall, John, unable to keep Virginia Federalist after Washington's
death, 282 ; member of Adams's
faction, 285.

Maryland, part played by its Catholic gentry in Revolution, 34; makes bargain concerning slave trade in Constitutional convention, 139.

Mason, George, denounces slavery in Federal convention, 138.

Massachusetts, its Revolutionary leaders compared to those of New York, 14; revolt in, 110; disunion movement in, 310.

Maury, Abbé, estimate of, by Morris, 215, 216.

Merchants, of New York, 13, 14.

Militia, its worthless character in Revolutionary war, 43; inferior to troops of Rebellion, 44; abandons army on eve of battle, 60, 61; its use by Greene in southern campaign, 98, 99; proves worthless in war of 1812, 304.

Mirabeau, Boniface R., advocates passage of Necker's loan scheme in order to ruin him, 174; disgust of Morris for, 193; not fairly estimated, 193, 194.

Mississippi navigation, demand of Americans for, opposed by Gérard, 79; willingness of Morris to abandon, 79; attitude of Spain toward, 97, 98; attempts of Morris to shake Jay's determination to retain, 98; Jay's yielding to Spanish claims, 115; renewed demand for, causes Louisiana purchase, 292-294.

Monciel, ——, plans with Morris the escape of king, 221; receives royal money from Morris, 222.

Monroe, James, his ability as diplomat, 255, 261; his career in Paris as revolutionary sympathizer, 261; recalled and rebuked by Washington, 261.

Montagu, Marquise de, urges Morris to help Lafayette, 275.

Montcalm, Marquis de, defeats Abercrombie, 3.

Montesquieu, Baron, meetings with Morris, 177, 178.

Montgomery, Richard, Irish leader against Quebec, 9; welcomes Washington in behalf of New York Assembly, 38.

Montmorin, Comte de, described by

Morris, 189; continually consults Morris, 217.

Moreau, General of French armies, 272; entertained by Morris, 297.

Morgan, Daniel, in campaign against Burgoyne, 63.

Morris family, origin, 1, 2; leads popular party in New York, 2; its eccentricity, 2; part of landed aristocracy, 12.

Morris, Gouverneur, birth, 1; aristocratic ancestry, 1, 2; inherits French traits, 2; fond of sport, 2; goes to school in New Rochelle, 2; studies at King's College, 3, 18; delivers commonplace Commencement orations, 19; studies law, 19, 20; early career at bar, 20; attacks proposed issue of paper money, 20, 21; desires foreign travel, 21, 22; his reasons, 22; dissuaded by William Smith, 22, 23; career as society man, 23; dislikes revolutionary attitude of "Sons of Liberty," 26; considers New York gentry to be in dilemma between English tyranny and democratic encroachment, 27; thinks union with England necessary, and proposes remedies, 27, 28; finally driven to join patriot party, 28.

In New York Provincial Congress. Elected delegate from Westchester county, 30; seconds motion to obey Continental Congress, 31; reports recommendation that Congress issue paper money, 32; marks himself a leader, 33; dissatisfied with proposed plan of reconciliation, 34; opposes article denouncing Quebec Acts, 35; in disgust writes letter to Jay and Livingston, 35, 36; succeeds by parliamentary ability in inducing Congress to leave the matter to Continental Congress, 36; opposes premature hostilities, 37; delegate to receive Washington, 38; denounces proposed invasion of Canada, 39; begins to think reconciliation hopeless, 39; leads bolder faction in Assembly, 40, 46; difficulties of his position, 42; advocates formation of a new government, 46; his argument

itary ability, 264; visits Madame
de Staël at Coppet, 264; on Swiss
sordidness, 265; visits Great Britain,
265; dealings with nobility and
with ministry, 265, 266; consulted
by Grenville and Pitt, 266; writes
to Washington in behalf of English
policy, 266; at court, 266; disgusted with French refugees, 267;
visits the Continent, 267; well received in Berlin, 267; not impressed
by royalty, 268; tries to refuse a
royal invitation, 268; relates conversations with Prussian king, 268;
condemns to Grenville Prussia's
foreign policy, 269; visits Dresden,
269, 270; meets diplomatists in Vienna, 270; bored by social devotion
to gambling, 270; considers Austria
on the decline, 270, 271; describes
court levees, 272; friendly relations
with English, 272, 273; laughs at
English fondness for uniforms, 273;
discusses diplomatic situation with
King of Prussia, 274; visits Brunswick, 275; meets General Riedesel,
275; makes friends elsewhere, 275;
interested in Rumford's reforms in
Bavaria, 275; vainly tries to get
Lafayette released, 275, 276; appealed to by Lafayette's family and
friends, 275; helps Louis Philippe
at Madame de Flahaut's request,
276; resents Louis's subsequent
meanness about repaying loans,
277; returns to United States, 277.

In United States Senate. Becomes
member of Federalist party, 278;
builds mansion at Morrisania, 278;
engages in suit as counsel against
Hamilton, 278, 279; chosen to fill
unexpired term in Senate, 285;
favors Hamilton rather than Adams, 285; begs Washington to accept a nomination, 285; disapproves of plan to elect Burr over
Jefferson in 1800, 287; describes
desolation of Washington in 1800,
287; not a strict party man, 287,
288; despises Jefferson, 288; favors
judiciary bill for partisan reasons,
289; opposes its repeal as unconstitutional, 290; comments on in-

consistency of Democrats, 291; advocates states'-rights doctrines, 291;
opposes constitutional amendment
regarding election of President, 292;
separates from party in advocating
Louisiana purchase, 293; thinks its
retention by France would cause
war, 293; advocates seizing territory and defying Napoleon, 293;
his reasons, 293, 294; approves the
purchase, 294; not reëlected to Senate, 295.

In Retirement. Originates plan
of Erie Canal, 295; chairman of
canal commissioners, 295; travels
in New York and elsewhere, 295;
habits of life at home, 295; friendship with Jay, 296; marriage, 296;
warns a friend against sending son
to college too early, 296, 297; visited by Moreau, 297; thinks American climate superior to English,
297, 298; high expectations of future American development, 298;
takes optimistic view of popular
government in America, 298, 299;
on republican government, 299; on
ultra-democracy, 299, 300; later
loses faith in the country, 300; feels
renewed jealousy of the West, 300,
301; bitter against Democratic government, 302; advocates secession,
302; defends British claim to impressment, 306; and rejoices over
British successes, 306; wishes to
repudiate war debt, 306, 307;
wishes to impede war taxation, 307;
derides fidelity to Union, 307; urges
Federalists to declare publicly
against it, 308; wishes New York
to join New England in a confederation, 308; disappointed in result
of Hartford Convention, 308, 309;
impossibility of defending his course,
309; proves himself inferior to the
mob he despised, 309; accommo-
dates himself after Peace of Ghent,
315; henceforward wishes country
well, 315; disapproves of tariff of
1816, 315; wishes Federalists to
abandon party organization, 315,
316; death, 316; estimate of his
character and services, 316, 317.